THE
MARSHALL
FIELDS

THE
MARSHALL
FIELDS

Axel Madsen

John Wiley & Sons, Inc.

ISBN: 0-471-02493-7

Printed in the United States of America

10 9 8 7 6 5 4 3 2 1

CONTENTS

ACKNOWLEDGMENTS

I CANNOT THANK ALL THE PEOPLE WHO TOOK TIME TO HELP ME prepare this story of the father of conspicuous consumption. First, let me thank my editor, Hana Umlauf Lane. In Chicago, I am indebted to Thomas M. Schroeder of the Field Enterprises, and Marshall Field V, for their diligent reviews of the first draft, and to my agent, Jane Jordan Browne, who put me up and put up with me. I also owe thanks to Jim Wells, to Diana Haskell of the Newberry Library, and to Caroline Nutley of the Chicago Historical Society. In Los Angeles, I owe thanks to Frederick Field and Suzanne Welch of Radar Pictures, and to my first reader, Paula Porter.

THE
MARSHALL
FIELDS

Founding father: Marshall Field I

*(Painted by Leon Bonnet;
photo by Thomas Schneider)*

INTRODUCTION

ONE HUNDRED YEARS AGO, MARSHALL FIELD WAS BOTH AN AMERican legend and a famously elusive figure. At a time when the average American's weekly salary was less than ten dollars, the annual income of this quiet, dignified, unemotional man—some thought him almost delicate—was $40 million (nearly $800 million in today's money). His son, Marshall Field II, was a Proustian figure of lassitude and mysterious illnesses who either committed suicide or was shot by a floozy. Marshall Field III was a Jazz Age playboy with a 2,000-acre Long Island estate who suffered the peculiar kind of public contempt reserved for idealists with money. After his brother died at twenty-three, Marshall Field III inherited the equivalent of nearly $4 billion in 2002 dollars and cleverly moved the family fortune from dry goods to publishing. *His* son added to the wealth, but family fragmentation splintered the fortune for the fifth generation when two half-brothers who barely knew each other dismantled the empire.

The Field chronicles are about the loneliness that comes with money. The drama of the founding father is the conflict between pride for his meteoric rise, his reticence, and the wish to be loved. Marshall Field made his fortune knowing what women wanted, but had no understanding of his wife's emotional needs. Too late, he wanted to discover the softer side of the life he had so industriously persuaded others to buy, but the mother of his two children chose to live apart. She died in France, possibly a drug addict. As adults his son and daughter followed their mother abroad, requiring the aging millionaire to cross the Atlantic to snatch time with his grandchildren. With remarkable foresight he drew up a will that, despite repeated attempts to break it, transferred the wealth intact for four generations. Yet no Marshall Field VI runs the landmark department store today.

The Fields' tale is the Jekyll-and-Hyde story of American capitalism, of drive and nerve, and moral stumbles, sometimes shocking, often absurd. What seems ingrained in the family genes is a sense of hurt, of feeling misunderstood, of being wronged by the world, by fate and circumstances. Marshall III's rebellion against his mother's Catholicism was, at least in part, an attempt to exorcise his father's apparent suicide. To please his dying mother, he married a Catholic, divorced her, and saw their children resent them both. The common thread running through the generations is a palpable sense of alienation and a deep fear of hereditary insanity.

The founding father was an acquaintance of John D. Rockefeller and a contemporary of the other overlords of triumphant capitalism—J. P. Morgan, Jay Gould, and Andrew Carnegie. Morgan, guru-like, proposed and disposed. Racier types clawed their way up in pursuit of dreams of wealth. Others used wits, backroom deals, and politics. High fliers like Charles Tyson Yerkes, the "cable czar" who made his money in urban public transportation, were always about to crash and burn, but while they soared, they lent the age a reckless flair. Marshall Field was the least flawed of the Gilded Age robber barons. In an age of shoddy merchandising practices, he stressed service, a one-price system, a money-back guarantee, and consumer satisfaction. He was a believer in the virtues of prosperity, a conservative in the Lincolnesque sense, willing to let any eager young employee try for the brass ring and to share earnings with worthy deputies. A century before compassionate conservatism entered the political vocabularly, he praised the ethos of wealth in the name of individual choice while seeing most of the changes in society with various degrees of alarm. His emphasis on character, self-improvement, perseverance and his admonition to his 20,000 employees that the customer is always right may sound trite or naïve, but he made the great shopping world accept his commercial uplift. He refined his customers' tastes and sold them on the necessity of fulfilling their newly acquired desires. He prospered not so much by maximizing profits as by riding out storms that sank less well-capitalized rivals. A rising tide of popular aspirations carried him to fame and fortune. A good part of his permanent reputation rested on people's trust in him, their belief that he would never stoop to anything at odds with his personal righteousness.

With its thirteen acres of Chicago floor space and a territorial army of spiffy salesmen servicing small-town dry goods establishments from Michigan to California, Field's department store operation was the largest in the world. Field profited enormously from the industrialization and general prosperity that swept the

North after the Civil War. Despite the labor upheavals and financial panics that punctured his heyday, he possessed a bullish faith in the future. He had risked and scored—and thought himself entitled to every cent of his winnings, even though success gave him little joy. What he left behind was human wreckage: a wife who lived abroad, a son whose death from a gunshot wound mystified the public and prompted his daughter-in-law to say American wealth is often a curse. A contemporary who knew the founding father well said Field never understood his own shortcomings. His daughter sank into depression. His grandson led a flighty, insouciant life until his early forties, when the waste of idle wealth began to haunt him. Two of the children of his first marriage were institutionalized as bipolars, and the third was murdered. The two daughters of his third marriage committed suicide. Yet unlike many men with colossal inherited wealth, Marshall III put his money to interesting use.

The Field chronicles tell us that it is not taxes or mismanagement that erode family fortunes, but multiple marriages. While it is often difficult for siblings to amicably take over the running of a huge enterprise, the situation becomes more challenging when divorce introduces half-brothers and stepsisters. Marshall Field's 22,000-word will was an extraordinary document, the longest ever probated in Chicago. He left the bulk of his fortune to his two underage grandsons, but stipulated that most of the money be kept in trust until they turned fifty. Like the great merchant princes of Europe, the Medici of Florence, the Rothschilds of Frankfurt, and the Fuggers of Augsburg, Field wanted to project his vast estate into the distant future. He was very careful drawing up his will. Because he knew banks could go bankrupt, commodities crash, and empires vanish, he followed the Old World example of patrilineal fortune-building to the point of making Illinois lawmakers wonder what would happen if his grandson in turn rolled over the accumulated wealth until the pyramid exceeded billions of dollars, and a not too distant descendant owned half the country.

What Marshall Field did not foresee was his male offspring's high turnover of wives. Of the six generations bearing the name Marshall Field, only Marshall II and, as of the present, Marshall VI (married in 1992) had one wife. Marshall Field III and IV each had three wives; Marshal Field V married twice and his half-brother Ted three times. The founding father's will that for sixty-five years carried the fortune forward collapsed in 1982 when Ted demanded his share of the Field Enterprises. Today, Ted is a player in the entertainment business, making film, music, real estate, and investment deals. His half-brother Marshall V is a successful real estate tycoon. His son, Marshall VI, who grew up with his mother in Philadelphia, is also in real estate and lives in New York. The Chicago landmark department store is today a subsidiary of the Target Corporation.

The history of American business is strewn with the wreckage of family firms, from RCA, where Robert Sarnoff turned his dad's electronics firm into a corporate patch quilt, to Wang Laboratories, which Frederick Wang destroyed by following all too closely in An Wang's footsteps. On the other hand, Ted Turner built his father's Atlanta billboard business and one UHF television station into CNN before he sold it to Time-Warner, which sold itself to AOL. Two exceptions, the Sulzbergers at the *New York Times* Company and the Grahams at the *Washington Post* Company, built their papers into powerful, lasting franchises. The *Los Angeles Times'* Chandler family quarreled and, after a ham-fisted and inept interregnum, sold the media group to the *Chicago Tribune*. Buying and selling nameplate corporations is the norm in today's economy, where, in a dizzying merry-go-round, every enterprise seems to be perpetually in play. Yes, in another exception, William Clay Ford Jr. is the chairman of the Ford Motor Company his great-grandfather built, but no great-grandson of Louis B. Mayer runs Metro Goldwyn Mayer, no Alexander Graham Bell VIII lords over AT&T, no scion of the Morgan family rules J. P. Morgan.

To Marshall III, money conferred responsibility and obligations. The family fortune was there to change the world. To Marshall IV, the smartest of them all, money was a chore. Ted Field saw money as a means to buy into fantasies; his half-brother felt he had to make money work. This book is the story of how different generations relate to money, the emotions of money.

CHICAGO

1

A PLACE TO LINGER

DRY GOODS—SILKS, SATINS, AND YANKEE NOTIONS. NOT EXACTLY the stuff of revolutions, yet the way one dressed could be seditious 150 years ago. When Amelia Bloomer created pantaloons and the loosely fitted tunic in 1851 and wore the ensemble at a Washington reception, she meant to give women a new freedom of movement. "Women are in bondage. Their clothes are a great hindrance to their engaging in any business, which will make them pecuniary independent," she proclaimed. The Bloomer costume, however, became the object of ridicule and personal martyrdom for those who wore it. Mobs of unruly men raided feminist meetings, newspapers and magazines printed satirical cartoons, and preachers fulminated from their pulpits against the scandalous costumes. Those who had adopted the new costume, including feminist Elizabeth Cady Stanton, soon reverted to crinolines and petticoats. Susan B. Anthony held out the longest, arguing the issue was too important to concede, but she, too, gave up, admitting she could no longer bear the emotional anguish that came with wearing pantaloons.

Victorian America was divided by gender as well as by class. City centers were a man's world. There were no beauty shops or tearooms, and no lady would dare venture unescorted into a restaurant, for she would not be served. If she was welcome at the new soda fountains, she was not expected to linger. A detailed code of behavior allowed a woman to go out alone during daylight hours, while nighttime excursions required an escort to see her safely to and from her destination. For the women of Chicago, there was one exception. Marshall Field's was a place where an unescorted woman was received with deference. She "might wander for hours through an exhibition of objects of beauty and value in endless variety from every land," Field's friend Thomas Goodspeed would write. "She walked among them as freely as though they were her own." It was a place where she could linger, where she could shop, compare, chat, and, without husband or father deciding for her, do her own choosing. It was a store where, if her credit was approved, she could charge her purchases; where, if she bought more than she could carry, delivery boys were sent along to help. The store worked out systems of credit and layaway plans, each with its own language and set of rituals that freed women of the responsibility of carrying and handling cash.

The way Field's treated customers was as famous as the quality of its goods, the honesty of its advertising, and its money-back guarantees. Here, instead of fawning salesmen, well-mannered clerks served customers with expertise and respect. Women shoppers were addressed as Madam, not My Dear or Lady. Clerks were taught to ask a customer, "Have you been served?"—a phrase later changed to, "May I Help You?" so as to make the employee feel less subservient. When addressing each other, staff members were told not to use their given names, but to refer to each other as Mr. X or Miss Y. Reciprocity was expected. Manuals on manners and etiquette dictated that a woman should speak softly in a department store, handle goods carefully, be courteous to other patrons, and never lean on a store counter. An 1885 book called *Our Deportment* told ladies they "should not monopolize the time and attention of salesmen in small talk while other customers are in the store to be waited upon."

Chicago profited enormously from the Civil War, and the city's nouveaux riches demanded selections worthy of Charles Frederick Worth and other Parisian couturiers. The store happily stocked silks in the most delicate colors, shawls costing $1,500 ($30,000 in today's money), frocks of grenadine moiré that sold for $225, a $300 gown in apricot silks with train. The upper floors offered yards upon yards of fabric in bolts for the majority of women who made their own clothes by hand or on a newfangled sewing machine.

Rich and famous ladies had their coachmen drive them to the 28 East Washington Street entrance. The two doormen, Eddie Anderson and Charlie Pritzlaff, knew who was who and helped the ladies alight and enter the store while directing their coachmen to find a place in the double line of conveyances waiting between Michigan Avenue and State Street. Pritzlaff reached notoriety on his own by writing down the names of customers in a notebook, checking the names against the society *Blue Book*. The notebook led to a bigger scrapbook, in which, once clients got comfortable with him, they in turn inscribed their signatures. The autographs scrawled in Pritzlaff's book ranged from Presidents Grover Cleveland, William McKinley, and Theodore Roosevelt to the Everleigh sisters. Minna and Ada Everleigh might have been the owners of Chicago's chic brothel, but when they arrived with their choicest girls, obsequious floor managers swept them toward the lingerie section. If a lady asked for the head of a department or a specific salesperson, either Anderson, who affected a Boston accent, or Pritzlaff snapped fingers to summon one of the half-dozen uniformed boys, who scurried off to fetch the requested individual.

Former First Lady Mary Todd Lincoln was a frequent shopper. She had been declared insane after the president's assassination and was usually accompanied by her son Robert and daughter-in-law Mary Harlan Lincoln. During one visit, the younger Mary was so pleased with the way a salesman treated them that she impulsively removed a rose from her gown and fastened it in the salesman's lapel. "I raised it in my garden," she told him, "and I want you to have it."

All eyes followed Bertha Honoré Palmer when she came to shop, usually on Mondays. The tall and energetic wife of Potter Palmer, Marshall Field's onetime boss, was very much the social leader. Her husband built Chicago's first luxury hotel, the Palmer House, with its magnificent roof garden, in her honor. "Whether the shopper bore the name of Bertha Honoré Palmer or that of an unknown dancer, or if a woman came in a hansom cab, on the cable car, or one of the West Side trolleys marked 'Field Special,' she was treated courteously," Lloyd Wendt and Herman Kogan would write in *Give the Lady What She Wants: The Story of Marshall Field & Company.* "The instruction was invariably the same to the doormen, the clerks, and the dapper floorwalkers who strutted about with their 5-cent carnations in their lapels: 'Utmost courtesy is required . . . Under no circumstances allow the customer to leave the store dissatisfied.'"

Chicago's men had their downtown clubs. Because the women had few places where they could meet, Marshall Field's became the place to socialize, to be seen socializing—and to answer nature's calls. Before Marshall Field's installed toilets, women went for a day's shopping with no hope of relief. An 1870s campaign in the *Women's Gazette* for ladies' lavatories resulted in the formation of women's clubs, and gradually led to amenities in hotels, restaurants, and tea shops. The Marshall Field's women's—and men's—lounges were elegantly appointed areas with sofas, chairs, writing tables, and reading materials. Out-of-town visitors, many of whom took in the store during a layover between connecting trains, were also frequent users of the lounges. Here they could send and receive telegrams, arrange hotel reservations, buy theater tickers, consult railroad timetables, and receive other travel information.

For women seeking employment, the store was a big step up from "teaching and the needle." The upheavals of the Industrial Revolution saw five million women, half of them under twenty-five, join the workforce. Although President Theodore Roosevelt condemned the tendency toward smaller families as decadent in 1905, the beginning of the birth control movement, the migration to the city, new opportunities for an education, the popularity of apartments and boardinghouses, and divorce (Americans had the world's highest divorce rate after Japan's) further widened opportunities and horizons and relaxed the codes of propriety. Field's hired female clerks so ladies would feel comfortable examining lingerie, and because the store was known to be a "respectable" place to work it was easy to recruit young women. Female employees had separate toilets, cloak, recreation, and lunchrooms, reported to work half an hour later than the men, and at the end of the workday left thirty minutes earlier. "We endeavor to throw about our young women an atmosphere of protection," Field explained. By 1880 Field's employed 600 women, paying them an average of $8 a week, a dollar more than the average for female workers, but two dollars less than men in comparable trades. When Field appeared, the men and women working for him came to attention and bowed slightly if he favored them with a nod.

Marshall Field brought to retailing the moral passion of an evangelist and wrapped himself in the mantle of his success. He never bored his dinner guests with stories of his early struggles, hardly ever spoke in public, and interviewers rarely got more than a sentence or two from "Silent Marsh." When Theodore Dreiser interviewed him for *Success* magazine and asked what drove him to become successful, the answer was unhesitating and straightforward: "I was determined not to remain poor." In his prime, he was an elegant man in hand-tailored suits and white gloves who, people said, looked more like a diplomat than a prosperous merchant. Erect in his bearing, he had steel-gray eyes and a full head of sleek dark hair. "When you came to see him at his desk," recalled his nephew Stanley Field, who worked for sixty years in his uncle's company, "he fixed you with the coldest gray eyes you ever saw. They read you through and through." Subordinates who sought his advice often left his office unsatisfied, but feeling pumped dry.

Field believed his employees were treated as well as they deserved to be, and if they objected, they were always free to seek employment elsewhere. The concept of trade unionism was deeply offensive to him. "The customer is always right" slogan was null and void if someone prominent in the labor movement entered the store, even if he came only to make a purchase. Before he could state his errand, he was ushered from the premises. Although the emporium was not in the crosshairs of worker anger, Field sided with his industrial friends, the railway car magnate George Pullman, Cyrus McCormick of reaper fame, and meat-packer Philip Armour when they faced strikes and riots.

2

SILENT MARSH

AS A YOUNG MAN, MARSHALL FIELD WAS RETICENT AND SHY. HE spoke little but listened hard, and fellow clerks called him "Silent Marsh." At his first job in Chicago, he often spent the night in the store at the end of an eighteen-hour day. When he slept at his boardinghouse, he arrived at the store long before it opened so he could help load wagons heading for the docks and the railway station.

He was born on September 18, 1834, in a one-and-a-half-story farmhouse a mile from Conway in the Berkshires in western Massachusetts. By family tradition, the Fields could trace their ancestors back beyond the Norman conquest of England to a De la Feld family in Colmar on the German-French border. Officially, a genealogy commissioned by Marshall Field in 1901 when he was the richest man in Chicago stopped at Roger del

Field, born in Sowerby Bridge, England, in 1240. The family of Marshall Field's mother arrived in the New World in 1637 when Thomas Nash and Margery Baker Nash, members of a Merchants of London trading company, landed at Boston. Twelve years later, the first Field crossed the Atlantic in the person of Zechariah Field, who settled in Hartford, Connecticut. Marshall's father, John, plowed and tended the 200-acre tract of land in Massachusetts that he had inherited. Marshall's mother was Fidelia Nash, a hometown girl of twenty-two, the daughter of Conway farmer Elijah Nash and Paulina Warner Nash, when she married John Field in 1828. She was a prim, sensitive woman who inspired her four sons and three surviving daughters to study. Marshall was the third child and third son of the eight children.

The family was Congregationalist. Congregationalism had its roots in the Reformation when its founders thought the Church of England too submissive to Parliament, prelates, and the law courts. Some tried to reform the Established Church from within, while others broke away, but they were all nicknamed Puritans because of their passionate desire for purity in worship, church government, and personal life. Those who left the Church of England split again when some congregations claimed the right of all worshippers to a share in the direction of church affairs. Congregationalists, as they were called, were far from isolationist as they found energy and attracted converts in "fellowship." Four successive waves of persecution and the martyrdom of three church figures only stimulated the elaboration of separatist principles. Congregationalists were among the passengers on the *Mayflower* setting sail for New England in 1620.

John Field's acres were a tract of rich loam, not the usual rocky soil of New England. Still, John drove himself from dawn to dusk and insisted on the same schedule for his family. The homestead was on the summit of a considerable rise known as Field's Hill. The view was one of woods, meadows, streams, and, below, nestling farms and the village of Conway. Two of Marshall's siblings died in childhood, but like his older brothers, Chandler and Joseph, younger sisters, Helen and Laura, and kid brother Henry, he was sent to school during the winter when farm work was slow. He was a quiet boy in school, fond only of mathematics. By the time he was ten, he was something of an athlete, usually playing the fox in a Fox and Hound hide-and-seek game. To play the fox demanded resourcefulness, and to avoid being caught he once ran eight miles to South Deerfield and back again.

He much preferred school to working on the farm. When he was fifteen he thought he could put the drudgery of farming behind him. His parents sold the farm, apparently because Conway abandoned the road running past the homestead. A year later, however, when Marshall's schooling was finished, John bought another farm. The only escape Marshall could think of was to convince his father that his knack for figures meant he was perhaps destined for the life of a shopkeeper. His older brother Joseph, who also wanted to leave the farm, helped convince their father to let Marshall go to Pittsfield to work for a Congregationalist church deacon and owner of a dry goods store. Marshall stayed five years in Deacon Henry Davis's establishment and, he would later say, studied storekeeping "with the dry passion of a genius." He was hardworking, courteous, and eager to please. He developed a memory for faces and names, a smooth sales technique, and an air of grave concentration. The eternal verities were his weapons: the sweat of his brow, thrift, and a sense of duty and avoidance of frivolity. Working with his father had given him a sense of responsibility and the confidence that he would be successful in whatever he chose to do in life. We do not know what his relationship with Deacon Davis's two daughters was, but he would remember them in his famous will sixty years later. His first brush with a young man of privilege came one day when Davis told him to entertain J. Pierpont Morgan, who was traveling with his father. The two young men would renew their acquaintance many years later.

In 1855, when Marshall was twenty-one, he made a major decision: he would go west. Several Pittsfield girls, including Marshall's two sisters, Laura and Helen, had left town and married ambitious young men in Chicago. Teacher Mary Eveline Smith had married Charles B. Farwell, a young official in Chicago's municipal government, and on a visit to her folks in Pittsfield stopped in at Deacon Davis's store to tell of her experiences out west. Years later she would remember Marshall Field for his quiet, intent manner as he waited on her, "a handsome young man with regular features and cheeks as red as a rose."

After five years, Marshall had almost a thousand dollars saved up. When he told Davis of his plans to go west, the storekeeper proposed to take him in as a partner if he would stay. Marshall thanked Deacon Davis, but declined the offer. Davis shook his head, but when Field was ready to leave, he handed him a letter, addressed "To Whom It May Concern":

> The bearer, Mr. Field, has been in my employ for nearly the past five years and now leaves me for the West. I can without qualifications commend him as a young man of unusual business talent worthy of the confidence of any who would employ him. His character and principles as well as his business qualifications are such I cannot doubt he will meet that success in life which usually accompanies industry, perseverance, and integrity when combined with strong energy of character. He has my warmest wishes for his success in whatever situation he may fall or business he shall engage.

The noise, commotion, mud, and stench of the undisciplined frontier town of 1855 Chicago shocked the orderly Marshall and made him wonder whether he shouldn't have gone to New York instead, or perhaps to St. Louis or Kansas City. Chicago was the center of the largest railroad network in the world. Almost a hundred trains entered and left every day, and wherever its trains ran, they changed everything. The prairies were becoming hinterland and the surrounding landscape suburban. His brother Joseph had preceded him to Chicago on his way to a job offer in a dry goods establishment in Omaha, Nebraska, and now dropped the idea of going to Omaha. He saw great potential in Chicago, even if the banks of the foul-smelling Chicago River swarmed with ambitious young farmers' sons like themselves. More important, he had great faith in Marshall's talent for business, his five-year experience with Deacon Davis.

Joseph and Marshall talked about the ten railroad lines that made the city a hub, and of ships arriving directly from Liverpool via the St. Lawrence and the Great Lakes. They also passed by the Lake Street retail and wholesale establishment of Potter Palmer, a Quaker from upstate New York, whose ads boasted that his prices were the lowest in the city, that he sold "at cost," and that "on approval," women shoppers could take merchandise home and, if less than satisfied, could bring the items back for full refund.

Before Palmer became Marshall's boss—and inspiration—the twenty-two-year-old newcomer with his letter of recommendation met a commercial traveler who explained how he covered the far end of the Mississippi Valley for Cooley, Farwell, Wadsworth and Company, Chicago's biggest dry goods wholesaler. The way to go was to become a traveling salesman. But Marshall wasn't sure he'd like life on the road. Nevertheless, Joseph knew a number of merchants, and he took the initiative of recommending his kid brother to Francis B. Cooley. Perhaps he had more confidence in his brother than Marshall had in himself or perhaps they thought it clever if, instead of showing up cold, Marshall arrived at senior partner's office at someone else's suggestion. Cooley prided himself on hiring only top prospects. With an appointment, Marshall presented himself. Cooley sized up the young man, read Deacon Davis's letter, and allowed that he was not impressed. Letters in the Marshall Field and Company archives show that Joseph returned several times to praise his brother's "unusual business talent" and "strict integrity." Cooley relented and hired Marshall on a trial basis—as a clerk.

Marshall Field in his twenties was a slender young man of quiet intensity and polite manners, five feet nine inches tall, with restless gray eyes, thin lips, and big ears. Invariably courteous and thorough, he kept his ambitions to himself. His annual wage for the first year was $400 ($7,200 in today's money), but he managed to save half of it by sleeping in the store and not buying new clothes. "As a young clerk he was not particularly impressive," said John Farwell, the junior partner whose brother had married Pittsfield's schoolteacher, Mary Eveline Smith. "It did not take us long to find out that he had no bad habits, that his word was always good, and that he was with us to make money. Yet these were the characteristics of many other good clerks." Some forty years later, when Marshall Field was Chicago's wealthiest citizen, Cooley would remember his young clerk: "He appeared to lack confidence in himself to an extent that could be surprising to those who have known him in maturer years." Marshall liked the store's location on the riverbank at 205 South Water Street, but nodded appreciatively when Cooley told him business was moving away from the waterfront and that the partners planned to open a new store on Wabash Avenue. A flair for divining exactly where to locate his stores would be the signature feature of Field's triumph.

Severe, formal, and with little interest in a personal life, Silent Marsh worked eighteen hours a day, acquired a thorough knowledge of the Cooley, Farwell, Wadsworth inventory, and made friends with out-of-town buyers. Farwell noticed that at the retail counter, Marshall had a talent for finding the right tone in dealing with women, that, in short, they might have acquired an extraordinary salesman. Marshall knew the merchandise and had none of the slick toadying of so many older salesclerks. "He seemed to have a wonderful comprehension of feminine nature," Farwell would recall. "He had the merchant instinct. He knew how to show off a stock to its best advantage, and he always knew what was in stock. He lived for it, and it only. He never lost it." According to Joseph, Marshall carried purchasing and selling prices in his head or in a small black book kept carefully in an inner pocket.

A credit crunch that panicked the Midwest in 1857 showed the partners another side of Field. He convinced his employers to tighten credit, borrow where they could, and slash inventory. The Cooley, Farwell, Wadsworth bookkeeper, a young man named Levi Z. Leiter, agreed. The company lost some customers by refusing to give easy credit, but rode out the storm that sent nearly three hundred other wholesale houses and stores into bankruptcy. Cooley awarded Marshall with a junior partnership. As his yearly profit sharing would be $3,000, he moved to a room in the comparative luxury of the Metropolitan Hotel at the corner of Randolph and Wells streets. His Congregationalist upbringing made him shun the city's social pleasures. If a buyer wanted to meet in a saloon, however, Marshall was there.

Levi Leiter.

He and bookkeeper Leiter had a lot in common and a lot that set them apart. Levi was Marshall's age and had come to Chicago to seek greater challenges than the ones afforded him after a dry goods apprenticeship in Springfield, Ohio. Marshall was painstaking, analytical, and measured; Levi talked things to death. Marshall fitted himself into the role he had laid out for himself, and was careful about what he said. Levi was generous, opportunistic, and had a hundred friends. Whereas Marshall was handsome and polished and grew a collar of a beard that made him resemble young Abraham Lincoln, Levi was burly and brusque, with a full beard that made him look like an Amish farmer. Some people were sure he was Jewish, but he said he was a native of the Maryland hamlet of Leitersburg, founded in 1760 by his Dutch

Calvinist great-grandfather James van Leiter. The two soon plot-
ted opportunities together and studied the methods of Potter
Palmer, Chicago's merchant with the golden touch.

The energetic and ambitious Potter Palmer was only eight years
older than Marshall, but four years after opening his dry goods
establishment on Lake Street, he was overtaking Cooley, Farwell,
Wadsworth. He was the son of Benjamin Palmer, a descendant of
1629 settlers in Massachusetts, and Rebecca Potter, the daughter of
a renowned Albany, New York, family. At birth, their boy was given
his mother's surname. He became a clerk in an establishment in
Durham, New York, when he was seventeen, and two years later
was in charge of the business. With $3,000 as an investment by his
father, Potter came to Chicago and opened P. Palmer & Co—the
sign painter charged by the letter and Palmer was content with only
the initial of his first name—and proceeded to reinvent retailing.
Instead of naming his price according to what he thought a shopper could afford or was willing to pay (traditionally followed by a bit
of haggling), Palmer had price tags on every piece of merchandise
in the store. He not only introduced the practice of sending goods
"on approval" to his customers' homes, where they could inspect
the merchandise at leisure and, if not satisfied, return it; he origi-
nated refunding upon request, no questions asked. The old New
York firm of Macy & Company sent an agent to investigate the
workings of Palmer's methods, and soon adopted his reforms.

Popularity and prestige allowed Palmer to go upscale. Instead
of catering to the coarse needs of pioneer settlers, he began stock-
ing silks, velvets, and laces. He laid out his merchandise in inviting displays, started home deliveries at no charge, invented "bargain days," and began aggressive advertising. In the midst of the

panic of 1857, he undersold everybody. An October 6, 1857, ad in the *Chicago Times* proclaimed:

GREAT SALE

In consequence of the
TIGHTNESS OF THE MONEY MARKET
and other
STARTLING CAUSES COMBINED,
and to enable me to
STAND FROM UNDER
the
PRESENT CRASH!
I shall offer my
ENTIRE STOCK
For the
NEXT 30 DAYS!
At a
GREAT SACRIFICE!

Palmer's instincts were unerring. He worked fast, on his own, and in less than ten years developed a business that grossed nearly $10 million a year—$200 million in today's money. His line of credit with New York banks exceeded one million dollars. Competitors took notice. Palmer was also innovative in wholesale. He told his salesmen traveling in the West to get cash if possible; if not, to get furs. Once a retailer proved himself reliable, Palmer made sure he kept him. "If I learned of a man two hundred miles away, buried in a clearing in the forest, who might buy, I got the name of my establishment to him and invited him in. After he once got acquainted with the store, we rarely lost him." Buyers from San Francisco began stopping in Chicago on their way to New York and soon switched to the reliable house on Lake Street. Palmer's biggest attraction, wholesale and retail, was of course his prices. To undercut competitors, he bypassed New York jobbers wherever he could. He worked directly with New England manufacturers and, with New York's fancy goods storeowner Charles Lewis Tiffany (father of the famous glassmaker), became the first American merchant to sell goods purchased on buying trips to Europe. In 1857, when he was all of thirty-one, his store burned to the ground. His Quaker tenets prohibited borrowing money, and he used his own capital to build a new and larger emporium near the ruins of the first.

The Civil War that broke out in April 1861 made Palmer a war profiteer. During the first weeks of the conflict, when his competitors panicked and unloaded goods below cost, he went on a buying spree and filled his warehouses with hundreds of bales of cotton, muslin, and flannels. He was one of several entrepreneurs to sense that the War Between the States would lead to an economic boom for the North. The complete lack of manufacturing took a heavy toll on the South. The North replaced the farm boys it recruited with Cyrus McCormick's reaping machines. The reapers of the South were slaves. The war sent inflation soaring. To Francis Cooley's consternation, Palmer continued to buy. Cooley was in New York in April 1863 when he wrote to Marshall Field that he had had lunch with a fellow merchant who didn't know what to make of Palmer. "I stoped [sic] buying & he [Palmer] is in no better shape than we are . . . I may be wrong."

Marshall was twenty-eight that year. Accepting a friend's party invitation, he met twenty-three-year-old Nannie Scott, visiting from Ironton, Ohio. Nannie, a delicate girl, was a well-turned product of Miss Willard's School for Young Ladies in Troy, New York. John Tebbel, the first biographer of the Marshall Fields,

would write in 1947 that Miss Scott drew out the timid, intro-
verted Marshall and inspired him to talk: "Perhaps she sensed his
future greatness; more likely it was sheer romance, for Nannie
Scott remained a romanticist until the day she died." The
"romanticist until the day she died" sounds dismissive in today's
ears. Romanticism emphasized feelings and individuality and, yes,
an idealized view of life and love, but the educated daughter of a
professional man, a young woman attractive and enticing enough
to exert a pull on a reserved business type, would not be a total
mooning dreamer.

Nannie was at the railway station for the train back to Ironton
when Marshall realized nothing except glances and gentle words
had passed between them and that he might never see her again.
For the first and maybe only time in his life he did something
impulsive. He raced to the station, jumped aboard the train as it
pulled out, found Miss Scott, and, while the train moved through
the yards, proposed. With her yes, he got off at the next station.

After a January 3, 1863, wedding, they set up housekeeping at
306 Michigan Avenue. As a conventional couple, they assimilated
the roles that Victorian rectitude assigned them: Marshall the triumphant breadwinner, she the dutiful wife devoted to husband
and hearth. Soon Nannie's dashing jumper of trains was lost forever. Marshall plunged into his business career and was buried in
it to the exclusion of everything human in his life. A son they
named Lewis died before his first birthday. Two years later, on
April 21, 1868, Nannie gave birth to a son they named Marshall.

We know little of Nannie's Chicago years. At her husband's
orders, his personal secretary burned all personal letters after his
death. Except for the formal record of a merchant's wife moving
up in society with him, few intimate details of Nannie's life exist.

3

PARTNERSHIPS

THE CHICAGO STORE'S HISTORICAL RECORDS ARE UNIQUE AMONG business archives. After perilous dispersal during the 1980s and cautious reassembly a decade later, twenty linear feet of catalogues, correspondence, advertisements, ledgers, employment records, and 30,000 illustrations are still extant. Before he died, Marshall Field ordered his personal secretary to burn all private letters, but the archival boxes still include letters showing how the twenty-nine-year-old would-be entrepreneur turned to Cyrus Hall McCormick, the city's leading industrialist, for financing, and how McCormick's brothers backed the idea of diversifying into dry goods retailing.

Field watched Potter Palmer's triumph and dreamed of imitating the tireless innovator of retailing. In the fall of 1864, Marshall decided to ask for seed money from the inventor of the mechanical reaper that had revolutionized farming. McCormick's two younger brothers, Leander and William McCormick, who managed the Blue Island Avenue plant, saw a partnership with Field as an opportunity to move beyond farm machinery. "Dear Brother," William wrote December 14, 1864, to Cyrus, who was in New York, "I have seen & talked with F [Field] here. Wm Dogget, Bowen & other good men here speak in strong terms of Mr. F as a close, calculating & safe business man . . . I am of the opinion that either you or C.H. McCormick & Bros. could take half the store & carry it along."

Cyrus considered William a dreamer and let a couple of months go by. Then, as the war ended with General Robert E. Lee's surrender to Ulysses S. Grant at Appomattox, Virginia, on April 9, 1865, Cyrus rejected the idea of investing $200,000 in a partnership with Field. The negative response, however, was couched in sufficient ambiguities to let Field believe the turndown might not be final. What in the end gave Marshall—and Levi Leiter—their chance was Palmer's deteriorating health.

Palmer was only thirty-nine, but the dozen years of unrelenting work and boundless drive had sapped his strength and vigor. There are two versions of what he did when he developed a severe cough. In one retelling, his doctor told him to take a very long vacation in a mild climate. In another, the physician warned that if Potter wanted to live he had only one choice: retire. No verdict could have been worse for a man of unflagging energy and boundless ambition. However, without a word of complaint, he began to look for a way to dispose of his establishment. His brother Milton had an interest in the firm but didn't have the brain and initiative to take over. As an alternative, Palmer selected Field and Leiter. At their first meeting, he didn't tell Marshall that his doctor had advised him to retire, but merely that the doctor had suggested a long rest. Were Field and Leiter interested in taking over the empire? They could have the business if they would take on Milton as a junior partner. As an incentive, Potter would leave $333,000 in the firm and remain a silent partner. Milton would contribute $50,000.

Field was cagey. War's end found the country exhausted, its finances in tatters. Conditions in the South were desperate and the costs of the conflict, when finally toted up, a staggering $30 trillion (in 2002 currency) for the Union and $18 trillion for the South. Surely peace would deflate the economy, meaning that Potter's inventory, acquired at wartime prices, would have to be sold at such discounts that the whole deal might not even be profitable. He approached the McCormicks again, only to be told to wait. How long would Palmer's offer be on the table?

Field and Leiter decided they couldn't wait out the procrastinating McCormicks, and on January 4, 1865, each signed contracts that gave birth to Field, Palmer and Leiter. The new firm acquired Potter's inventory and buildings for $750,000. As promised earlier, he agreed to leave $333,000 in the firm until such time as Marshall and Levi could afford to buy him out, and Milton Palmer retained a $50,000 stake. This left Field and Leiter to come up with $370,000—$250,000 for Marshall and $120,000 for Levi, they decided—money they didn't have. Confident that the business could generate that amount of profit in two years, they signed notes that would become due on January 4, 1867. When Palmer announced he was going to Europe for a vacation that would last three years, newspapers lamented that a fabulous era in the city's trade was coming to an end.

Wearing frock coats, the new partners greeted their patrons at the door on opening day. The reorganized firm's finances, however, were precarious. As Marshall had feared, prices began to plummet. Competing wholesalers with stocks acquired at inflated prices pleaded with their customers to buy the merchandise they had. Many went into bankruptcy. Field & Leiter discounted and attracted a lively business, but their losses were so heavy that they had no choice but to appeal to Palmer, who hurried back from Europe. They would have to throw in the towel, they told him, and ask him to take back the business. Potter wouldn't hear of it and recalled his own experience in the Panic of 1857 when he undersold his stock. "Why, boys," he shouted, "if I take it all back now, you'll lose 50 cents on every dollar. You listen to me and stay in business. This day of low prices won't last. Take my advice. Go into the market and buy all you can. Buy! You buy and think faster than the fellow down the street, and you'll come out all right."

Palmer put his money where his mouth was and invested a quick $50,000 in the operations. With the money came Palmer's bookkeeper, Harlow Higinbotham, whose astute business methods and persuasive ways with insurance companies would soon save his new employers. More personnel were hired. Each new employee was given specific duties and assured that attention to work, plus results, would win him a $200 bonus at the end of the year. On January 1, 1867, the partnership of Field, Palmer and Leiter dissolved and Field, Leiter and Company was formed. To competitor Farwell's irritation, some of his most promising employees jumped ship and went to work for Field & Leiter. They included the McWilliams brothers—John, a war veteran who showed up on the first day at Field & Leiter still in uniform, and Lafayette, only twenty-one but a clever salesman. Marshall's two older brothers, Joseph and Henry, also joined the company as salesmen. Since the time Joseph had gotten Marshall his first job in Chicago, he had been a cashier in the Omaha National Bank. Henry had clerked for Cooley, Farwell & Company. Both were married now, Joseph the father of six children, Henry the father of three daughters. Another new sales representative was Montgomery Ward, who was a few years away from starting his famous mail order house.

Posterity would call Marshall Field the greatest trader of his day, the merchant who applied artistic genius to business and not only gave people what they wanted, but educated their tastes, and at reasonable prices satisfied their increasingly sophisticated desires. What was forgotten in these panegyrics was how much he owed Palmer. Field and Leiter did not start on their own in a rented storefront, they took over a roaring success, and, after initial dif-

Marshall Field at forty.

ficulties, saw a winner flourish in a growing city and an expanding economy.

Palmer further smoothed their way by becoming a civic booster. Rested and energized, he plunged into real estate. If ever Chicago was to have a world-class shopping district to match the cosmopolitan capitals of Europe, he decided, the main thoroughfare had to be something better than the east-west running Lake Street, a poorly lit, dirty, and cramped street that was so close to the ill-smelling Chicago River that women held handkerchiefs to their noses. Chicago's main commercial artery, he felt, should run north and south, parallel to the lakefront. To change the city's axis of development, he bought land for more than a mile on either side of the narrow and ill-paved State Street, one of the longest streets, lined with one-story frame buildings occupied by saloons, blacksmith shops, and boardinghouses. Shopping was a middle- and upper-class activity, and whether they were buying or just looking—"window shopping" was the new expression— unescorted women in downtown settings were becoming the subject of considerable commentary. An 1881 editorial in the *New York Times* noted "the awful prevalence of the vice of shopping among women," a "purse-destroying [addiction] every bit as bad as male drinking and smoking." To attract and accommodate female clients, Palmer had the city council widen State Street twenty feet and devoted his capital, talent, and time to erecting commercial buildings. One of the first buildings put up by Palmer at the corner of State and Washington streets was rented to Field & Leiter for $50,000 a year—an enormous rent in the new street. Another new building was leased to Charles Gossage, Field & Leiter's competitor, whose stately establishment a block away was fronted by two brass lions. Ten years after Palmer started to rotate Chicago's business axis, the tide of the city's commerce was running north and south. State Street became Chicago's Fifth Avenue.

Fashion becomes a business when someone says, "This is what I want." The business of fashion is sociable and a response to ever-changing interactions of people, events, prevailing attitudes, and the ways in which all this rebounds. Fashion may be fragile and transitory, but as a mirror to its times, style and novelty are as much an indicator of the age as politics or the arts.

Fashion had become current events in the 1840s with the appearance of ladies' journals, but there were few top fashion figures until the rise in 1860 of Charles Frederick Worth. This English-born Parisian was the couturier of France's last crowned head, Empress Eugénie. Before him, couturiers had been tradesmen producing the clothes that the rich and powerful told them to make. With Worth, whose house on the Rue de la Paix lasted a hundred years, couturiers began telling the rich and the powerful how to dress.

Marshall had an instinct for discerning what women wanted. To keep the store's image current, Marshall moved himself, Nannie, and newborn baby Marshall to New York. Here he took charge of the purchasing office and for the next two years was a fashion buyer. He ordered the latest imports from Paris. To make women more at ease in purchasing lingerie, he ordered female clerks hired and got Leiter to open a new department—Notions. He kept an eye on Alexander Turney Stewart, the immigrant from Belfast who had turned a stack of Irish lace and linens into the beginnings of the world's largest retail store.

There was much to learn from A. T. Stewart. Born in Lisburn, County Antrim, in 1803, Stewart came to New York as an adolescent, only to return to Ireland a few years later to collect a legacy. With the $3,000 inheritance, he bought Irish lace, returned to New York, and opened a small dry goods store. Like Potter Palmer, he set standard prices on his goods and saw his business grow until, in 1846, he built a huge marble building for his retail and wholesale operations. The Civil War won him huge government contracts to supply Union army and navy uniforms, and in 1862 he built the world's largest retail store on Broadway. Here he could be seen greeting important customers at the door before turning them over to "floorwalkers." He employed courteous young men, and his store's second-floor Ladies Parlor with its full-length mirrors was the talk of women's magazines. Less admirably, he was autocratic, underpaid his workers, and instituted a system of fines for staff failings.

Stewart toyed with the idea of moving in on the home turf of Field, Leiter & Company. Blissfully unaware of this, Marshall and Levi concentrated their energy on making their emporium a success. They advertised aggressively. Tirelessly, they repeated, "Our intentions are to sell goods at the lowest possible price." "Cloth suitable for pants and suits, $1 to $2 a yard" or "Fancy linen for boys' wear, 25 cents and upward." They also became the biggest advertisers in the new *Chicago Magazine of Fashion, Music and Home Reading*, edited by the young matron Martha Louise Rayne. Sales climbed. UNDER NEW YORK PRICES, proclaimed Field & Leiter ads. A year after Palmer's rescue package, the partners had reason to celebrate and to pay bonuses. Harlow Higinbotham's carefully kept ledgers showed a sales volume for the year of $8 million, and some $300,000 in profits.

Field invested part of his earnings in a new railway venture.

It was an idea that had kept his friend George Pullman awake at night during long rides from his native New York to Chicago. Instead of sleeping upright on the uncomfortable train seats, why not install beds in railway cars? And for that matter, why not build rolling dining rooms? Distances were vast—New York Central's crack express trains made the New York-to-Chicago run in twenty hours. The rich traveled more than poor people, so why not build parlor cars? Pullman, who was three years older than Field and had operated a general store in a Colorado mining town, failed to convince Chicago & Alton Railroad to let him remodel three of their coaches. His startup capital was spent during the first year building one sleeping car. To gain publicity, he arranged to have it attached to President Lincoln's funeral train, and paid railroads a fee to hitch his cars to their trains.

Travelers loved sleeping cars and diners, but the railways wouldn't pay extra for passenger comfort and missed out on the next big thing. The construction of the first transcontinental lines made the sleeping car indispensable. In 1867, Pullman built a combination sleeping and eating car. Newspapers made much of the car's menu, which included steak and potatoes at 60 cents and sugar-cured ham at 40 cents. A year later he introduced a deluxe dining car, the "Delmonico," named after New York's famous Swiss-born restaurateur. Rich people ordered custom cars with stained glass, mahogany and chandeliers, observation lounges and pipe organs. The last word in rolling luxury was marble bathtubs, Venetian mirrors, hidden jewel safes, and English butlers. Mrs. Edward T. Stotesbury, wife of a Morgan partner, told a reporter, "The only thing that's economical about our car, is the solid gold plumbing. It saves polishing, you know!"

Pullman bought out his competitors and became the world's biggest builder of railroad passenger cars. During the 1870s and 1880s, however, Field's investments in the firm would grow so big that he spearheaded a stockholders' revolt that ultimately unseated his friend.

4

FIRE, PANIC, AND MORE FIRE

THE MAD DASH FOR RICHES THAT FOLLOWED THE CIVIL WAR LED
to speculation and the unparalleled growth of great fortunes. The
war itself had created profiteers, and a cult of opportunity produced a generation of empire builders with little regard for ethics.
Ironically, the factories, mills, and railroads they built produced
standardized products that in turn resulted in a more regimented
economy. Oil fields in Pennsylvania and Ohio and silver and gold
rushes in the West fed the inflationary bubble. In 1869 it was officially reported that "within five years more cotton spindles had
been put in motion, more iron furnaces erected, more iron smelt-
ed, more bars rolled, more steel made, more coal and copper
mined, more lumber sawn and hewn, more houses and shops constructed, more manufactories of different kinds started, and more
petroleum collection, refined and exported than during any equal

period in the history of the country." That same year, the rails of the United Pacific stretched east to meet the westward tracks of the Central Pacific, tying the immense country together. Chicago, whose population now exceeded 300,000, was hub, spoke, and springboard to western expansion. But the city of energy, arriviste jostling, chaos and creativity and graft nearly lost all its marbles one Sunday evening in 1871.

The historic disaster called the Chicago Fire started on October 8 in a stable at 137 De Koven Street on city's southwest side. Legend would have it that Patrick O'Leary's cow upset a lighted kerosene lamp. At 9:25 P.M. the alarm was sounded as a sudden wind fanned the flames and embers landed on other barns and flimsy cottages. As thousands fled to the North Division, the fire tailed them, jumping the neighborhood, scorching churches,

The Great Fire, fleeing across Randolph
Bridge in a sketch for *Harper's Weekly*.

mills, factories, and homes, reaching the business district by mid-night. For seventeen hours the fire raged out of control.

John Devlin, a heavily built Irish guard Field and Leiter had inherited from Palmer, was the first employee to reach the store. The night sky was yellow, but the fire was still far from State and Washington streets. Leiter and Field got there as the fire reached Courthouse Square, a few hundred yards west, only to turn north away from State Street. Before the little group could breathe a sigh of relief, other employees came running with the news that the flames were sweeping down both sides of Lake Street. Men carrying household treasures and women clutching babies in their arms ran from the flames. Looting started. Some broke into Lake Street liquor shops. The alcohol in overturned barrels that ran into the street caught fire and added to the inferno. People were heard shouting that the fire was divine punishment for the city's wickedness.

Buildings to the south and west of Field & Leiter were ablaze. The partners and their helpers managed to carry some of their merchandise out into the street, only to see pilferers reach for piles of silk. Men with coaches and buggies and teamsters with drays offered to haul goods to the lakefront for $150 cash a load, only to dump the consignment if someone offered more money. Field ordered their own teamsters to hitch up as many delivery wagons as they could. Employees working in bucket-style brigades removed bolts of silks, satins, velour, and lace and threw the wares into the wagons, which took off for the waterfront. By 3:00 A.M., some $200,000 worth of the best merchandise had been saved, but along State Street the flames crept closer. After flames engulfed the Allen-Mackay Carpet establishment next door, Field asked Devlin to form a seven-man crew, go up on the roof, and flood the side of the building with water from fire hoses. At 3:30

A.M., the city waterworks caught fire and the water suddenly stopped. Flying embers set the Field & Leiter roof on fire. Devlin and his men fought their way down the stairway. Partners and employees were trying a last stand with their own pumping engine when debris from the burning roof knocked the engine out of commission. An explosion rocked the building. By dawn only twisted steel framing was standing above the ruins of red-hot ashes. Around them stores, banks, hospitals, public buildings, railroad depots, hotels, and houses burned, including the Palmer House and the "fireproof" *Chicago Tribune* building.

By noon Monday the North Division fires reached North Avenue, advancing to the northern limit of the city. In the afternoon, Field joined Mayor Roswell B. Mason, elected officials, and prominent citizens at the still-standing West Congregational Church and turned it into a temporary city hall. They arranged to enlist citizens as special deputies to provide food and water to the homeless. Mason signed executive orders freezing the price of bread and banning smoking. Tuesday morning a saving rain began to fall, and the flames finally died out. The homeless gathered in dazed groups on open stretches of prairie west and northwest of the center city, in the South Division along Lake Michigan, and along "the Sands," a patch of lakeshore just north of the river. Here, rich and poor were thrown together. A Chicago Historical Society chronicle tells how "Mr. McCormick, the millionaire of the reaper trade, and other Northside nabobs, herding promiscuously with the humblest laborer, the lowest vagabond, and the meanest harlot. Once they settled themselves, there was little they could do but bear witness to this calamity beyond comprehension." Gone were eighteen thousand structures. Three hundred people were dead and 90,000 were burned out of their homes.

It was two days before it was possible even to survey the damage. Ruins were so hot that when anxious businessmen opened their safes among the rubble of what had been their offices, the banknotes that had survived the inferno burst into flame. The North Division was the hardest hit, and a major portion of the German community was wiped out.

Pessimists were sure the city's business and trade would trickle away to Cincinnati, St. Louis, and New York. Before the $200 million loss of property could be added up, however, boosterism took hold. CHICAGO SHALL RISE AGAIN! the *Chicago Tribune*'s owner Joseph Medill proclaimed in the Wednesday edition, its first after the fire. After reports of bravery and a story of a chubby woman selling apples from a handcart among the ruins and after notices from survivors seeking missing wives, husband, and children, the paper carried bold ads announcing resumed businesses and promises of no price gouging. On the West Side, where the fire had skirted Washington Boulevard, people set up tables to sell clothes and bedspreads, stores and sewing machines. Medill ran for mayor on a "fireproof ticket" and was elected. Deacon William Bross, the publisher of the *Daily Democratic Press*, himself burned out of his home, rushed to New York to assure bankers and merchants that Chicago would survive. "The capitalists, the mercantile and business interests of this country and of Europe cannot afford to withhold the means to rebuild Chicago," he told the New York Chamber of Commerce. "Women, send your husbands," he roared. "Men, send your sons. You will never again have such a chance to make money."

Potter Palmer was the biggest loser of property, but he, too, rebuilt. Ninety-two of his buildings on which the rents totaled $200,000 a year lay in ruins. As a Quaker, he had never mortgaged any of his holdings. To rebuild he disavowed his faith's tenet against debt and borrowed $1.75 million from the Connecticut Mutual Life Insurance Company, at the time the largest individual loan ever made in Chicago. Up went a new and more sumptuous 650-room Palmer House hotel, with silver dollars embedded in the floor of its barbershop. It didn't take long before the fire was seen as the best thing that ever happened to Chicago. As Everett Chamberlin put it in *Chicago and the Great Conflagration*, published two months after the devastation, the fire was preface to greatness.

Harlow Higinbotham took the Field, Leiter bookkeepers and the ledgers to his mother's home in Joliet, Illinois, and began assessing the damage and how much of the losses insurance could be expected to pay. A hand-scrawled sign, erected in the midst of the ruins, announced: "Cash Boys & Work Girls will be Paid what is due them Monday 9:00 A.M. Oct 16th at 60 Calumet Ave. Field, Leiter & Co." The bottom line was reassuring. Of the $2.5 million loss of merchandise, various policies covered $2.2 million. Fearing the insurance companies themselves would be bankrupt within days, Higinbotham traveled to Cincinnati, St. Louis, and San Francisco to adjust claims. He returned three weeks later after collecting only $1.275 million, but another $170,000 seemed certain to come in, meaning the net loss amounted to just over three quarters of a million, which, according to the *New York Evening Post* July 22, 1872, edition, was proportionately less than the injury most Chicago businesses suffered. Creditors were told the company would honor its debt 100 percent.

Less than five weeks after the fire, the partners wrote to reassure H. Greenbaum, an out-of-town retail client of theirs, who was offering to help:

November 15, 1871

Dear Sir

We have your kind note of this date and can assure you that we shall continue our business in the same manner as before the fire, making our purchases in the future the same as in the last.

We have suffered some loss by the fire as you are aware, but our capital is ample to continue our business in the same magnitude for the future as during the past. We had kept our affairs very snug, making our entire purchases for cash, never in a single instance having given a note for merchandise. We are therefore today in good shape.

Before we received any money from insurance, we met our obligations promptly. This was done exclusively from our daily receipts from collections.

Thanking you for your kind note, we are

Yours very truly,
Field, Leiter & Co.

Field, meanwhile, found a new location in a section that hadn't burned. One story has it that he borrowed $100,000 from Cyrus McCormick. Company records, however, seem to indicate the partners squeezed by on the insurance money and the salvaged merchandise. Marshall found one of the few buildings available—a trolley barn on State and Twentieth streets. On the theory that the first merchants to reestablish themselves would make the most money, he got crews to clean out the streetcar barn, varnish the floors, and the paint the interior. Six weeks after the fire, Field and Leiter reopened in the huge car barn.

The *Chicago Evening Post* sent a reporter to cover the opening:

> Down State Street to Twentieth, and here is the largest dry goods
> store in the city or the West—Field, Leiter & Company. Here are
> hundreds of clerks and thousands of patrons a day along the spa-
> cious aisles and the vast vistas of ribbons and laces and cloaks and
> dress-goods. This tells no story of the fire. Ladies jostle each other
> as impatiently as of old and the boys run merrily to the incessant
> cry of "cash." Yes, Madam, this immense bazaar was, six weeks ago,
> the horse barn of the South Side Railroad . . . Here where ready-
> made dresses hang, then hung sets of double harness. Yonder
> where a richly robed lady leans languidly across the counter and
> fingers point laces, a manger stood and offered hospitality to a dis-
> consolate horse. A strange metamorphosis—yet it is but an
> extreme illustration of the sudden changes the city has undergone.

The city healed quickly. Relief from all over the United States and
foreign countries included money, food, clothing, construction
materials, and books. President Ulysses S. Grant sent a $1,000
check to the relief committee, along with an invitation to his
friend George Pullman and family to stay at the White House.
Like the Fields's home, the Pullmans's house was unscathed, but
George and Harriet accepted the invitation anyway. New York's
department store magnate Alexander Stewart, whom President
Grant had made Secretary of War, sent funds just as he had lav-
ished money to the potato famine victims in his native Ireland
twenty-four years earlier. Jay Gould and William Vanderbilt organized relief trains. With winter approaching, skilled workers who
had lost their homes were given materials to build single-family
wooden "shelter houses," and makeshift barracks were built for

THE BOOK ROOM IN THE OLD WATER TANK.

Rebuilding after the fire: the Water Tower as a library.

former tenement dwellers. The response to the call for books was overwhelming. Books sent to Chicago from England numbered over eight thousand. Private donors included Alfred Lord Tennyson, Benjamin Disraeli, and Robert Browning. The success of the English Book Donation prompted Field to petition Mayor Medill for a public meeting to establish a new public library. Rebuilding began, and new buildings of stone and iron sprang up in the old, burned-out city center.

Merchants waited to rebuild until Field made up his mind where he would locate a permanent new store. Before the fire, Field and Leiter had agreed to pay $425,000 for a property with

240 feet of frontage on Wabash Avenue, but the conflagration ended the deal. When Field and Leiter rented the refurbished five-story Singer building on Madison and Market (now Wacker Drive), property owners in the old center shuddered at the thought of the potential losses facing them by this northward move. Some merchants thought the partners had made a major mistake.

The April 25, 1872, opening was neither as splendid as the 1868 affair nor as humble as the trolley barn event, but 25,000 people visited during the day and evening. The new store was a third larger than the pre-fire premises, and new departments were added. The main floor was reserved for fast-moving fashion items, from silks and gloves to notions. The second floor was devoted to cloaks, shawls, woolens, and intimate apparel. Shoppers found carpeting on the third floor and, one floor up, upholstery and house furnishings, while general retail workrooms occupied the fifth floor. In the first year, the Field & Leiter Company's turnover reached $25 million, with profits of at least $1 million. Clerks reported to work at 7:30, a half-hour before the store opened, and were required to stay until 6:00 P.M. Sales personnel working overtime received "supper money," usually about 50 cents. Many decided to forego dinner and added the money to their $10-a-week salary.

Marshall and Levi had been in business on Market and Madison just over a year when the New York banking house of Jay Cooke and Company, the financier of the Northern Pacific Railway, collapsed. The enormous cost of the war, excessive railway building, inflated credit, speculation, overexpansion, and capital outlays for new farmland provoked a crisis on Black Thursday, September 18,

1873, when, in a domino effect, railroad bankruptcies and bank failures—five in Chicago—followed. Over 18 percent of the country's railway mileage was in the hands of receivers, iron and steel works were devastated, and business failures led to massive layoffs. Wages plunged by 25 percent. In the downward spiral of economic contraction, Chicago recorded a rising number of deaths from starvation. Homeless men and women wandered the streets and lined up for kitchens set up in working-class neighborhoods. Over the next four years business failures reached $775 million ($155 billion in today's money), and the number of unemployed rose to nearly three million—in a country of forty-five million. Legions of tramps, for whom the *Chicago Tribune* prescribed "a little strychnine or arsenic," drifted across the country in search of work and shelter.

Field and Leiter were also wholesalers. When their competitors cut off retailers who couldn't pay their bills in full, Field and Leiter sent out circular letters assuring country storeowners it was business as usual. Their reason for optimism was western wheat exports. "We see no cause for general alarm," they wrote. "The partial failure of crops in Europe, creating such a large demand for our breadstuffs and provisions, warrants us in assuring you of our belief that no action of bankers can long retard their movements, and as the business of the West is almost wholly dependent on the money realized for its products, it cannot suffer to any great extent . . . We do not at present anticipate any immediate change in values or merchandise." When the *Chicago Times* sent reporters out to interview bankers, stockholders, industrialists, and merchants, they found Lake Michigan shipping at a standstill, the Union Stock Yard and the Board of Trade barely functioning, but Marshall Field in an optimistic mood. "Trade is fair. It is quite as good as we have any reason to expect." When asked if prices would drop, a sly smile creased his lips. "We like to sell cheap," he said. "It pleases our customers." What he didn't say but quickly implemented was to speed up the inventory turnover. With money scarce, it was suicidal to try to sell a $1 item at $1.20 when, in the meantime, the item's worth had fallen to 80 cents. The way to stay in business was to keep inventories low, stock new and often, and sell at modest margins.

Field became a civic booster of his adopted city, Leiter not at all. Tellingly, when a *Times* reporter remarked that the partners were fortunate in making their business start in Chicago and surviving the 1873 panic as well as they did, Leiter said that if circumstances had started them in New York, their foresight and mastery of retailing would have resulted in an even greater success. As it was, much of the Field and Leiter profits came from their out-of-town business.

To accommodate western storeowners, Field & Leiter employed a formidable contingent of energetic and persuasive "linemen," also known as "whizbangers." "The business of a salesman is to sell," Marshall told his young wholesale chief, John G. Shedd. "But I want to sell to the best merchant in every town, and if I cannot get the best merchant in every town, then I want to get the next-best merchant in every town. And if I cannot get him, I do not want to sell in that town."

The mostly young, fast-talking linemen would arrive in a railroad town with their big sample trunks and set up miniature trade shows in the lobby of the local hotel. To reach smaller stores off the rail line, they traveled over dirt roads by one-horse buggy, and by bobsled in some of the mountain states. For a 2 percent commission plus salary, a lineman covered thirty towns on his semiannual tours, traveling by train and sending his trunks of samples ahead. If he sold less than $80,000 worth of goods a year, he was told to find another occupation. The best of them averaged $100,000 in sales. Above that amount, they received an extra 10 percent bonus. A lineman's first job was to keep his customer satisfied, and work with him and Higinbotham's credit department. If a store got into real trouble, wholesale sales manager George Young would recall, Field frequently sent a manager—usually one of the house salesmen—to help the merchant and to attempt to put the store back on its feet. A lineman also gathered intelligence, and not only about the creditworthiness of his clients. He was supposed to report back whether the governor in his state was liked, what his chances for reelection were, what the crop prospects were, and whether the banks were sound. Also within a lineman's purview were such chores as advising on land prices. William F. Hypes, who traveled in the Dakotas, was famous for staging concerts and singing at prayer meetings and county socials. An unnamed whizbanger who covered Michigan once wired headquarters that it rained so hard he was unable to sell anything. By return cable, he was told to sell umbrellas. In a week, he had orders for $3,500 worth of umbrellas.

5

INSTINCTS

THE "NEW WOMAN" OF 1875 FOUND HER WARDROBE AND ACCES-
sories at Field & Leiter. The financial storm did not hurt the
store, as the partners had little debt and used their line of bank
credits cautiously. More important, a nouveau riche elite sprang
up after the Great Fire and in trickle-down fashion dictated the
trends, vogues, and lifestyles for the less prosperous. The age of
railway travel forced fashion to jump ahead. Women abandoned
the cumbersome crinoline, an impossible garment for anyone getting aboard or alighting from a train, and went all out for form-
fitting dresses. For a decade, the newest craze demanded the bustle, the wasp-waist bodice, plumed hats, and watered silks and
satins. Petticoats were of a new sheer muslin, so sheer, according
to the Field & Leiter advertising, "that it outrivals the finest web
ever spun by the cunningest old spiders, having embroidered all

over its frail surface the brightest of small red and yellow butter-flies." Illustrated Field and Leiter ads featured the "ideal beauty," usually copied from fashion magazines with her perfect figure, lovely features, and fashionable dress. Daring girls followed dash-ing young men in riding bicycles, and emancipated women wore form-fitting costumes and on summer lawns beat their menfolk at croquet. Golf and tennis further influenced fashions. To keep his daughter Alice happy at home on summer afternoons, Harlow Higinbotham built a tennis court. The introduction of chemical-ly produced dyes for cloth allowed for more colorful, elaborate garments. When fans became a must, the store advertised "Paris and Vienna Opera Party Fans." Cosmetics followed.

The New Woman was the wife of a man who inevitably was doing well. She made a pilgrimage to Europe at least once every other year. American women possessed a natural love of shopping, according to a London trade journal. London women's magazines, especially *Queen*, published shopping guides that warned against bringing husbands along. Not all novelties traveled east to west, as European women adopted American underwear. Exponents of the Rational Dress movement campaigned for more comfortable clothes and less underwear. American girls led a more active life than their friends across the Atlantic, going for energetic walks and showing interest in sports. Gradually they threw away their corsets and began to discard some of their underclothing. To be able to advertise "unparalleled foreign imports," Marshall sent his broth-er Joseph to Manchester, England, to open a purchasing office. Joseph was a solemn, frugal man, and he was dependable. Some British contacts regarded him as mildly eccentric for refusing to ride in cabs and for wearing his topcoat in the office. He bought judiciously and forwarded his goods by fast boats, even if his choice of merchandise was not always the latest in chic.

Could the department store do better? Marshall decided to personally scout the Parisian and London salons. We do not know whether he brought Nannie along. Marshall II was seven and their daughter, Ethel, was one year old. Great ladies routinely left young children with nursemaids, and accompanying Marshall on scouting-purchasing expeditions might account for Nannie's later extended sojourns in France. We have no proof either way. Neither personal letters from Marshall to his left-behind wife nor wish-you-were-here postcards from traveling Nannie to friends at home have survived. A surviving business note from 1880 did announce a deal to distribute the Fortin Fils and Deschamps famous "Alexandre" kid gloves.

Croquet players in a Marshall Field's advertisement.

As the depression dragged on, Marshall advised hundreds of retailers to imitate Field & Leiter, to figure orders closely and to move goods quickly. An ironic consequence of this recommendation was to restrain his linemen not to oversell to storeowners. The lean times suddenly sharpened the competition in 1876 when the great A. T. Stewart opened a large wholesale operation in Chicago. Stewart could boast of New York prestige, huge capital resources, its own mills, and an unsurpassed foreign buying strength, with offices and warehouses in six European countries. Stewart advertising stressed two points: its supplies came from its own factories and mills, and would sell in Chicago at New York prices. Finding top-flight salesmen proved difficult, and Stewart began raiding Field & Leiter staff, starting with offering to double Higinbotham's salary if he would defect. Field had the satisfaction of seeing Higinbotham and most of the sales force stay loyal.

To avoid being undersold—wholesale and retail—Field & Leiter had to match Stewart's prices. Other wholesalers followed. "Prices on some leaders fell so low that Field and Leiter found that their losses were less when they bought certain items from their competitors, Carson Pirie & Company and A.T. Stewart and Company, who were themselves selling at a loss, than when they attempted to supply their customers through their usual sources," Robert Twyman would write in *History of Marshall Field & Co.* "An attempt was apparently made even to buy up part of Stewart's stocks on some items merely to force up the price by creating a temporary scarcity. This kept up until Stewart's refused to sell to Field & Leiter."

What saved the Chicagoans was the death of Alexander Stewart. As is so often the case in the death of a founding father, the demise of the seventy-three-year-old merchant in April 1876 threw the giant wholesale and retail organization into turmoil. He had made no provisions for a successor, and his empire declined rapidly, surviving its founder by less than six years. A. T. Stewart Company was liquidated in 1882. John Wanamaker, the owner of the Philadelphia department store that bore his name, purchased the remnant of Stewart's New York emporium. Wanamaker and Field had much in common and were friends as long as they stayed out of each other's home turf. Seriously or, more likely, in jest, Wanamaker said he might open a store in Chicago, to which Marshall famously replied that *he* was thinking of opening a Marshall Field's in Philadelphia. They had both started as salesman. Both added wholesale and manufacturing—the Fieldcrest Mills, located mainly in the South, would become Marshall Field's most famous manufacturing division.

If someone was jealous of Marshall's savvy and winning streak, it was his friend George Pullman. It irked the builder of railway cars that the half-owner of a dry goods establishment had more money than he. Pullman's office matched the opulence of his Palace railway cars. An oft-told anecdote has it that when a visitor complimented him on his elegant office, he said nobody could hire him to work in a cubbyhole like Field's. They called each other George and Marshall and were often seen together in the late afternoon or evening. They played poker at the Chicago Club, a luxurious retreat opposite the Monroe Street entrance of the Palmer House.

Marshall's routine rarely varied. After eight o'clock breakfast, he rode only part of the way to the State Street store in a carriage. Five or six blocks from the store the conveyance stopped, and he walked toward the Washington Street entrance. A policeman always spied him coming and informed the doorman. Word swiftly passed through the building. Field stayed at the retail store for several hours, and lunched at the Chicago Club. Pullman was usually there. So was Judge Lambert Tree, who dabbled in politics and whose son would marry Marshall's daughter Ethel. N. K. Fairbank, the club's venerable president, and Lyman Gage, president of the First National Bank and later U.S. Secretary of the Treasury, also lunched at the "millionaires' table."

Calamity hit Field and Leiter on a rainy night in 1877. On the evening of November 14, a blaze started on the top floor. It was only when the flames shot through the roof that a passerby saw the fire and turned in the alarm. Firefighters hooked their hoses to the hydrants only to discover the water pressure petered out halfway up the five-story building. The fire spread down the elevator shafts, forcing back employees who tried to douse the flames with hand extinguishers. Field, Leiter, and scores of employees rushed to the store. To repeat the effective 1871 evacuation of expensive merchandise, he ordered the staff to save what they could and company teamsters to load the rescued goods onto their wagons. Too many policemen, firefighters, onlookers, and clerks with armloads of merchandise choked the doorways, and the operation proved less successful than six years earlier. By 2:00 A.M., when the last of the flames were extinguished, the outer walls were standing, but the upper floors were gutted and the unrecovered stock in the basement and ground floor was either burned or soaked.

Coming up on the Christmas season, the lack of a store was even more disastrous than the $800,000 loss. This time, however, Higinbotham had prepared himself, taking out insurance policies not only in the United States and England, but in France and Germany as well. The total insurance on the merchandise and fixtures—the building was leased and not a Field & Leiter liability—adequately covered the losses.

To cash in on what remained of the holiday rush, the partners leased the huge lakefront Exposition Building, built for the 1875 Inter-State Industrial Fair, for $750 a month. Members of the city council protested that it was unfair to allow a "rich and well advertised" firm to pay only a quarter of the going rate. The rent was later revised upward to 3 percent of gross sales. During ten frantic days that November, a hundred carpenters replaced exhibition booths and old furniture with counters and shelves. The weather was wretched on opening day, November 27. Customers not only had to find the out-of-the-way location and brave mud and pools of water, they also had to stand in line. Shoppers came in such numbers that they were admitted in batches. Cheers went up each time guards and policemen at the entrances led in another contingent. By December 10, Field & Leiter announced that the store was completely restocked. To draw Christmas shoppers away from rivals on State Street, free omnibuses ran every five minutes from State and Randolph streets to the Exposition Store.

The lakefront exile lasted two years.

On the assumption that Field & Leiter—or some other high-profile tenant—would want the original State and Washington site, the Singer Manufacturing Company had wasted no time tearing down the burned-out ruins of the 1871 fire and putting up a new building. Marshall was certain it was the best location in town and now began negotiations with Singer, not for a lease this time, but for an outright purchase of the new commercial structure. Singer wanted $700,000. Field and Leiter were willing to pay $500,000, but as the partners waited for the price to come down, rumors spread that the New York merchants Lord and Taylor were interested. Marshall was in New York hiring former A. T. Stewart chief of personnel C. P. Lyman to become the Field & Leiter personnel executive when the Singer negotiators asked

Leiter if he and his partner were ready to raise their offer. Thinking it was yet another ploy, Levi refused. The next thing he knew, their expanding rival, Carson Pirie Scott and Company, leased the building for $70,000 a year. Marshall rushed back, blamed Levi for being slow to see the threat, and huddled for days with the Singer people and the two industrious Scotsmen, Sam Carson and John T. Pirie. Field and Leiter ended up not only agreeing to pay $700,000, but also personally had to pay an additional $100,000 to break the Carson Pirie Scott lease.

On April 28, 1879, the public was once more invited to a Field & Leiter opening. "The general expression upon meeting an acquaintance connected with the store was 'Home again eh?' accompanied by congratulations," wrote the *Chicago Tribune* the next day. Home this time was a six-story French Renaissance building with a mansard-style roof crowned with eight cupolas. A huge skylight over the central well flooded daylight through all the floors down to the main aisle. Each floor around this shaft featured imposing columns, railings, and bracketed cornices. Sales aisles were wider, displays more intricate, and attention was paid to customer comfort. The second floor had waiting rooms for ladies and, behind potted palms, a first—lavatories. Under Lyman's vigilant eye, five hundred clerks greeted customers. Lillie Langtry, the English actress famous for her great beauty, patrician liaisons, and American tours, was among the customers.

Prosperity returned. The opportunities opened to capital in the West and South, as well as the general influence of machine production, led to economies of scale never seen before. Marshall Field and Levi Leiter emerged triumphant from fires and cutthroat competition. The leadership of their Chicago department store and their wholesale operations throughout the West was undisputed.

Field's next move was to get rid of his partner.

6

MARSHALL FIELD & COMPANY

THE KINDEST SPIN ONE CAN PUT ON LEVI Z. LEITER'S DEPARTURE
is to say he wanted to do what so many of Chicago's *nouveaux*
riches did—"retire" and go into real estate. A less charitable view
of the end of the fourteen-year partnership is to acknowledge that
the two men had grown apart, that Marshall increasingly found
Levi wanting. We do not know what Leiter thought of Field, but
there can be no doubt that the uneven partnership grated on him.
Marshall always owned the larger share of their company. On the
strength of his sixty-thirty majority—and his talent for retailing—
he took the initiative and arrogated major decisions for himself.
Not that either partner could complain about the rewards of their
success. Both were freshly minted millionaires. Both had invested
excess capital in real estate.

During the two years at the lakefront, property values rose

and fell on rumors that they might or might not move back to the State and Washington location. When they did and the two men personally bought the renovated Singer building, they leased it to Field & Leiter Company for $50,000 a year, escalating to 6 percent on $700,000 for the land and 8 percent on $300,000 for the building. Leiter's inattention to Carson and Pirie had almost cost them the building, but it was not the only reason Field wanted to end the partnership. Levi never shared Marshall's enthusiasm for the retail end of the business. Nor did he possess his partner's suave manners. Coming back from a business trip, Marshall realized that Levi's brusque personality was losing them business. One customer, he learned, had entered the store and ordered $700 worth of goods. The client was paying cash, but Leiter shoved the man toward the door, saying, "Your record is bad." Levi suspected the worst of anyone who dyed his hair, barring the way of one patron, saying, "You are a thief. Your mustache is dyed—so get out of here!"

When Leiter made an argument for abandoning retail, it seemed, on the face of it, unassailable. Why bother displaying wares to a snobbish and fickle clientele in a store that required a workforce of five hundred? Indeed, why bother with a retail store at all? The big money was in wholesale. Thousands of storeowners from the Alleghenies to the Pacific depended on Field & Leiter Wholesale for their seasonal stock. While retail sales climbed steadily, the wholesale business went through the roof. In 1867, retail sales totaled $1.4 million while the wholesale figures climbed to $7.6 million. This seven-to-one ratio was the same five years later, when retail sales reached $3.1 million and wholesale sales topped $14 million. Unfortunately for Leiter, the senior managers, from Harlow Higinbotham to Henry Willing and Loranzo Woodhouse, the head of the busy New York office, thought the argument naïve and lined up behind Field. The store was the locomotive that pulled the whole train. It was the façade that gave glitz to the back office operations. The ostentatious display of big-city fashion was the straw in the wind, the novelty the linemen traveled on, the tonic storeowners in turn offered their customers. Not only that, the store's reputation allowed them to charge more for what they sold, retail *and* wholesale. Take away the cachet of the department store and a bolt of Field & Leiter gingham was no better than the bolt of tissue sold by their State Street neighbors Charles Gossage and newcomer Edward J. Lehmann or the Mandel brothers—Simon, Leon, and Emmanuel—on Clark and Van Buren. Without the flagship store, they were warehouse jobbers, no better than their lowliest competitor.

Field had little trouble persuading Higinbotham, Willing, and Woodhouse to see things his way and, with Leiter's consent, made them junior partners. At the time of the three men's promotion, Field contributed 55 percent and Leiter 41 percent of the working capital. The trio of junior partners was further enlarged to include Marshall's two brothers Henry and Joseph. Investment bankers thought the five junior partners were something of a joke insofar as they never put money into the firm. An anecdote that survived them all had it that when asked what he would do if one of the junior partners were to leave, Field replied, "Hire another office boy."

The partnership agreement Field and Leiter had signed in January 1867 included the following proviso: If for any good and just cause Marshall Field and Levi Z. Leiter shall become dissatisfied with either of the other partners, the remaining partners may at their election take their interest in said firm by paying them its cash value. Their agreement, always set for a limited number of years, was coming up for renewal in January 1881. In a tactical move stage-managed by Field, his brothers, Higinbotham, Willing, and Woodhouse asked for a larger percentage of the profits. Marshall endorsed the five individual demands. Next, he canvassed members of the sales staff, telling them he intended to either buy out Leiter or sell out to him. After key employees said they would leave if Leiter became the owner, Marshall confronted Levi. He offered to name a figure at which either of them could buy or sell the business to the other. Levi agreed, having no choice. With the junior partners all pledged to Field, Leiter would have to buy out all of them. Marshall's $2 million figure was so low that Levi smelled a rat, and asked for time to consider. Field gave him twenty-four hours. Levi discovered what his partner no doubt wanted him to discover: that none of the key men would stay if Field left.

Opening his copy of the *Chicago Times* the next morning, Levi discovered a detailed analysis of the partnership, including real estate figures that he had supposed were confidential and now appeared in blunt type, with each partner's estimated share in the company to be worth $3 million. Field swore he had not leaked the figures. In Marshall's presence, Levi telephoned Wilbur Storey, the editor of the *Times*, requesting an interview with the man behind the figures. The culprit was Frederick F. Cook, the paper's real estate editor. No doubt staged for the benefit of the two partners, Cook was hauled into Storey's office to face his boss, Field, and Leiter. Levi wanted to know what possessed Cook to give out details of their business. Cook answered that it was legitimate news. Perhaps to mollify Levi, Marshall said, "We have been large patrons of the *Times* and you should have considered our interests." Cook shot back: "Mr. Storey does not expect his reporters to consult the counting room before they report the news. But tell me, why, specifically, do you object to publicity about your real estate holdings?" Field thought for a moment. "Because, I don't care to be made a target for socialists to fire at."

Had Field read the *Chicago Tribune*'s interview with Karl Marx? Two years earlier, the newspaper had sent a correspondent to interview the sixty-year-old author of *Das Kapital* in his Haverstock Hill villa in northwest London. To the question, Did socialists favor assassinations and bloodshed, Marx answered:

> No great movement has ever been inaugurated without bloodshed. The independence of America was won by bloodshed, Napoleon captured France through a bloody process, and he was overthrown by the same means. Italy, England, Germany and every other country gives proof of this, and as for assassinations, it is not a new thing, I need scarcely say. Orsini tried to kill Napoleon; kings have killed more than anybody; the Jesuits have killed; the Puritans killed at the time of Cromwell. These deeds were all done or attempted before socialism was born. Every attempt, however, now made upon a royal or state individual is attributed to socialism.

Closer to home, Henry George's trenchant indictment of land speculators and absentee landlords was capturing the imagination of many Americans. The economist and one-time Democratic candidate for mayor of New York asked: Why should increasing poverty accompany increased civilization? Back in the 1820s, the egalitarian ideas of Robert Owen, the pioneer of British socialism, had enjoyed an American following when Owen founded the cooperative community New Harmony in southern Indiana. In the 1840s, the social system advanced by François Fourier got a foothold in Brook Farm, a utopian community in West Roxbury, Massachusetts, which attracted support from Nathaniel

Hawthorne, Margaret Fuller, and Albert Brisbane. Socialism was predicated upon communal or government ownership and control of production and distribution of goods and services, yet it didn't necessarily imply the abolition of private property. Early Christians believed that all property should be communally owned, and the societies advocated in Plato's *Republic* and Thomas More's *Utopia* were also socialist in nature. George campaigned for a single-tax doctrine and saw his 1881 book *Progress and Poverty* go through a hundred editions in twenty-five years. It inspired single tax colonies, including one in New Jersey where Upton Sinclair would later live.

The socialism that agitated Field and his friends George Pullman, Philip Armour, and the McCormicks was not the theories of Anglo-Saxon intellectuals, but seditious theories coming into the country in the baggage of the huddled masses. To Field—and to a majority of native-born Americans—socialism suggested furtive immigrants with Central European accents, sinister facial hair, and bombs. The rich, the privileged, and the successful rarely emigrate. Why should they? It is the poor and the adventurous with little to lose who uproot themselves and seek a better life elsewhere. New York and Chicago were the twin magnets for immigrants, but Chicago was also the stronghold of revolutionary anarchism. Almost all the German and Czech immigrant workers were either socialists or anarchists (by 1890, persons of German parentage in the Midwest reached four million). Chicago had five anarchist newspapers—one daily and four periodicals. Various groups fused into the Workingmen's Party of the United States in 1877, the year the Socialist Labor Party was founded. Farmers resented railroads and moneylenders, and Joseph Pulitzer's *New York World* consistently criticized the powerful and the wealthy and drew attention to the poverty and suffering in the cities. Field was not the target of organized labor; Pullman and McCormick were. However, within a few years of gaining control and renaming the emporium Marshall Field and Company, he would arm his own employees against angry workers.

Levi Leiter walked away from the partnership with $2.7 million—over half a billion in 2002 money. He had many more millions invested in stocks and real estate, and happily joined the leisure class. While Marshall went to the office every day, Levi and his family enjoyed themselves. The social aspirations of Mary Carver Leiter soared with her husband's wealth. She was determined that her three daughters should marry aristocrats. Not well-educated, she was given to malapropisms. After one stormy Atlantic crossing, Mrs. Leiter declared herself pleased to be "back on terra cotta." On another occasion she announced that her husband would attend a fancy-dress ball "in the garbage of a monk." When the Leiters weren't in Paris, London, or St. Petersburg, they entertained at their big house on Calumet Avenue or spent time at Linden Lodge, a $200,000 showplace they built at Lake Geneva, Wisconsin, the fashionable summer community seventy miles north of the city.

The major aggravation for Levi and Mary was their son. Joseph Leiter spent millions of his father's money to corner the wheat market during the winter of 1897–1898, a dream of many commodity brokers. Unfortunately for young Joe, Philip Armour, the meatpacker who was also a spectacular plunger in the wheat market, decided to bring in extra wheat. A mild early winter allowed Armour to buy and ship in Canadian wheat. When the Sault Ste. Marie Canal finally froze over, Armour had it dynamited. Joe lost $6 million—some claimed $10 million—of his father's money, forcing Leiter Senior to sell some of his real estate holdings to Field.

Levi and Mary moved to Washington, where they rented the grand Blaine House on Dupont Circle. Mary was a special friend of Frances, the wife of President Grover Cleveland, and invited to parties given by the Theodore Roosevelts, the Hays, and the Whitneys. Levi's pride was his three daughters, Irene, Mary, and Nancy. Their parents followed the fashion among rich Americans of marrying off the daughters to British nobility. Eldest daughter Irene became the Baroness Ravensdale, and Nancy married the nineteenth Earl of Suffolk. Mary married George Nathaniel, Earl Curzon of Kedleston, in 1895, and her father's $1 million dowry brought a welcome relief to his lordship's heavily mortgaged properties. Three years later, when he was named viceroy of India, Lady Curzon was called the most beautiful vicereine when, on a cool, clear December morning in 1898, she stepped off the ship in Bombay. A generation later, George Nathaniel and Mary's daughter Cynthia was to marry Sir Oswald Mosley, founder of the British Union of Fascists. Her death at thirty-five would spare her a divorce from a philandering husband and the news that his marriage to Diana Mitford, sister of author Jessica Mitford, took place in Berlin, with Hitler in attendance.

7

PAID TO THINK

THE "OFFICE BOY TODAY, PARTNER TOMORROW" APPROACH
yielded spectacular results. For everyone of ability, Marshall Field
proffered the opportunity to scale the ladder of promotion to any
of the higher positions, including partnership in the firm. His
poise and energy as a merchant were an inspiration to ambitious
young men, and he began to write brief and pithy essays, advising
newcomers never to give a note, never to buy a share on margin,
and never to mortgage their holdings. He counseled young businessmen to hold their customers to a strict meeting of their obligations. Give the best quality for the least money, he suggested.
Sell on shorter time than competitors. Twice a week, he toured
the wholesale division, carrying a small writing pad and a pencil.
When he strode through the retail store, he passed out advice to
his employees. Quality is remembered long after price is forgot-

ten, he admonished. And, of course, remember, the customer is always right.

Department heads were told to reward employees for showing initiative. "Marshall Field and Company was in Chicago to make money, and each employee was expected to contribute directly or indirectly to that end," the store's historian, Robert Twyman, would write in 1954. "According to the degree to which he succeeded he might expect promotions. If he failed he was either released or transferred to another position. But in any case he could not expect continuous directions from above as to what moves to make. Field employees, within the limits of their responsibilities, were hired to think and to act, not simply to take orders. This independence of action was especially apparent—and most conspicuously success-ful—at the department head or 'buyer' level." Contracts with John G. Shedd, who rose from salesman to department manager, and Dixon Bean, head of the wholesale and retail carpet departments, show how the company financed its expansion, how departments were assessed for the floor space they occupied, how they paid 6 to 8 percent interest on the capital, and how the department heads could price their goods as they saw fit. If they miscalculated, they had to cover any loss. If they made profits, they received a percent-age of their department's earnings. The retail buyers worked on a straight salary, but their duties were much the same.

Shedd was a replica of the boss, down to the New England origins, first job in a Rutland, Vermont, store, and, following his older brothers, the westward exodus, and a $300 stake when he arrived in Chicago in 1872. "Sir, I can sell anything," he answered when Field asked what he could do. Shedd got to prove it in the wholesale division. After selling $10,000 worth of merchandise in seven months, he saw his salary raised from $14 to $17 a week ($280 to $340 in today's money). He managed to put aside $5 a week and at the end of his first year proudly showed Field that his bankbook savings had reached $260. Shedd had a passion for work and believed profitable business should be equated with high ethics. He was an omnivorous reader of inspirational literature and, like his boss, spouted epigrams. "The great highway to success lies across the summit of enthusiasm," he admonished, quoting Emerson's saying that nothing great is accomplished without enthusiasm. "The way to health," he said, "is in keeping the mind young by a new and greater interest in each day. There must be no catchpenny tricks to boost inferior wares." He studied management techniques and manuals, and was allowed to go through the books to check sales in various lines for several years back. This led to planned inventories and seasonal purchases. He worked with manufacturers to select what colors and sizes should be produced and in what quantities, and surrounded himself with top-notch assistants. By 1890, he was the head of the wholesale operation and earning $5,000 a year ($100,000 in 2002 money).

Field thought of himself as an enlightened employer, and compared to his friend George Pullman, he was. Department store employees and builders of railway cars were rarely recruited from the same labor pool. Salaries at Marshall Field's were slightly above average, and the incentives for advancement were a powerful motivating force. The boss, John Shedd would remember, "had an amazing faculty for reading character and could gauge a man with extraordinary accuracy. Occasionally he would make a mistake in his man, but the instances were extremely rare. He would look a man in the eye, ask a few questions, talk a little, and he seemed to have plumbed the depth of his character. 'I don't think he's just our kind,' he used to say when examination of a man was unsatisfactory. The phrase in itself was significant of the standard required."

Neither Field nor Pullman tolerated organized labor's growing efforts to improve workers' condition. They were convinced that the ten-hour workday—let alone an eight-hour day—would ruin the country, that efforts to unionize were criminal. To them and to most nineteenth-century empire builders, the idea of employees having a say in how long they should work and how much they should earn was outrageous. Marshall was horrified in June 1877 when railway workers struck because the New York Central and Pennsylvania Railroads reduced wages by 20 percent. Baltimore & Ohio followed suit and provoked a general railroad strike that degenerated into one of the bloodiest battles in American labor history. In Pittsburgh alone, union vandals torched locomotives, cars, and buildings and fought pitched battles with the police and militia. Coming in the fourth year of an economic depression, the strikes brought the country closer to class revolution than at any time before or since.

The job action started in Martinsburg, West Virginia, and swept across the country with explosive suddenness. Tens of thousands of angry workers closed down packinghouses, lumberyards, rolling mills, and foundries, attacking strikebreakers, setting fire to railroad property, and fighting pitched battles with police. Chicago's newest newspaper, the *Daily News*, churned out Strike Extra! editions and doubled its circulation. Field told his Chicago Club fellow members that the railway rebellion was no doubt the first skirmish of a socialist takeover of the country and the *Daily News* was fanning the flames of anarchy. He got Levi Leiter to lead a deputation to the offices of Victor F. Lawson, the owner of the *Daily News* and its morning sister paper, the *News-Record*, and, with the *Tribune*'s Joseph Medill, the city's most powerful opinion-maker. Lawson proved less than accommodating when Leiter asked him to suspend publication, at least temporarily. Leiter insisted that by printing extras, Lawson was playing into the anarchists' hands. Lawson refused. Two days later, workers at McCormick's plant walked out. The action spread to the slaughterhouses and meatpacking plants on the West Side. Rumors flew that meatpackers were marching on downtown, meat cleavers in hand. Field, Leiter, and J. V. Farwell put up money to hire Allan Pinkerton and his private detectives and guards. Pinkerton liked to tell how he had been "a poor lad in Scotland, buffeted and badgered by boorish masters," and his career for some years after his arrival in Chicago in 1842 had shown sympathy for the underdog. In 1850, the chief purpose of the Pinkerton's Detective Agency had been to help runaway slaves escape to Canada. During the Civil War, President Lincoln had assigned Pinkerton to organize the United States Secret Service. After the war his agency turned to guarding industrial property, protecting strikebreakers and spying on trade unionists.

What frightened Field, the McCormicks, Pullman, Armour, Mayor Monroe Heath, and the civic leaders was that in Chicago the strike was spontaneous, hotheaded, and leaderless. Mayor Heath deputized and armed thousands of men, closed the city's saloons, cabled Washington for federal troops, and rang the city's fire bells to summon militia companies to duty. Marshall ordered all employees in the wholesale building to be drilled in handling weapons, and put the firm's dray horses and delivery wagons at the disposal of police and armed deputies for dispatch to trouble spots. At home on Prairie Avenue, he and his neighbors formed street patrols, fearing that mobs would fan out to attack and loot the privileged. A massive show of force that exacted the death of hundreds of workers—thirty in Chicago—caused the uprising to fizzle. What started on a Tuesday was over by Friday.

There was more to come.

* * *

Field's knack for putting together a superb workforce and his forward-looking strategies impressed businessmen far beyond Chicago. By 1890, his wholesale and retail company grew to become an organization with a workforce of twenty thousand. "Despite this rapid increase, the firm had an amazing ability to retain throughout the years the loyalty and devotion of its employees," Robert Twyman would write in *Marshall Field & Co.* in 1954. "The paternalistic interest in their subordinates which caused the partners of the firm to provide for illness and retirement compensation, clean locker rooms, recreational facilities, and medical care was only a small part of the store. For the increasing numbers of women hired by the store Field's provided a 'respectable' place to work. Consideration was shown for their limited physical capacities, need for somewhat shorter hours of labor, and desire for clean, attractive restrooms and dining facilities."

Three-day strikes notwithstanding, the times were, for men like Field, splendid. There were no wars, no natural disasters. There were no income taxes, and the federal government's biggest problem was what to do with a huge Treasury surplus. The general prosperity of the 1880s offered businessmen inducements to grow. The opportunities for fortunes to be made were irresistible, while all attempts to organize labor were undercut by immigration. Half a million newcomers came through Ellis Island every year, ready to replenish the labor pool. Forty percent of them never got above the poverty line of $500 a year. To survive, they, their wives, and their children all worked twelve or more hours a day.

Field believed Chicago was on its way to international prominence, and readily echoed the "Aim high" motto of Daniel

Burnham, the master city planner, architect, and greatest builder in Chicago's history. Skyscrapers were invented in New York, but Chicago was the nurturing ground of the first theorist of high-risers. In 1885, the architect and engineer William Le Baron Jenney designed the ten-story Home Insurance Building at LaSalle and Adams streets (now demolished), thereby earning the title Father of the Skyscraper. Burnham, Louis Sullivan, and many of the Chicago School architects served their apprenticeship on the staff of Jenney, a New Englander like Field who had opened his Chicago office in 1868. It was his development of a fireproof steel skeletal structure capable of withstanding the attendant loading of a tall building that established the skyscraper as an identifiable form.

Burnham's partner, William Root, had studied at Oxford and taken an engineering degree at the University of New York. The 1873 panic had hit the partners hard, but they had managed to keep their young firm afloat, doing business, as he said, with a couple of pencils, a piece of rubber, a few boards, two stools, and a dozen thumbtacks. After a number of commissions from various Chicago millionaires, they built skyscrapers, including the twenty-two story Masonic Temple on State and Randolph streets—the world's tallest building in 1890—and in 1903, New York's Flatiron Building. After Root's premature death at forty-one, Burnham embraced classicism and was asked to offer plans for improving Cleveland, San Francisco, Chicago, and Baltimore. He wanted Chicago to emulate the grand boulevards Georges Haussmann had carved out of medieval Paris. His plan called for broad avenues, museums and theaters, a series of islands just offshore, and a lakefront civic center. Famous for getting things done and for moving projects forward, he was entrusted with planning the 1893 Chicago World's Columbian Exposition. Here, he transformed sandy, clay-filled tracts on the south shore of Lake Michigan into the "White City" of faux-marble expo palaces and exotic carnival streets. Thirty-seven-year-old Louis Sullivan designed the fair's Transportation Building, soon to be seen as the beginning of modern architecture. Christopher Columbus's descendant, the Duke of Veragua, came from Spain. So did replicas of the *Santa Maria, Niña,* and *Pinta.* Paderewski gave piano concertos, Sousa's band thrilled. A pair of gasoline-powered buggies staged a twenty-mile race to Evanston. Neither made it to their destination.

To coincide with the Fair, Field opened a new addition. Success meant new customers, and the 1879 store had to be enlarged. When it came time for yet another expansion in 1902, Burnham designed the new, present-day block-long and block-wide Marshall Field and Company store. The store was a temple of allure, luxury, and conspicuous consumption.

Largely out of sight, the wholesale division was transforming the company into a giant distributor. It also outgrew its back office space. In 1885, Field had commissioned Henry Hobson Richardson, the prolific architect called the father of modern architecture, to design a square-city-block wholesale building. A Louisianan of Field's generation, Richardson had studied at Harvard and the Paris École des Beaux Arts and designed the Trinity Church in Boston, and the Allegheny County buildings in Pittsburgh. For the seven-story Marshall Field Wholesale Store, he used massively modeled stonewalling and semicircular arcading to produce a vigorous geometric design. He repeated the arcades design inside the building to give it open spaces. While the finished granite and brownstone structure was massive, its

lines were clean. There were no exterior ornaments or roof pen-
dants. Louis Sullivan pronounced the building a work of great
strength and coherence.*

Field didn't forget Burnham. In 1893, Marshall was among
the society guests who honored the architect with a spectacular
banquet at New York's Madison Square Garden. Burnham made
plans for the Gimbel brothers, John Wanamaker, and Edward
Filene, and although his plans for their stores were much alike,
the Marshall Field and Wanamaker buildings especially echoed
the Roman and Renaissance palazzo traditions. Aesthetics and
environmental reform, he told Field, had benefits for commercial
and financial growth. There were no contradictions among beauty, efficiency, and material prosperity.

Joe Girard and Lou Bachus were the new doormen greeting
out-of-town merchants on opening day, June 20, 1887, of the new
wholesale building. Inside, storeowners not only found the goods
that had made the Marshall Field brand famous, but such novelties as carpet sweepers, cutlery, musical instruments, diapers and
baby strollers, opera glasses, and mattresses. Several department
heads were legendary. Dan Hill, in charge of the silks, was a
showy salesman. In contrast to Field's insistence on studied courtesy and staid formality, Hill would buy five thousand pieces of
silk at his own expense and send COME AND GET IT invitations to
merchants. In three days the entire stock was sold. Roland P.
Marks was another star of the sales floor. Famous for his actress
girlfriend and flashing diamond rings, he did $2 million a year in
black cotton and silk stockings. Frank Ames, who came to work
on horseback, headed the thriving carpet section.

The victims of Marshall Field and Company's triumphant

---

* The building was torn down in 1930.

growth were smaller competitors. On a very minor scale compared to John D. Rockefeller's predatory elimination of rival oil-
men, Field dealt a mortal blow to small-scale merchants and
altered the size and scope of retailing. Each new department put
retailers out of business, since Marshall Field's inaugurated cutlery, jewelry, hosiery, millinery, gloves, and men's underwear
departments with splashy advertising, cut-rate prices, and, on
occasion, so-called loss leaders, items sold below cost. Already
profitable departments soaked up the red ink the new sister
departments incurred in selling below cost. A contemporary
observer noted that "Chicago is honeycombed from end to end

The competing advertisers of the day on January 4, 1883:
Marshall Field's, Schlesinger & Mayer, and Mandel Brothers.

with elderly men who twenty years ago had businesses of their own in retail stores by which they expected to make a living of their own and to have a competence on which to retire in their old age."

Field lured retailers too big to be put out of business to congregate on State Street. He offered the Mandel Brothers a lease on the property on the northeast corner of State and Madison, which he had owned since 1873, and encouraged the Schlesinger and Mayer store to move to a building that Leiter had acquired in the breakup of the partnership on the southeast corner of State and Madison. Next, he acquired the remaining property on the block bounded by State, Washington, Wabash, and Randolph streets, and in 1887 bought Leiter's remaining interest in the State and Washington land and building. After six additional purchases were recorded in 1892, he began a vast construction program that led to the expansion of the Marshall Field store over the entire block and to a twenty-story Field annex building on Wabash and Washington. Leiter twice sued his former partner—in one case requiring Field to physically divide into two halves a jointly owned building. The lawsuits did not change the course of history, but Marshall wouldn't forget.

8

MILE-A-MINUTE HARRY

BEFORE HARRY GORDON SELFRIDGE CROSSED THE ATLANTIC AND
opened London's first American-style department store, he spent
twenty-five years at Marshall Field's. He thought of himself as
God's gift to women, and certainly was an inspired contributor to
the store's renown, distinction, and bottom line. He teemed with
ideas, talked for effect, and understood that the way to sell was to
excite the mind's eye. Ten times a day, he rushed through the aisles
and, if he liked what he saw, dangled a gold chain. If a shopper
complained, he listened patiently, and assured the lady she was
absolutely right. By 1887, when he was twenty-nine, he was made
"retail general manager" and occupied an office more elaborate
than Field's. Selfridge's presence and celebrity permeated the
store. Chicago's new millionaires' wives, many of them accus-
tomed to shopping in London and Paris, knew what they wanted.

Harry Selfridge.

Field knew *what* to sell them. Mile-a-Minute Harry knew *how*.

Born in Jackson, Michigan, the son of a widowed school-teacher (his father had disappeared after the Civil War), Selfridge was a handsome bespectacled bachelor with a rakish mustache and sideburns who dressed in a wing collar and expensive frock coat with a gold chain attached to his vest. He presented himself as a supporter of women's emancipation and called the department store "a comfortable resting place in which urban women's bodies could be satisfied, indulged, excited and repaired." Shopping should be a pleasure, he said, not a chore. He invented imaginative advertising and modern displays, ripped out counters and high shelving, piled assortments on tables in the center of the ground floor, and started the practice of annual sales. When shoppers arrived for Selfridge's "special sales," they found the show windows he had decorated looking exactly like his full-page advertising in the *Chicago Tribune* and the *Daily News*. He set up workrooms where a shopper could leave her glasses to be ground, her gloves to be cleaned, her jewelry and shoes to be shined. Field's had been the first major store in Chicago to switch from gaslight to electric illumination. Harry installed many more electric globes. He tripled the number of telephone lines and installed a central switchboard with lines to every department. When the Democrats and Republicans held their 1884 conventions in Chicago, he printed souvenir booklets with space for tallying votes and invitations to delegates to visit the store.

His smartest brainstorm, copied by department stores the world over, was the bargain basement. The store cellar had been used to sell marked-down goods that had gone out of fashion or didn't sell well. Transforming the basement to a vast "bargain center," Harry told Field, would not only lure people of modest income but, as they and their children climbed the social ladder, turn them into upstairs customers. He tinkered with names like Annex Department and Branch Department before settling on Budget Floor. To eliminate any perceived stigma of shopping on the cheap, his advertising proclaimed that Field's was keeping up with the times. Shoppers by the thousands inundated the bargain basement when it opened in 1885. The campaign marked a turning point in retail marketing. The lure of styling made Selfridge drop conservative and dignified advertising for exuberant, eye-catching come-ons. He wrote much of the copy himself. He also persuaded Field to spend $25,000 on newspaper space, a fivefold increase. Not all of Harry's ideas met with approval. Field vetoed the idea of an in-store restaurant until 1890, when Harry was finally allowed to open a tearoom. Within a year the seventh-floor tearoom had to be enlarged as fifteen hundred customers a day clamored for corned beef hash, chicken pot pie, orange punch in an orange shell, and Field's ice cream, Rose Punch, which featured a red rose on each plate.

He brought his mother, Frances, to Chicago and found an exclusive apartment for her at 1430 Lake Shore Drive. He was all neatness and elegance, and retail employees loved to be on the Selfridge team. He knew how to inspire people, made his staff feel part of the store's success, and never criticized a salesperson in the presence of customers or other clerks. "There was no big front to Selfridge with the help," said Homer Buckley, who had started in the shipping department. "He was dashing, impressive, and cut quite a figure in the town, but he'd let young men, especially, in the firm argue with him. He would drop in at your desk, sometimes all of a sudden, sit there and talk ten minutes, ask about this

A Marshall Field's advertisement for fans, circa 1890.

and that, debate a thing with you, never talk down to you—and the result was you'd be thrilled for a week. I would literally walk on air for two weeks after he'd done this at my desk. I never met a man capable of putting such inspiration into his employees." Recrimination was not his style. A much-repeated anecdote had him showing a friend through the glassware department when a cleaner fell from a ladder into a showcase of Bohemian stemware. Every glass was smashed. When the man scrambled to his feet unhurt, Harry turned back to his companion, saying, "As I was saying."

Stories of his appealing ways with customers accumulated over the years. He accompanied Glover Cleveland and Theodore Roosevelt through the store, and knew how to placate and win back ladies who, after perceived slights or real misunderstandings, swore never to shop at Field's again. Eighteen-year-old Isadora Duncan, newly arrived from San Francisco with her mother, one trunk and $25, was told that if she wanted to perform her Greek dances at the Masonic Roof Garden she should get herself some frilly costumes. When she entered Field's, asked to see the manager and told Selfridge her Masonic engagement depended on her wardrobe, he gave her material for petticoats and lace frills with which, billed as The California Faun, she scored her first success.

He used his considerable persuasive powers to make Field agree to an expansion and to let him travel to Europe for inspiration and ideas. The Bon Marché department store in Paris impressed him the most, and he sent back a flow of reports to Field. Back in Chicago, he sent underlings to Macy's in New York and Wanamaker's in Philadelphia, which carried everything that could be sold for a profit. The cost of buying, advertising, selling, and delivering did not seem to increase in proportion to the quantities of goods sold. If new merchandise could be introduced and sold without an equal increase in expense, Harry argued, it added to the profits. Besides, they had to keep up with the times.

The store had inaugurated free delivery service in 1872. In 1897, Field ordered a clock large enough to be seen for blocks to be mounted above the State and Washington corner entrance. When the eight-ton clock was installed by clockhangers dressed in black suits and dignified bowlers, the *Chicago Tribune* took notice. "Projecting as it [the clock] does, several feet from the building, it will be very conspicuous, especially at night when it will be lighted from within." It gave birth to the phrase "Meet me under the clock." The *Saturday Evening Post* immortalized it with a Norman Rockwell painting in its November 3, 1945, issue.

Field was stingy with praise. Said Harry, "Often I prevailed upon him to do things, take chances, much against his will, and when they came off, he seldom was inclined to unbend and confess that, perhaps, he had been wrong. I fancy he always regarded me as a young man in a great hurry."

Selfridge was earning $20,000 a year in 1889 when he asked to become a partner. Perhaps the reason was that he was contemplating marriage. His fiancée was Rose Amelia Buckingham, a Chicago girl who was accorded debutante standing in the *Elite News*. Field was not amused by the audacity of Selfridge's demand. "To say that Mr. Field was astonished and delighted," Harry recalled, "would be a gross misreading of that famous man's feelings. He was dumbfounded and rather angry." Harry's two-year term as retail general manager expired on December 31. To his surprise, when the new partnership was announced on New Year's Day 1890, he found himself included and given 9 percent of profits. The following November he married Rose. A thousand guests attended the wedding in the imposing Central Music Hall. The stage was covered with chrysanthemums and white roses, and a fifty-voice chorus, accompanied by organ and harp, intoned the nuptial music.

Harry's flamboyance provoked jealousies that Field was quick to slap down. The mocking was loudest in the wholesale division. Trying to ingratiate themselves with the boss, several managers ridiculed Harry's flashy work methods. To which Field pointed a finger at the ledger and said, "He may not be doing things to your liking, gentlemen, but he's making a lot of money for us. Are you?" Perhaps to mollify the head of wholesale, Shedd was also allowed into the partnership in 1893, the year Selfridge outdid himself luring World Exposition visitors to the store with hefty advertising and a block-long red carpet. Shedd's share was slightly ahead of Selfridge's. By 1900, Selfridge owned 9 percent of the business and Shedd 10 percent. Yet retail earnings were catching up with wholesale.

Urban America was expanding. In 1880, Chicago had a population of 500,000. Ten years later it had doubled to one million. Ahead of his competitors, Field realized that the railways and manufacturing in the West meant storeowners needed general wholesalers less and less. Stanley Field, Joseph's son, who started as a messenger in wholesale at $5 a week and stayed with the company sixty years, would remember his uncle telling him wholesale "is a dying business; the trend is to retail." The insight proved prophetic. John V. Farwell and Company's wholesale section collapsed in 1925, and Carson Pirie Scott and Company closed its wholesale division in 1941.

9

NANNIE

THE BEST KNOWN OF CHICAGO'S BARGAIN BAZAARS WAS THE
Boston store. A popular 1890s ditty spelled out the difference:

> All the girls who wear high heels
> They trade down at Marshall Field's
> All the girls who scrub the floor
> They trade at the Boston store

With Selfridge in inspired control of the store and John Shedd
running the wholesale division, Marshall Field wanted to redis-
cover the wife he had neglected in pursuit of success. His early
years had been hard and self-denying, but now he had the means
to be a man of leisure. His emotional makeup, however, prevented him from discerning his wife's needs and aspirations, and her

timid rebellion against Victorian rectitude had already set them apart. Very much a Madame Bovary romantic, Nannie was unhappy in the marriage to a man who bent everything in his life to making money and was never there for her. The conventions of her day left her with few options. She dutifully bore him two children, Marshall Junior and Ethel, and was a capable and popular hostess. Her mercurial nature, however, was a disappointment to her husband, who wanted his wife to occupy a position commensurate with his rank. For the title of Chicago's First Lady, Nannie readily conceded that role to Bertha Palmer.

Mrs. Palmer, as she was known, was a remarkable woman, ahead of her time, regally beautiful and dazzling in her gowns and diamond tiaras. Born into an aristocratic Louisville, Kentucky, family that had relocated to Chicago, she was twenty-one, a radiant, convent-educated socialite, when she married the forty-four-year-old Potter Palmer in 1870. His wedding gift to her was the much-talked-about Palmer House nearing completion on State Street. The eight-story hotel was the tallest building in Chicago, and with 225 rooms, one of North America's largest. It was decorated with marble from the Carrera quarries in Italy, and featured hand-woven Axminster carpets and French chandeliers and candelabra. Over the years Bertha Honoré Palmer remade the city socially, as her husband had reconstructed it physically. An acquaintance of Mary Cassatt, she was introduced to Claude Monet and the leading Parisian art dealers and started a collection with a Renoir and a Degas. The Palmers began buying art in earnest in 1891, when she was named chairwoman of the Columbian Exposition's Board of Lady Managers. From Paris she brought back the most extensive collection of Impressionists in the New World, including paintings by Pissarro, Corot, and Sisley, and over thirty Monets. To have a place to hang the paintings, the Palmers built an addition to their home. The brownstone on the North Side was a forest of balconies and turrets. It had no doorknobs on the outside; nobody could enter unless a servant opened the door. Mrs. Palmer's friends were required to write for appointments.

Nannie was less flamboyant, but she, too, traveled and became a patron of the arts. The Palmers' marriage was cheerful enough for Potter to joke that should his younger wife remarry after his death, she would surely need his entire inheritance because no new husband could possibly afford her. The Fields's marriage was a slow-moving train wreck that went from heated words to alienation and separation. Migraines were the proverbial excuse for ill-loved wives to elude matrimonial duties and to retreat into fantasy, imagination, whim, or absence. After the Great Fire, Nannie went to Europe, ostensibly for her health. To keep her home, Marshall made her pregnant and built a $100,000 mansion. A daughter they named Ethel was born in 1873. Marshall Jr. was five when his little sister was born. More is known about the Prairie Avenue mansion than about the early childhoods of Junior and Ethel.

The site was on the lakefront, south of the city center. Philip Armour; financier Ferdinand Peck; pianomaker W. W. Kimball; International Harvester director John Glessner; President Lincoln's son, Robert Todd Lincoln; General Philip Sheridan, the commander of the Western Army Headquarters; N. K. Fairbank; and other plutocrats built on what was little more than a cow path running through sand dunes. Field envisioned South Park as a new residential district laid out with ornate boulevards and hired the architect Richard Morris Hunt to build a three-story French-style mansion at 1905 Prairie Avenue.

Hunt was the first American to study at the École des Beaux Arts in Paris. His facility with historical styles earned him com-

1905 Prarie Avenue.

missions designing the luxury dwellings that William H. Vanderbilt and John Jacob Astor III erected on New York's Fifth Avenue, and the Breakers, the Italian Renaissance palace the Vanderbilts erected in Newport, Rhode Island. Marshall hired him because he thought a fellow New Englander would know the virtues of frugality and common sense. Field told the architect he wanted no frills, that he deplored the ostentatious splendor of Pullman's home a block away and Cyrus McCormick's huge residence. The end result did sumptuous justice to the brocaded decorum of Belle Époque affluence. Nannie found it bleak and depressing. The residence, the first in Chicago to be wired for electricity, felt like a dressed-up monastery, she said.

Arthur Meeker, the son of the Fields's immediate neighbors at 1815 Prairie Avenue, who wrote his first book when he was seven, would publish a lively memoir of growing up on "the street of the stately few" and, without naming names, tell how a number of the street's most respected matrons "had queer histories attached to them." "One of the most dignified had been a cigar-stand girl in a 'downtown' hotel before her marriage; others had even more lurid secrets. A certain fabulously prosperous widow was said to have owed her prosperity less to her late husband's acumen than to the generosity of the husbands of her friends," he wrote in *Chicago with Love: A Polite and Personal History*. "Men went quietly insane in several of these grim old houses and took their lives for business or personal reasons. More marriages were failures than not; since divorce was unheard of, there was nothing to be done except bear one's lot as gallantly as one could. In their old age the millionaires' relicts were liable to take to drink or drugs; I myself have seen antique wrecks, with staring, myopic eyes, tottering in and out of their carriages, up and down those perilous flights of front steps, on their nurses' or companions' arms."

Young Arthur's mother, Grace, and Nannie became friends. Arthur and his two sisters were the same age as Marshall Junior and little Ethel. Here is how young Meeker remembers Nannie:

Tall and willowy, she was the first woman in the Middle West to wear a teagown. Chicago considered it unconventional. She had, furthermore, a penchant for asking celebrated actors and musicians to her parties, not primarily as artists engaged to perform for a fee, but as personal friends. Chicago considered that Bohemian, or worse. When annoying society palled she could always, apparently, fall back on the reliable amusement of quarreling with Mr. Field . . . As time went on the scenes became more frequent and painful till finally Mrs. Field, unhappy, at loose ends, hopelessly estranged from her husband, went abroad to live.

If a teagown was considered unconventional on corseted Prairie Avenue, it was no doubt because this long dress, usually made of silk and lace-trimmed, was loose-fitting. A teagown evoked intimacy, Bohemia, and the influence of Japanese art. Whistler, Beardsley, Van Gogh, Toulouse-Lautrec, Renoir, and Bonnard were all inspired by the *Japonisme* and liked to paint women in intimate scenes.

Field's no-frills directive to his architect didn't extend to the interior, where Nannie had her say. A circular staircase of carved wood spiraled upward from the end of the central hall. Visitors remarked that the ivory and gold drawing room with its high ceiling would form an appropriate setting for state receptions.

Arthur Caton, a noted lawyer and the son of a chief justice of the Illinois Supreme Court, lived one street over at 1910 Calumet Avenue. His wife, Delia Spencer Caton, was pretender to the throne of Bertha Palmer. George and Harriet Pullman lived at 1729 Prairie Avenue. The widow of the economist Edward P. Kellogg resided at 1923, and the Armour family at 2115. Phillip Armour, a brusque, hard-edged big man with a volcanic temper and mercurial moods, was, with Gustavus Swift, the most famous of the Union Stock Yards meatpackers. What Pullman's sleepers and dining cars did for travelers' creature comfort, Swift's and Armour's refrigerated cattle cars did for national food distribution. Railroads were reaching the cattle-rich range states, and urban populations were growing. Swift had seven of his sons join him in the business, and his daughter married a supplier's son. Armour expected his two sons to follow him into the roaring business. The younger, Philip Danforth Jr., did as he was told, but the quiet and bookish elder son, Jonathan

Ogden, went to Yale and Oxford to study architecture, and wanted to live in England. As his father told his stockyard crony John
B. Sherman, "Ogden was impressed with the fact that so many
Englishmen had a leisurely life on a small income, with a lot of
worthwhile things to do . . . [things] he would like to do instead
of grubbing for money, when we already had more than enough.
He thinks he should retire. I told him to be at the Yards in his
working clothes at 7 on Monday morning." When Philip Junior
died suddenly at the age of thirty-one, the first son reluctantly
agreed to take over a business he never developed a feel for. We
do not know whether Jonathan and Marshall Junior were friends,
but their stories were eerily parallel. Perhaps to foreclose any
ideas of evasion in his own son, Field bought the lot at 1919
Prairie Avenue for Junior's future home.

Nannie Field, 1882. *(Chicago Historical Society)*

As wife, mother, and hostess, Nannie valiantly tried to breathe life into the house. She welcomed leading personalities to dinner parties. When Oscar Wilde came to Chicago in 1882 and permitted himself to be lionized, Nannie was among the select people invited to a reception. Other celebrities she got to know were a pair of visiting actresses, Sarah Bernhardt and Helena Modjeska. Two things impressed la Bernhardt: the hospitality of Potter Palmer and the "butchering of the hogs, a horrible and magnificent spectacle."

Chicago's society women formed a Fortnightly Club whose purpose was to be the spread of both "social and intellectual culture." Their husbands joined the Chicago Literary Club, but as the founder of the Fortnightly Club said, when a distinguished foreigner and people from other parts of the country come to Chicago, they wanted to meet the representatives of society people. "They don't care about being bored with a lot of men who have a local reputation as men of genius. They want to meet persons whose names are known as men and women of fashion." Mrs. Herbert Ayer was one woman who dared rebel against the city's prim conventions. Harriet Ayer was a student of ceramics and antiques who, it was noted with disapproval, read French novels in the original and at parties at her home staged French plays. She entertained unconventially at Sunday morning breakfasts where she served *omelettes aux fines herbes*, chicken livers *en brochette*, black coffee and wine. Her guests included such stage celebrities as Edwin Booth and Lawrence Barrett, the matinee idol of the 1870s. When her husband's business failed, it was felt that his downfall carried a moral for the eccentric behavior of his pretty wife.

On Sundays, the Fields occupied the front pew of the First Presbyterian Church. The *Sunday Herald* sent a reporter to the church once to do a "pen portrait" of the great merchant:

The wonderful executive ability of this man is reposed in a figure compactly built, firm and of medium weight, some five feet nine inches in height, with an excellently developed head over which has blown more than two score winters. His bright-blue, restless eyes, his keen, bargain-driving New England nose, his erect carriage, quiet manners, impressive silence and stylish getup have made him for years a remarkable man.

One of the social centers of the Prairie Avenue set was the Washington Park Race Club. On the annual June running of the American Derby, the first fashionable event of the summer, Field, Palmer, Pullman, and others gathered with their families to form a cavalcade of shining carriages making their way to the racetrack.

Bertha Palmer.

"In the grandstand, before the betting began, all eyes would be on the line of landaus, stanhopes, drags, victories, and tandems that rolled off the boulevards onto the club's carriage drive," Donald L. Miller would write in *City of the Century*. "Potter Palmer was always the scene-stealer, arriving one year in a French charabanc, with leopard skins covering its seats. The tails of his slim and majestic horses fashionably blocked, their heads reined high, their curried bodies shining."

Bertha and Potter Palmer found Prairie Avenue too close to the Illinois Central shunting yards and to the new steel-rolling mills further south and on their own created a new "Gold Coast" north of downtown, a move that set Prairie Avenue on its eventual course of decline. Potter bought a stretch of Lake Michigan dune and marsh on the North Shore, had clean sand pumped in from the bottom of the lake, convinced the city to run a through street—later called Lake Shore Drive—and invited friends to form with him "a community where there had been wilderness." It took two years to build his residence at 1350 Lakeshore Drive. Finished in 1882, the sumptuous Italianate castle of turrets, towers, and minarets was by far the largest, most expensive home in Chicago. The interior centerpiece was a spiral staircase rising eighty feet into the main tower and completely superfluous, as the house included two private elevators, the first ones installed in a Chicago residence. After the huge castle was finished, Potter built a row of magnificent graystone houses and rented them to those of wealth and taste who might wish to become Bertha's and his neighbors.

Social life on Prairie Avenue was stuffy. The same families invited each other to soirees of gossip and formal dancing. Chicago's historian Donald L. Miller retells how a number of society women described the conversations at these gatherings as all about books and "ideals," but led by the men, which meant the talk invariably turned to business. To be up on the latest schottische, waltz, polka, and quadrille of local origin known as the Prairie Queen, Mrs. Pullman organized private dancing lessons in her ballroom. The instructor was Eugene A. Bournique, the master of Chicago's most fashionable dancing school, and the students the city's first couples, including the sons of two presidents, Frederick Dent Grant and Robert Todd Lincoln. General Philip Sheridan, the commander of the Potomac Cavalry and the victor in the Shenandoah Valley battle that led to Confederate General Robert E. Lee's surrender, carried his military steadfastness into the ballroom. Jennie Otis Counselman confided after a series of turns with the general that "as he stepped on my toes and did not reverse until I was dizzy, I concluded many who were not heroes danced better."

On New Year's Day 1886, Nannie gave a memorable party for eighteen-year-old Marshall Junior and thirteen-year-old Ethel. The Richard D'Oyly Carte company's production of Gilbert and Sullivan's *Patience* had been a phenomenal success in Chicago the year before, and with the tunes of Gilbert and Sullivan's *The Mikado* on everybody's lips, Nannie christened her event a "Mikado Ball." As the young guests, all in Mikado costumes, and their parents dashed up Prairie Avenue toward the dazzling electric lights, they were redirected from the front door. Coming in by the side, they saw the reason: a life-sized copy of the backdrop for the second act of *The Mikado* filled the entrance hall. Young Marshall's guests numbered two hundred of his own age; Ethel's equaled that number, and the assortment of parents brought the crowd to over five hundred, some from the upper-crust families of Baltimore, Boston, and New York. Nannie scored a social and diplomatic coup by persuading James Whistler, who distilled Japanese influences in his paintings, to design two of the favors that were distributed along with toy animals, lanterns, parasols, Japanese slippers, and ornamental storks.

Police records and newspapers kept Chicagoans informed of life in bordellos and gambling houses and of the criminal doings, but the society pages were limited to fawning reports on who was seen where, dressed how, and giving which teas and parties. The 1905 Prairie Avenue household was doubly shielded. Not only was its owner the richest man in town, his store was the biggest advertiser. Not too coincidentally, the *Chicago Tribune*, the Chicago *Daily News*, and the Chicago *Examiner* augmented their women's pages with profiles of society leaders, professional women, girl athletes, and household hints. The *Tribune's* fashion, gossip, society news, marriage advice, and various "special services" such as meal planning first appeared on Saturdays, then on Sundays, and finally throughout the week. The parties and balls that Bertha Palmer and Nannie Field gave sometimes made the front page.

What was *expected* of a Mrs. Field can be gleaned from a series of advice books. The sisters Catherine Beecher and Harriett Beecher Stowe's *The American Woman's Home, or, Principles of Domestic Science; Being a Guide to the Formation and Maintenance of Economical, Healthful, Beautiful and Christian Homes* was the most noted of all household manuals. From the middle of the nineteenth century until 1930, titles such as Mary Elizabeth Sherwood's *Manners and Social Usages* and Irene Davison's *Etiquette for Ladies* went through edition after edition. The Harris & Morrow publishing house brought out *The Bon Ton Directory: Addresses and Hours of Reception of the Most Prominent and Fashionable Ladies Residing in Chicago and its Suburbs*. A wife should never act contrary to her husband's inclinations. She should receive his wishes with attention, and execute them as quickly as possible. She should act promptly, and in affectionate manner, if she had allowed herself to run into an ill humor.

Nannie never had control of family finances. Marshall was not ungenerous in supporting his wife when she traveled, but didn't think a woman should be in control of a fortune. He was scandalized when Potter Palmer left his fortune to Bertha. "Imagine, leaving her everything," he said. "A million dollars is enough for any woman."

Bertha Palmer might have the Swedish impressionist Anders Zorn do her portrait in the manner of John Singer Sargent, but she, Nannie, and the wives of the other merchant princes and robber barons were not the grand ladies in Sargent paintings or in the fiction of Henry James and Edith Wharton. They exuded little of the mystery, power, privilege, and conceit of the Vanderbilt and Astor women, whose houses, wardrobes, and affectations the parvenus tried to copy. Industrialists were often awkward in glittering surroundings and did not encourage their wives to join the "champagne aristocracy." John D. Rockefeller might control 85 percent of the country's oil business, but Laura Spelman Rockefeller never outgrew her devotion to duty and thrift and, as her husband became the richest man in the world, retreated into her strict Baptist religion. Helen Miller, the daughter of a prominent New York merchant family, was shocked when she married Jay Gould and found her husband vilified in the press, hounded by sheriffs, and linked with the most famous and infamous men of the time. Like Nannie, Helen suffered from a "nervous disposition," and her health began to fail. A pulmonary disease killed J. P. Morgan's first wife, Amelia Sturges, four months after they were married. He and his second wife, Frances Tracy, lived in dif-

ferent worlds and she grew increasingly unhappy. Andrew
Carnegie waited until he was fifty-two to marry twenty-eight-
year-old Louise Whitfield, a woman he called a Connecticut puri-
tan. Millicent Willson Hearst, the wife of newspaper tycoon
William Randolph Hearst, stuck to her assigned role and never
publicly rebelled against her husband's thirty-year affair with
Marion Davies. Adelaide Childs Frick figured only in her taciturn
husband's chronicles as a nursemaid after his ruthless union-bust-
ing in Pittsburgh led to an assassination attempt.

Ironically, Nannie had a shining example of feminine power
among her friends. She was Nettie Fowler McCormick, the first
American woman to assume leadership of a major business. Cyrus
was forty-nine when he married twenty-six-year-old Nettie. Both
were devout Presbyterians who taught their children to give to
the poor. Cyrus died in 1884 and Nettie lived another forty years,
presiding at business conferences and unofficially directing
Harvester International even after their son Harold was named
president and married John D. Rockefeller's daughter Edith.
Nannie got to know Nettie when both they and their husbands
were in New York. "Nannie Scott Field had leaned on Mrs.
McCormick's sympathy in her despairing grief over the death of
her first child," Nettie's biographer, Stella Virginia Roderick,
would write in 1955, adding that Nannie poured out her suffer-
ings to "Dearest Nettie" in letters and calls.

The Fields were guests at the affairs of influential
Chicagoans. On the occasion of the 1889 opening gala of the
Auditorium Theater, Mrs. Field was one of the social arbiters
consulted by the Chicago *Tribune* on the suitability of low-cut
evening gowns. Edith Harrison, the mayor's wife, told the
enquiring reporter that a plunging neckline no longer suited a
woman by the time she became a grandmother. Diplomatically,

Nannie said every woman would have to decide for herself, but that she didn't wear décolleté. "As I never wear jewelry of that kind myself I always have the necks of my dresses cut high," she added. "Of course it is all right for women who have handsome necklaces to cut the dress low enough to display them," she added. "I never wear a low-necked gown myself and hold that a slender woman's appearance is vastly improved by the Bernhardt style of dress. I really think that quite as dressy an effect can be produced by omitting the sleeves."

We find Nannie curiously absent from the excitement that followed the act of Congress that decreed a Women's Building should be part of Chicago's 1892 World's Columbian Exposition. Sophia Hayden, a twenty-three-year-old architect, submitted the winning design for the building, dedicated to "direct attention to [woman's] progress and development, and her increased usefulness in the arts, sciences, manufactures, and industries of the world during the past four hundred years." Bertha Palmer was the president of the Board of Lady Managers, and Daniel Burnham was the Chief of construction. After President Grover Cleveland opened the expo on May 1, 1893, Bertha inaugurated the Women's Building.

Upper-class women who felt trapped by boredom sometimes took to bed and religion in self-defense. Contemporaries described Nannie as "ailing," but instead of bed and religion she turned to art and travel, and spent months convalescing in southern France. The Victorians had a term for her supposedly medical condition—neurasthenia. The ill-defined condition was characterized by lassitude, fatigue, headaches, and irritability.* Nannie

---

* Modern medical dictionaries translate "neurasthenia" as chronic fatigue syndrome with a variety of causes, including fibromyalgia characterized by encephalomyelitis occuring after a viral infection.

was reported to be a dope addict, banned by her merchant prince husband to avoid disgrace. The condemnation seems exaggerated insofar as Nannie's contemporaries in Chicago puffed on "Coccarettes," made of Virginian tobacco and Bolivian coca leaves, and acclaimed as a "nerve tonic and exhilarator, absolutely not injurious." Narcotic drugs were readily available in patent medicines, and were neither well regulated nor widely regarded as a social problem.

Not surprisingly, Nannie barely figures in the Marshall Field literature. John Tebbel spends thirty-one lines on Mrs. Field in his 1947 book *The Marshall Fields: A Study in Wealth*. While the 1954 *History of the Marshall Field & Co. 1852–1906* is the story of the department store, author Robert Twyman managed never to mention the tycoon's wife. Stephen Becker's 1964 biography of grandson *Marshall Field III* calls her "weak, debilitated in spirit and easy prey to a succession of minor ailments." Stephen Longstreet, writing eighty years after her death, would suggest Marshall and Nannie's marriage was a living hell. Without giving sources, the author-painter would write in *Chicago 1860–1919*:

> Their loud excruciatingly shrill battle scenes (even before the servants) were really something no good society would expect of them; so violent, such malice. Mrs. Field not only had actors and singers in as friends, those devastatingly common Bohemians, but she was the first respectable woman to wear a tea gown. Mr. Field got the harsh side of her tongue when he objected. The scenes became so violent that it was clear the Fields were destroying their marriage. No divorce, of course, but Mrs. Field went off to live in France.

A more sympathetic portrait appears in Arthur Meeker's 1955 memoir, *Chicago with Love*, although he, too, would mention

painful scenes between the Fields. Meeker would remember his
mother having long conversations with Mrs. Field. The Meekers
had two daughters and the talk was often about Nannie's daughter, Ethel. The last time the two women met, they agreed Nannie
had been born twenty years before her time.

Before Nannie went to France permanently, Marshall and the
children sometimes accompanied her to Europe. On such occasions the family always traveled on the White Star liner *The Baltic*
and occupied staterooms formally known as the Field Suite.
Mostly Nannie traveled alone. Like her husband, she was a
Victorian Presbyterian and, as far as we know, sublimated sexual
yearnings with a passionate interest in the arts. She liked the arts
of the Mauve Decade, the art for art's sake esthetics espoused by
Oscar Wilde, and, in France, the Art Nouveau and Impressionist
movements. One acquaintance who realized that Field's success
had somehow stunted his potential as a human being was Dr.
Thomas W. Goodspeed, the financial secretary of the Baptist
Theological Seminary. An astute judge of people, he persuaded
John D. Rockefeller to give $600,000 toward the construction of
a university in Chicago and got Field to contribute $361,000.
Field's personal tragedy, Goodspeed believed, was that he never
understood his own shortcomings. "He did not measure up to his
opportunities and his obligations," Goodspeed wrote in *University
of Chicago Biographical Sketches.*

Going on sixty, Field was still a graceful figure. Heavy dark
eyebrows that contrasted with his hair and mustache, which had
turned from chestnut brown to gray in his fortieth year, now
topped his steely gray eyes. "In repose, his features were sad; his
smile, when it appeared, was quick," Lloyd Wendt and Herman
Kogan would write in *Give the Lady What She Wants.* "The fore-
finger of his right hand was crooked slightly, and he habitually

kept this hand in his right vest pocket, hiding the stiffened finger. In this pocket he also kept a roll of one and five-dollar bills, with larger ones in the other pocket or in linen-lined envelopes in his coat. He was slightly bowlegged and a little stoop-shouldered, but he affected the walk of a military man, stiff and firm." He accepted his social position as something that was due him by virtue of his wealth.

His pleasures were those of his fellow capitalists—golf, travel in style, lunches in private clubs, not that he particularly enjoyed his club. It was merely a place he could be when he was not in the store to discuss the problems of commerce and worry collectively about the imminence of anarchist revolutionaries.

The great disappointment of his life was Marshall Junior, so different yet, all things told, so similar to the sons of his friends. The widowed Nettie McCormick was the power behind Harold's throne at the International Harvester. George Pullman was convinced that neither of his twin sons had what it takes to run a major corporation. Philip Danforth Armour never developed a feel for his father's business, and Joseph Leiter's failed attempt at cornering the wheat market had cost his father millions. If there was one bright exception it was young William Borden, the son of John Borden, with whom Field was a partner in a mining enterprise in Leadville, Colorado. The two investors had chosen Borden's engineer son to run the Colorado mine. The venture had yielded Field and Borden more than $1 million each. Marshall and Nannie's son, Marshall Junior, suffered by comparison.

Ignored and disliked by his father and cosseted by his mother, young Field grew up close to Nannie. He was certainly no Harry Selfridge, who was only nine years his senior, nor was he a second William Borden. To his father, he was a figure as pathetic as his mother, a neurasthenic who failed to take advantage of his oppor-

Marshall Field II.

tunities. Worse, he showed no interest in business. In young Marshall's own eyes, what he could look forward to was a life of complete subservience to a self-made millionaire father who was already a legendary figure. Junior, who turned eighteen in 1886, was a young man of fine mind for whom there seemed to be no place, no activity that required his presence. He shared his mother's delicate constitution, and was almost always described as "sickly" or "unwell," but the debility was never specified. If pressed, he admitted he suffered from asthma. He absorbed his mother's interest in the arts. At twenty-two he drifted off to Harvard, not because he wanted an education but because there seemed nothing else to do. This was in deep contrast to the father-son relationship of Senior's partner in a 20,000-acre iron ore deal in Vermillion, Minnesota, John D. Rockefeller. Young Rockefeller idolized his father and was loved in return. On his son's twenty-first birthday, Rockefeller Senior sent twenty-one dollars and a note saying, "We are grateful beyond measure for your promise and for the confidence your life inspires in us, not only, but in all your friends and acquaintances and this is of more value than all earthly possessions."

Daughter Ethel was the first to escape the stultifying atmosphere of Prairie Avenue by marrying and living abroad. Her husband was Arthur Tree, the son of her father's acquaintance Judge Lambert Tree. The young couple honeymooned in Great Britain and liked rural England so much they stayed.

In 1890, Marshall Junior made the acquaintance of Albertine Huck, the dark and lovely eighteen-year-old daughter of a Chicago brewer. Her father, Louis Huck, and his family had come from Baden-Baden in southwest Germany. The Hucks were not only "German" in Chicago's stratified society, they were Roman Catholic, and Albertine marrying the heir presumptive to the Field realm was enough of a first to be remarked upon. On their wedding day the bride had her husband promise they would bring up their children as Catholics.

Their honeymoon took them to Europe. On their own they thrived. After seeing how his sister and brother-in-law had settled in England, Junior and Albertine followed their example and leased a nearby estate. The two couples' choice was the rich valley of the Avon in Warwickshire and its spa resort of Leamington in Warwickshire. Ancient forest and pasturelands surrounded Leamington, where a 900-year-old oak traditionally marked the center of England. Queen Victoria enjoyed the waters of Leamington's saline springs. Ethel and Arthur lived at Compton Verney, near Warwick, and were devoted to English country life. They hunted with the best packs, and she in particular was well known as a first-class rider to hounds.

Nannie, too, decided to remain abroad, moving permanently to France in 1892. She found that the Riviera suited her delicate constitution, and satisfied her romantic impulses in art galleries, occasionally buying paintings. "Field's enemies circulated the rumors that she was a dope addict and that he had sent her away to avoid disgrace," John Tebbel would write in *The Marshall Fields* in 1947. "The truth was almost as pathetic. Nannie was simply a romantic whose dreams ended at the altar. She had everything in the world a woman could want, except what she wanted and needed most—the warmth of love."

Once a year, Marshall came to Paris for a few weeks to see her. His letters to friends were filled with reports on her health, sometimes sad and rather bitter, occasionally expressing the hope that her "chronic headaches" might vanish.

10

HOSTILITIES

TWO LABOR CONFLICTS IN WHICH MARSHALL FIELD AND COMPANY
was not the target turned its owner sharply to the right and made
him toy with the idea of running for president of the United
States in the 1900 elections. The first was a riot that became a piv-
otal event in the history of the labor movement, the second a
strike that paralyzed George Pullman's railway car company.
Marshall's fear of anarchy turned him into a heavy contributor to
the cost of maintaining the National Guard in Chicago and made
him twist the Citizens Association into an antisocialist alliance.
Ironically, the Citizens Association was started after the Great
Fire to improve city government and had attracted a handful of
liberals, including young Clarence Darrow, who would defend
John Scopes, the Tennessee high school teacher charged with
teaching the theory of evolution. Field's intervention in the

A generic photo of the founder that was handed
out to inquiring journalists at the store.

Pullman strike was energetic. As principal stockholder he took
control of the company and despite his hostility toward labor
unions, raised salaries and pushed through quality controls.

His enterprises grew astronomically during the 1880s. More
than three thousand employees swarmed over the thirteen acres
of wholesale floor space on Madison and Market. The retail store
covered all but one small corner of the State Street block. Besides
heading Marshall Field & Co., he was a primary influence in thirty corporations. Since the fortune he amassed in retailing, real
estate, railroads, banking, and manufacturing was only one-tenth
of Rockefeller's wealth (the Standard Oil founder's net worth
peaked in 1913 at $900 million, $190 billion in today's money), he
liked to say he wasn't really rich. Asked whether it was true that
he dominated thirty corporations in which he had interests, he

said, "'Dominate' is too strong a word. I own stock in all of them, and I am an officer in practically all." The reply prompted the enquiring reporter to say he'd characterize Field as a financial genius and a builder. To which the great man replied. "I'm a merchant, that's all you need to say."

In its campaign to win an eight-hour workday, the newly formed Central Labor Union, whose declaration of principles proclaimed that all land was a social heritage and all wealth created by labor, called a strike against McCormick in the spring of 1885. Sixty thousand workers responded. McCormick declared a general lockout and brought in three hundred armed Pinkerton guards to protect non-union new hires. For months, pickets clashed with the Pinkertons and policemen along a section of Blue Island Avenue near the McCormick plant. "It became a pastime for a squad of mounted police, or a detachment in close formation, to disperse with the billy any gathering of workmen," according to the *Centennial History of Illinois*. "It was the police, aided by the 'Pinkertons,' who added the great leaven of bitterness to the contest." The strike was a year old when, on May 3, 1886, police and Pinkerton guards opened fire on a meeting and left a number of demonstrators dead. A protest was called for the Haymarket Square the next day. The May 3–4, 1886, Haymarket Square bombing and the trial that followed turned Marshall Field into a champion of muscular law and order. After eight anarchists were sentenced to death for the bombing, he cowed fellow businessmen into opposing calls for clemency.

The rally started out peacefully enough, and a number of speakers addressed the crowd. Things got ugly when two hundred policemen moved in to break up the rally. Somebody in an alley threw a bomb into the crowd, killing some of the protesters. The police opened fire and hit demonstrators and fellow officers. Some

Mayor Carter Harrison.

of the workers who were armed returned fire. The shooting spree left seven policemen and more than twenty workers dead.

All known anarchists were rounded up, and ten men were indicted for the murder of a police officer. One of the accused turned state's evidence, while another proved he had left the Haymarket before the bomb went off and, after being released, fled the city. The trial of the remaining eight took place in an atmosphere of hysterical prejudice. "The newspapers, which had convicted the anarchists of murder before the proceedings had even begun," Paul Avrich would write in *The Haymarket Tragedy*, "demanded that the noose come quickly and with little ado. Public opinion, inflamed by the press, was at fever pitch against the defendants. It was said that neither person nor property would be safe until they were hanged."

The socialist activist and journalist Albert R. Parsons was the only native-born defendant, but, as the *Chicago Times* pointed out in its May 6, 1886, edition, he was "the husband of a negress." The other seven were German immigrants—August Spies, Michael Schwab, Samuel Fielden, Adolph Fischer, George Engel, Louis Lingg, and Oscar Neebe. William Perkins Black, a decorated Civil War veteran and corporate lawyer, headed the defense team. He had Mayor Carter Harrison testify that the demonstration had been orderly, with the wives and children of anarchists sprinkled among the crowd. State Attorney Julius Grinnell brushed such arguments aside by declaring that the law itself was on trial. "Anarchy is on trial," he declared in court. "These men have been selected, picked out by the grand jury and indicted because they were leaders. Gentlemen of the jury, convict these men, make examples of them, hang them and you save our institutions, our society."

The jury foreman and a witness for the prosecution were Marshall Field employees. M. M. Thompson testified he had attended the Haymarket demonstration and in the alley overheard snatches of conversations between Spies and Schwab. Spies had mentioned pistols and police, and Schwab had wondered whether one bomb was enough or whether they should go and get more. On cross-examination, Thompson admitted he did not understand a word of German. Another eyewitness told the court he had seen who lit the bomb, who threw it, and who was with whom, yet had not shouted a warning. Others contradicted him, including ten prominent citizens who testified that the witness was an inveterate liar and a police snitch. Parsons had brought his wife and their two children to hear him address the rally. As defense attorney Black pointed out, no sane person would bring his wife and children if he were going to set off a bomb.

Before the trial, Grinnell had discussed with friends the difficulty of convicting eight men as accessories when the murderer could not be found. Melville Stone, editor of the *Chicago Daily News*, had the answer: "The identity of the bombthrower was of no consequence, and that inasmuch as Spies and Parsons and Fielden had advocated over and over again the use of violence against the police and had urged the manufacture and throwing of bombs, their culpability was clear." The prosecution failed to show any connection between the eight and the unknown bomb thrower, or that any of them had ever seen or heard of him. No spectators were admitted when the jury returned with its verdict. Under Illinois law, the jurors were required not only to decide guilt or innocence but in the case of a guilty verdict, to set out the penalty. The jurors found Spies, Schwab, Fielden, Parsons, Fischer, Engel, and Lingg guilty as charged and sentenced them to death. The jury fixed the penalty for Oscar Neebe, a labor organizer, at fifteen years' imprisonment.

The *Chicago Tribune* echoed Marshall Field's sentiments—and those of newspapers throughout the country—when it proclaimed: "Law has triumphed. Anarchy is defeated." The journalist Henry Demarest Lloyd, who had married the daughter of the wealthy co-owner of the *Tribune*, William "Deacon" Bross, put it differently. The defendants had not been prosecuted for their deeds, but "for the violent insanity of their public speeches." This slap at the law-and-order rectitude so infuriated Lloyd's father-in-law that the Bross family cut him off. Undeterred, Lloyd began a national campaign for clemency. Nina Van Zandt, a Vassar-educated Chicago socialite, married August Spies by proxy after attending the trial.

Potter Palmer and Field's lunch companion and future U.S. Secretary of the Treasury Lyman J. Gage joined William C. Goudy, head of the Chicago bar; Stephen S. Gregory, future president of the American Bar Association; and Lyman Trumbull, Abraham Lincoln's old law partner, in signing a petition in favor of clemency. Clergy of national renown such as James Huntington, prior of the Order of the Holy Cross, and Rabbi Sabato Morais of Philadelphia also raised their voices against the executions. After the Illinois Supreme Court upheld the verdict, William Dean Howells, the country's leading literary figure, led the intellectual charge to save the seven from the gallows. Howells appealed to Governor Richard J. Oglesby for a commutation. Samuel Gompers, president of the American Federation of Labor, and twelve other labor leaders signed a public appeal and spoke to a rally in New York. Appeals, including a British petition signed by sixteen thousand, flooded Governor Oglesby's office. Sharing a London platform with Annie Besant of the National Secular Society and George Bernard Shaw of the Fabian Society, socialist William Morris said the Haymarket affair demonstrated that any hope of social betterment founded on existing American models was a pernicious fallacy. Karl Marx had died in 1883, but Friedrich Engels wrote to feminist Florence Kelly, "I only wish Marx could have lived to see this, the breaking out of class war in America."

For a governor of Illinois to commute a death sentence, state law stipulated that the condemned had to submit a formal appeal for clemency. After the United States Supreme Court denied a writ of error, thereby refusing to review the case, defense lawyers persuaded three of the eight to do just that. During the last days before the scheduled hanging, thousands of appeals deluged the governor's office. Many urged him not to spare the men's lives because the anarchists posed a challenge to society. During the last week before the scheduled execution, Oglesby told Lyman Gage that if the business community requested commutations, he was willing to pardon four of the eight.

As a supporter of clemency, Gage immediately called together fifty business leaders, including Field, informed them of the governor's offer, and urged them to join him in support of clemency insofar as the inviolability of the law had been vindicated. More important, he added, to hang the men would make martyrs of them and poison labor relations for years to come. Field spoke next. In one retelling, he merely said Illinois Attorney Julius Grinnell would speak for him. Grinnell, who in the hours after the Haymarket riot had advised police to arrest first and look up the law later, merely repeated what he had said during the trial: the anarchists should pay for their misdeeds with their lives. In another version of the meeting, Field himself stood up and said he was totally against commuting the sentences.

"After Field spoke, the meeting broke up," Avrich would write in *The Haymarket Tragedy*. "None cared to take issue with him. 'It was terribly mortifying to me,' said Gage. 'Afterwards many of the men present came around to me singly, and said they had agreed with me in my views and would have been glad to join in such an appeal, but that in the face of the opposition of powerful men like Marshall Field they did not like to do so, as it might injure them in business, or socially. In spite of the setback, public sentiment continued to shift in favor of the prisoners." Petitioners came away from meetings with Governor Oglesby believing he would commute the sentences. It was understood that he would announce his decision on November 10, the day before the scheduled execution.

On the morning of November 10, Louis Lingg used dynamite smuggled into his cell to blow himself up. Three hours after he died, Oglesby commuted the sentences of Fielden and Schwab to life imprisonment. He could do nothing for the remaining four, since they had not requested commutation. On November 11 at high noon, Parsons, Spies, Engel, and Fischer were hanged.

The funeral procession was the largest Chicago had seen. A crowd of more than two hundred thousand people watched twenty thousand mourners march behind the burial carriages to the Waldheim Cemetery on the far West Side. Police forbade banners and flags, but as the procession made its way down Milwaukee Avenue, a Civil War veteran in uniform stepped in front of the marchers and unfurled a small American flag bordered in black crepe. A police officer tried to pull him from the procession, but a group of workers knocked the policeman down.

Like the Dreyfus affair in France a decade later, the Haymarket hangings quickly led to reform. While President Grover Cleveland was not successful in encouraging a labor commission to mediate disputes, state legislatures began providing for arbitrations and passed laws regulating factories and child labor. While radicals embraced the martyrdom and in many cases dedicated themselves to easing suffering, socialist ideas spread, even among Western farmers, who resented the railways' powers. In rural minds the railroads were a single monster monopoly, "a great ring that wrings the sweat and blood out of the producers of Illinois," as *Chicago Tribune* publisher Joseph Medill had told a state convention in 1870. Howells published *A Hazard of New Fortunes*, whose villain is a greedy businessman rising to great wealth and whose hero is beaten to death during a transit strike. Edward Bellamy reached bestsellerdom with his utopian science fiction novel *Looking Backward: 2000 to 1887*, in which he invented a benevolent collectivist society. Sales were phenomenal after Bellamy's ideas became one of the leading subjects of conversation. A number of imitations followed, including Brackford Peck's *The World: A Department Store*, which told the story of life under a cooperative system.

By the 1888 election campaign, agrarian reformers agitated

against the railroads and urban anarchists and socialists denounced predatory economics. Henry Demarest Lloyd wrote the first serious expose of Standard Oil. He accused Rockefeller of controlling two U.S. senators and of corrupting the Pennsylvania legislature. "America has the proud satisfaction of having furnished the world with the greatest, wisest, and meanest monopoly known in history." With protests against oil, whiskey, sugar, and other cartels growing, politicians realized there were votes to be had in opposing big business, and although there was no shortage of clergymen ready to bless the piling of huge fortunes, Protestant ethics still viewed fast money to be distasteful if not immoral. Evangelicals deplored the lopsided distribution of wealth and denounced gilded avarice. The Sherman Antitrust Act followed the election of General Benjamin Harrison as the country's twenty-third president. The full force of the antitrust law—sponsored by Ohio senator John Sherman, brother of General William Tecumseh Sherman—would not be seen until the famous breakup of the Standard Oil in 1908.

Farm and labor votes gave Illinois its first Democratic governor since the Civil War in 1892. Born in Germany, John Peter Altgeld was three months old when his parents brought him to the United States and settled in Ohio. After a stint in the Union Army during the Civil War, Altgeld read the law and was admitted to the bar in 1872. His ambition was to become a senator, the highest office to which a foreign-born citizen can aspire. A few months after the Haymarket riot, he was elected a judge of the Cook County Superior Court. There was nothing he could do, since the trial was not in his courtroom, but what he saw was an appalling miscarriage of justice. Field would repeatedly clash with Governor Altgeld.

*   *   *

Pullman and Field were a study in opposites. Where Marshall was reserved, reticent, and methodical, George was loud, domineering, only at ease when talking about himself, and, in business, most often acted on emotions. What they had in common was attention to detail. After establishing plants across the country, Pullman built a whole town on the edge of Chicago for making railroad cars and named it after himself. The site he chose was an empty stretch of marshland on the northern shore of Lake Calumet. The unpromising-looking location had three advantages: the land was cheap; trains coming in and leaving the city from the east and south ran directly through it; and the federal government had begun dredging the river and improving the harbor site on Lake Michigan, making it possible to land big ore and lumber boats. Completed in 1881, the City of Pullman (later part of Chicago) was designed as a model industrial town. In contrast to the workers' slums in most industrial areas, Pullman offered sturdy brick houses on paved streets with modern gas, sewer systems, water, and electricity and company-approved stores for his four thousand workers and their families. Socialists and liberals were not the only ones denouncing Pullman's workers' paradise. Marcus Hanna, the pudgy campaign manager and architect of Ohio Governor William McKinley's Republican victory in the 1896 elections, called Pullman a cold-hearted, cold-blooded autocrat. "Oh, hell," he said, "go and live in Pullman and find out how much he gets sellin' city water and gas 10 percent higher to those poor folks." In the depth of the slump, the town became the focus of one of the country's bitterest labor disputes.

Railroads burned money on a colossal scale. Textile mills, the country's largest manufacturers, rarely cost more than $1 million ($18 million in 2002 money), whereas the capitalization of the four big east-west trunk lines—Pennsylvania, Erie and Northern

Pacific, New York Central, and Baltimore & Ohio—reached $140 million (over $25 billion today). E. H. Harriman, the boldest proponents of the spend-money-to-make-money strategy, poured a rousing $240 million ($4.8 billion today) into expanding and modernizing the Southern Pacific Railroad. Three months after President Grover Cleveland began his second Democratic term in 1893, railway overexpansion provoked a cascading collapse of the economy that, until the 1929 Wall Street Crash, was known as the Great Depression. The 1893 slump brought down the Erie, other debt-ridden railroads, and six hundred banks. It embittered the already discontented farming regions, and exhausted the silver-mining states. Massive layoffs brought poverty and suffering, sharpened class tensions, and took George Pullman totally by surprise.

With railways canceling orders, he dismissed most of his workforce and slashed the wages of his remaining workers. What he didn't cut was the laid-off workers' rent in the city of Pullman. In May 1894, the workers went out on strike. Within a month, members of the American Railway Union, led by Eugene Debs, refused to work on trains that had Pullman cars attached to them. This action extended over twenty-seven states and territories from Cincinnati to San Francisco. The *Chicago Tribune* scolded Pullman for refusing to negotiate with his workers and berated Governor Altgeld for initially sympathizing with the strikers. Rioters in Chicago burned millions of dollars in railroad property. Altgeld mobilized a regiment of Illinois troops, but when he refused to use his militia against the workers, President Cleveland's Attorney General, Richard Olney, himself a former railway lawyer, ordered federal troops to the scene, on the constitutional grounds that they were necessary to prevent interference with interstate commerce and the postal service. National

Guardsmen, who were paid by the railroads, stormed Pullman's workers' paradise. Seven strikers were killed. Union leader Debs was jailed. The courts issued a sweeping injunction requiring all American Railway Union members to return to work.

George Pullman rehired only workers who signed a non-union pledge and had the rest blackballed throughout the railway industry. Field was appalled at the way his friend treated his workforce. He was no less a conservative than Pullman, but he was steeped in work ethics and his approach to business was unemotional. Where Levi Leiter and Potter Palmer had chosen to rest on their laurels, he continued to labor. He believed that with a talent for making money came obligations to reward those who applied themselves. Over George's bitter objections but with the backing of fellow stockholders, Marshall assumed control of the Pullman company. He hired accountants, investigators, and experts who unearthed corporate fraud and outstanding contracts that couldn't be met. When he had all the facts in hand, he raised wages across the board and told the workers that management would reciprocate reasonable actions on their part. Adapting his give-the-lady-what-she-wants dictum (he was a director of three railroads: Chicago and Northwestern, Chicago Rock Island, and St. Paul, Chicago, Burlington and Quincy railroads), he offered to build rolling stock to specifications and introduced quality control. "The result seemed pure magic," Tebbel would write in *The Marshall Fields: A Study in Wealth*. "Almost overnight the labor revolts ended, new construction contracts were made, the company absorbed its chief rival and entered a period of exceptional prosperity."

Pullman himself came away a sick and resentful man. Half of his $40 million fortune was squandered on the labor strife, and he died three years later. Paranoid about revenge from his workers, he had ordered that his grave be lined with concrete to foil grave robbers. He didn't trust his wife, Harriet, or his four children any more than his former employees. He left his twin sons an annual income of $3,000 each, commenting that neither had the talent "for wise use of large properties." Harriet successfully sued to claim the principal of the fortune.

Nannie died. No death certificate has survived detailing the cause of her death far from her husband and children in Nice in 1896. She was fifty-six. We do not know how Marshall felt about this absent wife to whom he had been married for thirty-three years. She had lived within the confines of many nineteenth-century women, even those in favored circumstances. Not counting the rumors of her addiction, she had never disgraced her husband. Her remains were brought back to America and buried in the family plot at Graceland Cemetery, the resting place for many prominent Chicagoans. What we do know is that Marshall remained alone in the big mansion on Prairie Avenue, and that he distanced himself somewhat from the Prairie Avenue social set.

There were the children and grandchildren, of course. Marshall Junior and daughter-in-law Albertine were the parents of two boys, Marshall III, who was three years old when his grandmother died, and one-year-old Henry. Two of Ethel and son-in-law Arthur Tree's three children, Gladys and Lambert, died in infancy. Their third son, Arthur Ronald Lambert Tree— Ronald to everybody—had survived and would live to be seventy-nine. The marriage was not a happy one, and in 1898 Ethel met and fell in love with David Beatty, a twenty-eight-year-old Royal Navy officer. Ethel found accommodations in Compton Verney

Ethel Field.

away from her husband, but there was no official separation. She and David were discreet—only his sister knew. The lovers met on hunts and, with Edwardian decorum, made sure they were never seen alone at social occasions.

The idyll was cut short when David was appointed captain of the small battleship *Barfleur* and ordered to sail for China. The Boxer Rebellion, the violent Chinese uprising to oust all foreigners, saw forces led by the secret Boxer society murder Europeans and Chinese Christians and lay siege to Beijing's foreign embassies. Marines from the *Barfleur*, anchored at Tianjin, were dispatched to the capital to guard the British embassy. Beatty, however, stayed onboard his ship and wrote frustrated letters to Ethel. One of them read:

> Darling mine, if something doesn't happen soon to clear the air and bring us closer together, I feel like going off my head and becoming a raving lunatic and the burden of it all seems more than

I can bear and I am in that state you quoted from Longfellow. Do you remember? It has been in my head ever since:

> *My heart is hot and restless*
> *My life is full of care,*
> *And the burden that is laid upon me*
> *Seems greater than I can bear.*

It is so dreadfully applicable . . . one cannot live on hope alone. It is such small comfort after two long wearisome years, and without an active useful life to occupy the mind it lies like a lump of lead across my heart without the symptoms of a silver lining anywhere.

In a letter announcing that a promotion had made him the Royal Navy's youngest captain, he wrote of wanting "your dear arms round my neck." Back from China, he was so lovesick he didn't care for London. He went to a fortuneteller who not only told him his hand showed the most extraordinary line of success, but that he would be married within twelve months. When Marshall Field was informed of his daughter's liaison, he was so upset he rushed across the Atlantic to have her tell him to his face that she wanted to leave her husband and children for a man who signed his letters "Jack, the Sailor." Like many children born to wealth, Ethel expected to have her way. She engaged her father to talk Arthur into granting his wife a divorce. The father's appeal apparently convinced the cuckolded husband. In March 1901, Arthur instructed his American attorneys to sue for divorce on grounds of desertion. The decree was granted on May 12. Ten days later, Ethel and David were married by special license at the St. George's, Hanover Square, Registrar Office.

Because Ethel enjoyed a large income from her father, she and her new husband kept up appearances in sporting and social circles. They acquired a country place in Leicestershire, southwest of Warwickshire, and a house in London. To show interest in the sea, Ethel bought a steam yacht. Once a year her father journeyed to England to play with his grandchildren—Ethel bore David two sons. Marshall Senior bought a house near Junior and Albertine's in Leamington and turned up unannounced, telling Junior and Ethel he had come for no other purpose than to bounce the grandchildren on his knee. Marshall III would remember the romps with his grandfather as the happiest of his childhood memories. Junior and Albertine were reluctant to make trips to Chicago, and Ethel wanted to be there for David's irregular furloughs while at the same time resenting his absences on naval duties. Both couples lived off the widower's generosity, but showed an aversion to the raw bustle of American industry. Their moneyed existence in England was built around the social calendar of Edwardian landed gentry. When Nannie was still alive, Junior and Albertine had made occasional excursions to France to visit art galleries with her. Albertine was a doting mother who took charge of her children's upbringing—she and Junior had two more children, Henry, born in 1895, and Gwendolyn, born in 1902.

Was Junior totally the ineffectual Proustian dilettante, victim of exhaustion and migraines, uninterested in his father's crasser world that nevertheless afforded him and Albertine the life of leisure they enjoyed? Intriguingly, in 1904, when Harry Selfridge sold his partnership back to Marshall Field for a million dollars and went to London to explore a Chicago friend's suggestion that the British capital might be just the place for him to succeed on his own, Mile-a-Minute Harry carried with him an introduction from Junior to Harry (later Sir Harry) Brittain, head of the

English branch of the Pilgrims' Society. Junior's letter earned Selfridge an invitation to Brittain's residence. Here, Selfridge spread his plans for a proposed London store on the dining room table.

In Chicago, the patriarch ruled in solitary majesty. His widowed younger brother Henry died in 1890, leaving a $2 million estate to his three daughters. With mournful regularity, Marshall's fellow millionaires passed away—Philip D. Armour in 1901, Potter Palmer in 1902, Gustavus Swift the following year, and Levi Leiter in 1904. Prairie Avenue was a street of widows. Stanley Field, Marshall's nephew, worked for his uncle, but their leisure time together was largely limited to playing golf. Field's friendship with Robert Todd Lincoln, who became a president of the Pullman Company, was also confined to the golf course and occasional dinners. There was the poker circle at the Chicago Club, but Field indulged less and less. Gambling, in his opinion, was a weakness. Peter Funk, a salesman who after thirty years in Field's employ had earned the right to call the boss by his first name, one day found him in his office, silent at his desk. Said Funk: "Marshall, you have no home, no family, no happiness, nothing but money."

A journalist got a glimpse of the great man's existential qualms. At the end of an interview, Field expressed the thought that newspaper work gave reporters a chance to meet interesting people. The newsman murmured something appropriate, but Field was lost in his own musings. The journalist waited respectfully. In the end Field asked the reporter if he found life interesting. It was said of Field that few men ever had less fun out of their money.

11

GIVING BACK

JOHN D. ROCKEFELLER WAS HOUNDED BY PEOPLE TRYING TO CADGE loans from him and by institutions wanting endowments. "The good people who wanted me to help them with their good work seemed to come in crowds," the country's richest man complained. "They brought their trunks and lived with me." The supplicants who pestered Marshall Field were proportionately smaller in numbers but so insistent that in making donations to churches he asked for anonymity. Notes saying, "I beg you will not allow anyone to know that I send it to you" accompanied his checks. Back in 1871, he had taken a leading part in the effort to merge the old Chicago Library Association into the Young Men's Christian Association, and after the great fire had contributed freely to the city's recovery. He was a member of the Chicago Historical Society and aided in founding the Art Institute and establishing the Chicago Musical Festival, the Chicago Manual Training School, and the Chicago Symphony. When it came to raising funds for a new University of Chicago, he was asked to match Rockefeller.

A University of Chicago had started under Baptist auspices in 1856. Debt and mismanagement had closed the institution thirty years later, leaving the city with little in the way of higher learning. Augustus H. Strong, an eminent Baptist theologian who feared young Baptists were losing their faith going to Harvard, Yale or Princeton, tried to convince Rockefeller to put up a breathtaking $20 million to build an elite Baptist institution on Morningside Heights in New York City. The Reverend Strong harassed Rockefeller at every turn, overplayed his hand, and in the end saw two Baptist lobbyists from Chicago lure the millionaire away. The Chicago clergymen were Dr. Thomas W. Goodspeed, the silver-haired financial secretary of the Baptist Theological Seminary, already supported by Rockefeller, and Frederick T. Gates, an articulate young Baptist minister. Where Strong was bold and ambitious, Goodspeed was practical and modest. Building in Chicago was cheaper, he told Rockefeller. Gates argued demographics. The fastest-growing part of their church was in the Mississippi Valley and the Great Lakes, not in Congregationalist New England and New York. And where in Chicago would they build? Rockefeller asked. On ten acres that Marshall Field was donating near Midway Plaisance on the South Side. To Strong's mortification, Goodspeed and Gates won the day. In May 1889, Rockefeller agreed to put up $600,000 if another $400,000 could be raised. In January 1890, Field offered $100,000, eventually donating a total of $361,000, one-thirtieth of Rockefeller's contribution.

Gates came to Chicago to help Goodspeed raise the remaining funds. It was not easy. Rockefeller insisted that two-thirds of the trustees and the president of the new school be Baptists. But there were few rich Baptists in Chicago. The fundraisers, however, received support from an unexpected corner. In June 1889, Andrew Carnegie, who fancied himself the friend of the working man and was in fact an open-handed philanthropist, published an influential essay entitled "Wealth" in the *North American Review*. The diminutive Scotsman was a prolific autodidact who authored eight books and seventy magazine articles. The brute realities of his Pittsburgh steel mills, where men worked 12-hour days seven days a week, clashed with Carnegie's ideals, but in "Wealth" he warned against the widening gap between the new capitalists and the toiling classes. Instead of letting heirs fritter away the builders' fortunes, industrialists should give away large sums to worthy causes during their lifetimes. Rockefeller was greatly influenced by Carnegie and in turn told Field, Armour, and other Chicago capitalists to make bequests before they died. Goodspeed gently echoed Carnegie's ethos in his dealings with Field, persuading the department store millionaire to add $136,000 to his original $100,000 gift to the University of Chicago project. More was still to come.

Max Weber, a German sociologist and historian, not only puzzled over amassed wealth and philanthropy, American style, but also wondered what the factors were behind the rise of Northern Europeans in the modern era. In "The Protestant Ethic and the Spirit of Capitalism," a seminal essay he published in 1904, he theorized that what had kick-started the capitalist revolution was the Protestant Reformation and its emphasis on individual responsibility. Carnegie, Rockefeller, and the rest of America's entrepreneurs were all Protestants and shared the moral value of fulfilling their worldly duties. To explain Latin America's economic lag behind North America even though the Spanish and Portuguese empires started more than a century before the Pilgrims landed at Plymouth Rock, Spanish intellectuals saw the difference in the two strands of Christianity. Where the supreme expression of faith for the darker Spanish tradition of Catholicism celebrated in El Greco's paintings was Jesus's moment of self-doubt in the garden of Gethsemane, Protestantism, they said, was a cash-and-carry religion admirably adapted to capitalism. The Protestant God rewarded work, in the here and now, and, if you didn't make your pile, in the next world. Capitalism and thrift were two sides of the same coin, Weber said. To become rich, a man had to be frugal and perhaps even cautious, traits that Carnegie, Rockefeller—and Field—had in common. They would no doubt agree with Weber when he wrote, "Capitalism *may* even be identical with the restrain, or at least a rational tempering of the irrational impulse."

Vanity was not among Rockefeller's vices. He refused to have any building of the new university named after him. Other rich men were less reticent. The railroad barons Johns Hopkins and Leland Stanford let their names grace the portals of the universities they endowed. Goodspeed was named secretary of the new University of Chicago. William Rainey Harper was chosen as president. Dr. Harper was a biblical scholar with a gift for tapping Rockefeller for money. By 1892, Rockefeller donations had soared to over two million. "I investigated and worked myself almost to a nervous breakdown in groping my way, without sufficient guide or chart, through the ever-widening field of philanthropic endeavor," he would remember. The experience led him to hire Gates away from his ministry and make him the organizer and planner of future benefactions.

The University of Chicago gifts were not Field's largest dona-

tions. After much persuasion he made his largest single contribu-
tion to keep open the 1892–93 Chicago World's Fair Museum.
Edward E. Ayer, a timber executive with a passion for American
Indian artifacts, thought something of the fair should survive, and
approached Field about a museum. Marshall declined, but Ayer
persisted and, by appealing to the great merchant's vanity and
sense of stewardship, got him to reconsider. Imitating
Rockefeller's approach to philanthropy, Field pledged $1 million
if another $500,000 was raised in the business community and $2
million in World's Fair stock assigned to the new museum's
trustees. The money was raised. In June 1894, the Chicago
Natural History Museum, later renamed the Field Museum of
Natural History, opened in Jackson Park. In his will, Field
bequeathed $8 million more to build a new museum (completed
in 1921) to house exhibits, research collections, and a library.

12

POLITICS

HE WAS THE WEALTHIEST CITIZEN OF A CITY THAT HAD THE WORST government. Sprawling over two hundred square miles, Chicago at the turn of the century made its living from steel mills, slaughter-houses, and scandal sheets. "It was first in violence, deepest in dirt, loud, lawless, unlovely, ill-smelling, irreverent, new, an overgrown gawk of a village, the 'tough' among cities, a spectacle for the nation," wrote Lincoln Steffens in 1902. Field was the biggest tax-payer in the city and perhaps the country. John D. Rockefeller was the richest man in the land, but Field paid the highest taxes. He was assessed on an estimated $40 million worth of real estate and personal property in Cook County alone, and was said to pay taxes on a greater amount of property than any other U.S. citizen.*

---

* The runner-up was John Jacob Astor III, New York's aristocratic slumlord, with property valued at $35 million.

The railroads and the layout of the city—hemmed in on one side by Lake Michigan—made him ever richer by boosting the value of downtown. Only one square mile of land at city center was free from the tracks that elsewhere ran down the main streets. Long freight trains blocked intersections for hours, choked traffic, and blighted entire neighborhoods. Moreover, the huge terminals and railway yards on the southern end of downtown prevented any southward expansion. The result was mounting prices for center city real estate. To maximize land use, businesses built ever-taller office buildings.

Field's Cook County taxes alone were more than half a million dollars a year, and he paid $250,000 in states outside Illinois. He deplored the fact that tax revenues never seemed enough to keep the city's streets clean, the public buildings in repair, its water sanitary. Why wasn't government run like a business? A city that couldn't maintain decent elevators in its own buildings, he told reporters, was not fit to operate the streetcar system.

Chicago's unlikely Jeremiah was William R. Stead, an Englishman who had arrived in the 1890s and denounced the sins of what he believed could be America's shining city on the hill. His laments led to ladies' clubs sessions, businessmen's lunches, and church gatherings where Stead appeared and declared himself appalled by the city's slumlords, venal politicians, gambling dens, brothels, saloons, and pawnshops. There were threats on his life, but also calls for reform. Stead's thunder—itemized in a national bestseller titled *If Christ Came to Chicago*—led to the creation in 1894 of the Civic Federation. Field was a founding member. Lyman Gage was elected president, Bertha Palmer vice-president, and $135,000 was raised. The Pullman strike tested the group—and Field, when it sided with Eugene Debs and recommended that the dispute be arbitrated. We do not know whether Field intervened, but the Pullman Company refused arbitration. Next, the Civic Federation hired special constables to raid gambling dens, where they seized and destroyed the gaming tables.

Field was a conservative because to him to be otherwise meant to admit defeat to violence, vulgarity, and disrespect for authority. Wanting to save the country from the "trashy" challenges seeping up from society's lower rungs also burnished his self-image. He and his Chicago Club friends saw no inconsistency in supporting civic reforms directed against gamblers, prostitutes, and corrupt aldermen while working hand in glove with Charles Tyson Yerkes Jr., the only Chicago capitalist with a prison record. This former bond salesman had earned his prison term for a municipal bonds swindle in his native Philadelphia. The governor of Pennsylvania had pardoned part of the sentence, but Philadelphia's Society Hill couldn't forgive Yerkes for leaving his wife and six children for a younger woman. Urban transportation became his ticket to riches. On a January morning in 1882, he helped inaugurate Chicago's first cable car system, running from the store to Twenty-first Street, four miles south. A crowd of three hundred thousand lined the tracks of the Chicago City Railway Company to watch local history being made. By Christmas engineers made the cablecars turn around in a loop near Marshall Field's, making the term "Loop" synonymous with downtown fifteen years before the completion of the elevated railway system around the central business district that still remains a Chicago landmark. Five years later, this and a parallel line on Cottage Grove Avenue reached the once-secluded village of Hyde Park.

To lay streetcar tracks Yerkes needed city franchises. By the early 1890s, he controlled a sizable block of alderman, including Johnny Powers, the "Prince of Boodlers." Powers and other alderman on the take rammed through right-of-way concessions that effectively gave Yerkes a monopoly on new streetcar lines. Newspapers cried fowl. Field was of two minds. He benefited from the Loop trolley turnarounds but found Yerkes sleazy. In 1895, however, he held his nose long enough to back a series of monopoly bills rushed through the Illinois legislature. Governor John Altgeld's veto and refusal to accept a $500,000 bribe to change his stand provoked Yerkes to say he admired the governor's uprightness. When a new governor took office, however, Yerkes bribed the legislature to pass a law that gave the Chicago City Council the authority Altgeld had vetoed. Three years later Yerkes built the elevated railway system, subcontracting, padding bills, and pocketing huge profits. Field was not a party to Yerkes's scams and froze in disgust when he heard Yerkes brag of his special talent for corrupting aldermen. But Field was a director and leading stockholder of the Chicago City Railway Company and made a great deal of money on the crowds the elevated railway and streetcars brought downtown.

The Randolph Street–Wabash Avenue elevated station featured a direct entrance to the second floor of Marshall Field's, allowing passengers from the Northwestern, Oak Park, Metropolitan, and South Side elevated trains to go shopping without descending to the street level. Many surface trolley lines had their terminals at Randolph and Wabash. Between 1899 and 1903 there were Marshall Field Specials running from Harlem to Randolph and Wabash. Wrote five-time mayor Carter Harrison in his memoir *Stormy Years*: "The fact—too significant to be accidental—is that the people who constitute the most desirable class of buyers in the city of Chicago and its suburbs are deposited at the doors of Marshall Field & Co, or within sight and easy walking distance of the big store."

Harrison, who was the publisher of the Chicago *Times* before he became mayor, brought down Yerkes in 1897. Harrison owed much of his popularity to having come out flatly—and alone—for the workers in the bloody Pullman strike. His re-election and the glare of newspaper exposure caused the city council to defeat, 32–31, the municipal version of Yerkes's eternal monopoly legislation. Field had clashed with the mayor in the aftermath of the Haymarket riot when Harrison refused to forbid anyone to address a public meeting unless allowed to do so by the police. Field had led a delegation of capitalists to the mayor's office. The November 5, 1893, edition of the *Chicago Times* quoted Field and the mayor verbatim.

Field: "Mr. Harrison, we represent the great interests in Chicago . . ."
Harrison: "Mr. Field, any poor man owning a single small cottage as his sole possession has the same interest in Chicago as its richest citizen."

Now Field applauded the Harrison administration's cleanup of the worst city hall graft.

On the national level, reformers picked up on the rumblings of unhappiness with Grover Cleveland's leadership. Governor Altgeld might be branded a dangerous radical, but Cleveland's use of army troops to break the strike brought his nomination for a third term in doubt. Progressives in the Democratic Party thought Altgeld was the man to unseat Cleveland, but of course his foreign birth meant he could never be president. Party liberals began focusing on the rising star, William Jennings Bryan. An Illinois native and a graduate of Chicago's Union College of Law, he had served as a member of the U.S. House of Representatives from Nebraska and was a formidable speaker. Marshall Field was a Cleveland Democrat, as opposed to a Bryan or Altgeld supporter. And the reason was money and monetary policy. Bryan's answer to depressed Western farming was to propose the free coinage of silver, an idea that was anathema to conservative Democrats. They wanted a nominee who endorsed the "hard money" policies favored by eastern bankers and industrialists.

Since the founding of the republic, the jealous states had distrusted the federal government with printing money, and for a hundred years gold and silver were the only trusted legal tender. "Bimetalism"—monetary policy based on the use of the two metals—tended to stabilize the prices of commodities and to simplify foreign exchange. Many economists opposed it on the grounds that the cheaper metal, silver, valued commercially at less than its face value, drove the more precious gold from circulation. They were proved doubly right when gold was discovered in Australia and California and the price of gold fell relative to silver. Adherents of bimetalism, however, got a boost when the Civil War ruined whatever confidence people had in paper money. After the war, the notes issued by the Confederate treasury and the southern states became worthless. U.S. notes (greenbacks) and other paper money also lost value, especially after the federal government stopped redeeming its paper money for gold or silver in 1873. Events proved the government right. Greatly expanded production of silver in the West caused its value to plummet. The silver in a silver dollar was worth 89 cents in 1877, 72 cents twelve years later. Paradoxically, the slide in the value of silver led to agitation by silver interests for restoration of the free coinage of silver dollars.

Marshall Field thought the Democrats should nominate a muscled supporter of the gold standard. He sensed that the United States not only stood on the threshold of economic expansion and consolidation but that the country was becoming a power so great that in industrial might it exceeded all other nations. Unfettered capitalism had victims, however. Farmers were unhappy with bankers' and industrialists' dominant role in Washington. The gold standard had forced prices and wages down. Manufactured goods, shielded by high tariffs and corporate practices that limited competition, fell only slightly in prices while farm commodity prices slumped sharply.

Not surprisingly, given the Western silver rush, Bryan championed the unlimited coinage of silver. He was a fiery orator adored by socialists and populists. At the 1896 Democratic Convention, held in Chicago, the balding, thirty-six-year-old Bryan delivered his famous "cross of gold" speech: "You shall not press down upon the brow of labor this crown of thorns; you shall not crucify mankind upon a cross of gold."

Field did not break with the party when Bryan received the party's presidential nomination. Nor did Field join a dissident faction of breakaway "gold Democrats," who held a convention of their own and nominated General John McAuley Palmer of Illinois on a platform that extolled Cleveland and attacked free coinage. Out west, the Populist Party had made great strides with a platform of extensive reforms. The most important demand of the populists, as well as of Western Democrats and Republicans, was the free and unlimited coinage of silver at the legal ratio of 16 to 1 with gold. After the Populists also nominated Bryan, he toured the country making fiery speeches for free silver and against wealth, privilege, and business control of government.

The Republican presidential hopeful, Ohio Governor William McKinley, was a tireless advocate of hard currency and protectionist tariffs on imports. Feeling threatened by Bryan's populism, big business interests energized the McKinley campaign by contributing an unprecedented $3.5 million to the Republican campaign. Marc Hanna, McKinley's campaign manager, got Standard Oil to give $250,000—Rockefeller sent a personal check for $2,500—and spent large amounts of campaign funds to rally voters to the Republicans' commitment to the gold standard. Bryan made six hundred campaign speeches in twenty-seven states, traveling an unprecedented eighteen thousand miles. The Republicans counterattacked by frightening small entrepreneurs and their workers: a vote for Bryan would mean another wrenching depression. McKinley's election victory was a squeaker, with fewer than 600,000 popular votes over Bryan.

The President-elect and Marc Hanna accompanied Mrs. McKinley to Marshall Field for fittings for her inauguration gown, "a dress of silver wrought brocade of Parisian texture combined with point d'Alençon lace and silver passementerie threaded with tiny pearls, with lace edging and a taffeta skirt and many frillings and French shirrings." Field was not at hand to greet the President-elect, the soon-to-be First Lady, and campaign manager Hanna. McKinley and Hanna nevertheless scrawled their signatures in doorman Pritzlaff's book next to that of brothel owner Carrie Watson.

McKinley's election renewed business confidence. The Republicans passed the Gold Standard Act, which ensured the maintenance of this standard by reserving $150 million of gold coin and bullion to redeem United States notes—the Federal Reserve System would not come into existence until 1913. Silver mining collapsed, and prospectors sought and found gold in Canada's Yukon Territory and Alaska. Chemists discovered cheaper and more efficient ways of extracting gold from low-grade ores. In the five-year period 1897–1902, the United States coined $437 million in gold—double the output twenty years earlier. In a repeat of silver's devaluation, too much gold sent its value down. McKinley stifled demands for reforms. Sympathetic to the plight of farmers and laborers victimized by the growing power of big business, he nevertheless believed government had no right to interfere. Monopolies and giant new corporations grew at a frantic pace and reached nearly two hundred quasi-monopolies in timber, coal, and sugar. Bryan continued to hammer away. "One of the great purposes of government is to put rings in the noses of hogs," he told a Chicago audience in 1898.

In exchange for their support, business leaders had obtained high tariffs to keep out foreign competition. Now they wanted to acquire new markets by expanding overseas and wanted Washington to arm-twist other countries to lower their tariffs. While McKinley was no war hawk, he nevertheless failed to rein in his assistant secretary of the navy, Theodore Roosevelt. The result was the quick Spanish-American War that gave independence to Cuba and economic concessions to American business, along with the annexation of Hawaii, Guam, Puerto Rico, and the Philippines. Filipinos no more wanted American imperialism than they wanted Spanish domination, and McKinley faced rebellion against American occupation.

What Bryan had in mind for the 1900 election campaign, if the Democrats chose him to run against McKinley, was to attack both the Republicans' imperial adventures and the tariff walls that kept consumer prices high. No nation, he said, could endure as half republic, a form of government in which all citizens had the same representation, and half empire, under which many people might have no voice at all. To Field's dismay, Bryan planned to balance the attacks on Republicans with one positive: If elected, he would revive the silver doctrine.

Could the nomination be wrested from Bryan? A number of party stalwarts thought Marshall Field was the man to deny Bryan the nomination. The *South Bend Times* endorsed a Field for President campaign. While he weighed his options, he coyly allowed, "I have a little reputation now. I might not have any if I became a candidate." He would have made a terrible candidate. He was much too wooden for the stump. His pronouncements were doctrinaire defenses of private property combined with critiques of public services. Municipal ownership of water, power, streetcars, and sewers was an aberration because however much taxpayers contributed, governments managed to spend more. What weakened the country was permissive law enforcement. "The trouble is that the young people of the land are growing up to have no respect for law and order, and why should they have, when they are not made to respect it?" The subtext of his declarations was no doubt that he had no talent for the bartering of smoke-filled rooms, the jostle of nominating conventions, and the rough-and-tumble of a presidential campaign. The question of his candidacy was rhetorical anyway. Bryan was elected to head the Democratic ticket.

McKinley's running mate was the ardent interventionist and reformer Theodore Roosevelt, who had returned a hero from the Spanish-American War to become governor of New York. McKinley defeated Bryan, winning by a more comfortable 849,000 majority and taking twenty-six states, leaving Bryan only the South and four silver-mining states. McKinley moderated his protectionist stance and to promote reciprocity in trade arranged to speak at a Pan-American exposition in Buffalo in September 1901. While greeting visitors at the fair, he was gunned down. The assassin was Leon Czolgosz, an anarchist. The crowd pounced upon Czolgosz. The president underwent immediate surgery in Buffalo, but gangrene, then incurable, set in, and eight days after the shooting he died. Teddy Roosevelt became president.

13

DELIA

THE 1900 CENSUS COUNTED SEVENTY-SIX MILLION AMERI-
cans—a century later the U.S. population would reach 281 million—and over a million of them lived in the Second City, the heart
of the heartland, which drew eager young people from towns and
farms. Like Dorothy in *Chicago Evening Post* reporter L. Frank
Baum's new book *The Wonderful World of Oz*, newcomers were
warned of the city's wickedness but also told that a person with
heart and courage could prevail. If Baum's Dorothy was too good to
believe, Theodore Dreiser published a darker tale of the city. *Sister
Carrie* was the story of a young country girl arriving in cruel
Chicago, to be rescued by a traveling salesman; she later takes up
with a wealthy married man. Short-time visitors were more optimistic. As he passed the stockyards on his way out of Chicago on
the Pennsylvania Limited, H. G. Wells mused that the future was

in America and its center of energy Chicago. The French novelist Paul Bourget, who visited during the 1892–93 Chicago World's Fair, found Burnham's make-believe White City less meaningful than the Union Stock Yards. The big ideas of America, he wrote, were business ideas and Chicago was the capital of big ideas.

No other city could boast of so many breakthrough industries. Besides the big ideas of George Pullman, Gustavus Swift, and Philip Armour, there were the nationwide mail order houses of Richard Warren Sears and Aaron Montgomery Ward. But the living fairy tale was Marshall Field's, a man rich beyond anyone's wildest dreams, since his annual income was $40 million, or seventy thousand times the average Chicago family's earnings.* He had risen from farm boy by dint of hard work. He was influential and respected by his peers, and understandably defended his wealth and the acquisitive society that allowed him to keep it. The new century gave him trouble, and, on a personal level, happiness and tragedy. Two teamsters' strikes in 1902 and 1905 set his blood boiling, and in 1904 he lost Harry Selfridge. Fifteen years after he had made Mile-a-Minute Harry a partner, Selfridge quit. Other partners retired because of illness or old age—Harlow Higinbotham retired in 1901 with $2 million in accrued profits. Why Selfridge left was the object of endless

---

* The average family income was $553 a year ($11,000 in 2002 money). Food was reasonable (chuck steak was 8 cents a pound, coffee 14 cents, rice 6 cents), and housing the most crippling item in a family budget. Rent in Chicago's slum districts was $8 to $10 a month, communal toilet down the hall and heating not included. Older houses in more fashionable neighborhoods rented for $25 to $60 a month, with certain Lake Shore Drive palaces going for $1,000 a month. The 5 cent fare was almost universal for public transportation. *Source:* Chicago Public Library.

speculation. One report had it that he had "demanded his name over the door," that the store be renamed Field, Selfridge and Company. A second story had it that he walked out after Field vetoed Selfridge's idea of going nationwide, with stores in all major cities. Selfridge created a mild sensation when, ahead of Carson Pirie Scott and Company, he bought the Schlesinger & Mayer partnership and put his own name above the door. The store was located in the State and Madison building that, twenty years earlier, Field had persuaded Schlesinger and Mayer to occupy. Selfridge's go-it-alone in Chicago lasted exactly ninety days. He sold out to Carson Pirie Scott and Company. Because the seven Scotsmen, as he called the Carson Pirie Scott partnership, had wanted the Schlesinger & Mayer location, Harry came out all right. He and Rose retired, and on the shores of Lake Geneva, Wisconsin, where Levi Leiter had already built his dream castle, spent $100,000 on Harrose (Harry and Rose) Hall, and proceeded to live the life of a man of leisure, growing orchids and white roses. But Harry was too full of energy to stay retired. He resurfaced in London five years later and applied all his talent to make his emporium an Oxford Street landmark. Rose died in 1918. The Selfridges had three daughters and a son. Levi Leiter's daughter was now Lady Curzon, and Marshall Field's Ethel the wife of Admiral Sir David Beatty. Not to be outdone, Harry married Rosalie, his eldest daughter, to Serge de Bolotoff (later Prince Wiasemsky) at the Russian embassy. Harry's store was London's high temple of allure and he the lord of the aristocratic Lansdowne House, associate and friend of some of the wealthiest men of his time. He became a social lion, a first-nighter at theaters, a friend of industrialists, artists, and monarchs (son-in-law Prince Wiasemsky was an adviser to Britain's premier movie producer Alexander Korda).

*   *   *

Labor unrest hit Marshall Field & Company in 1902. At the time
of the railroad strike in 1877, Field had ordered that all employees in the wholesale building be drilled in handling weapons. The
guns were kept ready in a rack installed in the carpet department.
At the height of the crisis he had posted men behind bales of cotton at the entrance to repel any mob attacks. In 1902, when the
newly organized Chicago department store drivers' union target-
ed Marshall Field & Company, he was determined that no union
was going to interfere with his business. He asked employees to
volunteer for deliveries. The strike was settled quickly due to the
intervention of the new Illinois State Board of Arbitration. James
Simpson, Field's personal secretary, nevertheless hired spies from
the McGuire Agency to attend his shipping room employees'
union meetings.

Marshall had been a longtime friend and frequent guest at the

Delia.

house of Arthur and Delia Caton—gossips would have it that he had been secretly in love with his neighbor's wife for nearly thirty years. Arthur had always had money. His father was one of the first men in the West to take an interest in telegraphy and in 1857 had become the owner of all the telegraph lines in Illinois and Iowa. Eight years later the elder Caton sold out to Western Union on terms that made him rich. Delia Spencer Caton was the daughter of a founder of Hibbard, Spencer and Bartlett's hardware store. A reigning beauty of her day, she had what the English painter Edward Burne-Jones called the sweetest smile. Arthur and Delia had met at her father's estate in Ottawa, Illinois, under romantic circumstances. Out riding, Delia came upon an injured fawn and was binding its leg with her handkerchief when Arthur appeared, got off his horse, bent down, and replaced her handkerchief with his larger neckerchief. They were married in 1876, but remained childless. They entertained sumptuously at their 1910 Calumet Avenue home, which was located directly in the back of Field's Prairie Avenue home. At one dinner party everyone made a speech except Marshall, who never gave speeches. So Delia made one for him: "Mr. Field just wants me to remind you that the White Sale starts next Monday."

Arthur Meeker thought the (soon-to-be) second Mrs. Field more remarkable than Nannie. "In one respect she surpassed her predecessor, for she knew, not only what she wanted, but also how to get it," he would write. "Chicago remembered her best as Mrs. Arthur Caton, the name she bore during all but the last few months of her life there. In our drawing-room for years stood a photograph of a lady in an evening gown wearing a towering feathered headdress and seated on a glittering throne made to look like a peacock's spread tail: this was Mrs. Caton at some charity *tableaux vivants*, I suppose. Even then she had a comfortable embonpoint; in later years she became very large, very large. I have been told of an unfortunate foreign diplomat for whom she gave a party in Washington. Seated between his hostess and another equally stout matron, he found himself unable to eat as they inclined their majestic busts towards him in turn to make polite conversation, and he ended up dinnerless in a shockingly bad temper. But it is horrid of me to take up anecdotes from the declining years; at the height of her fame she must have been an extremely attractive woman."

Was it true that Marshall was the lover of his friend's wife? The gossip of the day insinuated as much and passed on rumors that an underground tunnel connected the Catons' house on Calumet and the Field house on Prairie. Meeker asked his mother at the end of her life if she didn't find it odd that the woman the Prairie Avenue matrons looked up to was married to one man while generally supposed to be another man's mistress. "What did you think of it, really?" To which his mother replied, "Why, no, dear, we didn't find it odd; we never thought about it all." In *Chicago with Love*, Meeker would write that he couldn't quite make up his mind whether the reply was extraordinarily naïve or sophisticated "to a degree unknown amongst us now."

Arthur Caton had died unexpectedly in the Waldorf-Astoria in New York in 1904. His death opened honorable possibilities for the seventy-year-old multimillionaire and the fifty-year-old socialite. Marshall persuaded Delia to come to England with him to meet his children. Friends said they had never seen him as happy as when Delia and he boarded his private Pullman for New York—and left John Shedd to deal with the second teamsters' strike in three years. The walkout was essentially a sympathy strike—the teamsters' had no direct grievance against Marshall Field's. The strike turned ugly when Field and other merchants of the Chicago Employers' Association decided to break the union. "Thousands of Negroes and professional 'toughs' were imported and added to the force of volunteer employee strikebreakers and deputy police in the pay of the employees," Howard H. Myers would write in 1929. "Both sides were armed and Chicago became a virtual battleground. Over twenty persons were killed and over four hundred others injured."

Marshall and Delia crossed the Atlantic in the set of "Field Suite" staterooms on the White Star liner the *Baltic*. By July, when the strike was entering its fourth month, Marshall read in the London press that the Chicago teamsters were ready to capitulate. On July 4, he wrote to Shedd: "I see by Morning papers that the drivers are beginning to want their old places . . . it took them a long while to find out Shedd."

A month later, Marshall and Delia were married in St. Margaret's Church. Reverend Herbert Hensley Henson, canon of Westminster Abbey, officiated at the September 5, 1905, ceremony and U.S. Ambassador Whitelaw Reid headed the guest list. Marshall looked grave pronouncing the ritual "I do." The bride exchanged a smile of reassurance with Ethel, and her stepdaughter broke out in tears. The wedding party was whisked off to Claridge's for a wedding breakfast, which offered *sole diablée* and melon shipped express from France. The newlyweds vacationed briefly in Switzerland before returning to a whirlwind of social engagements in New York and Chicago. We do not know whether the groom thought it becoming to have his son and family accompany him and his bride or whether Junior and Albertine decided a visit was due. In any case, Junior and Albertine returned with twelve-year-old Marshall III, ten-year-old Henry, and three-year-old Gwendolyn. Given Junior and Albertine's long-honed talent for creating distance between themselves and the paterfamilias, it was no doubt Senior's idea that they should stay with him and Delia at Prairie Avenue. Perhaps he merely wanted to hear children's laughter enliven the mansion.

Delia's debut as Mrs. Field was eagerly awaited. *Le tout Chicago* had expected to be introduced to the new Mr. and Mrs. Field at the theatrical evening that traditionally opened the season. The Fields did not show that night or the next. After the house lights went down on the closing night, they were ushered to their box. At the end of the play, they walked down toward the carriage entrance and were greeted by smiles and bows. Marshall lifted his hat and Delia graciously inclined her head.

It was to be the only time they appeared together in Chicago. As the *Tribune* recalled after the death, seven weeks later, of Marshall Junior, "None who beheld the pleasant scene guessed that in many cases it was to be a farewell passage of courtesies, or realized how soon disasters were to settle their crushing weight upon the house of Field."

14

SON AND FATHER

MARSHALL III WOULD REMEMBER HIMSELF AT TWELVE, CONVA-
lescing from the measles and playing in the nursery, when he
heard a shot down the hall, and a cry from his father. The family
butler and several servants rushed to Marshall Field II's room
while a French maid scurried back to the nursery, grabbed young
Marshall, and carried him off, bewildered and protesting. The
servants found Marshall II on the floor. At his feet was an auto-
matic pistol he had recently bought from a Wabash Avenue sporting goods store. His father and Delia were in New York when the
news reached them. Marshall Senior telephoned the New York
Central for a private train, which took him and Delia to Chicago
in the near-record time of nineteen and a half hours.

The accident happened on November 22, 1905. The following days turned the septuagenarian's hostility toward the press

into hatred. A barrage of flash pans greeted the Fields as they stepped off the train at the 31st Street Station, where Laura and Henry Dibblee, Marshall's sister and brother-in-law, greeted them. Reporters chased them to the doors of Mercy Hospital, "The meeting between father and son at the hospital was pathetic," the Chicago *Daily News* reported the next day. "At a signal from the attendant physician, Mr. Field and his wife, Mrs. Field, Jr., and Mr. and Mrs. Dibblee entered the sick chamber. An unsteady white hand was extended to greet the father as the pale face resting on the pillow turned toward the door. The father's feelings were suppressed with effort as he sank into a chair beside the bed and bent over the form of his son. After remaining in the sick chamber for fifteen minutes, Mr. Field and his wife held a consultation with other members of the family."

Photographers' flashes nearly blinded Field Senior when they came out. Trembling with indignation, he shook his walking stick at them. The next morning when Senior visited again, doctors told him the next eight hours would be critical. As he left, a reporter asked whether his son had told him how he was shot. "No, he did not," Field replied. The press could not believe that a father's first question hadn't been, How? The police were equally flabbergasted.

Detectives were refused access to the hospital room and to Prairie Avenue, leading the police to tell reporters they had been unable to obtain details. The press quoted Chief of Police Collins as saying he was anxious to learn "whether the shooting was accidental or otherwise." The family's wall of silence and noncooperation with police inflamed the press. At the *Tribune*, reporters told managing editor James Keeley that Marshall Junior had botched a suicide and had been wounded at the Everleigh Club.

Owned by Minna and Ada Everleigh, daughters of a well-to-do Kentucky lawyer, the Everleigh Club catered to the sons of Chicago's respectable families and visiting dignitaries. Minna and Ada were adroit entrepreneurs who, after trying out a whorehouse in Omaha, bought the lease of Effie Hankins, the madam of a downtown establishment, and her stable of girls. The spinster sisters launched a lavish facelift of the South Dearborn Street establishment and turned it into the country's most elegant brothel. It was said that it was as difficult to get into the Everleigh Club as Buckingham Palace. Once accepted, however, a visitor was enfolded in sybaritic allure. Two mahogany staircases swept grandly upward, flanked by palms and busts of Greek goddesses. "There were fourteen parlors on the first floor alone and a library crammed with the writings of Plato, Montaigne, Lamartine," Dana Thomas would write in *The Money Crowd*. "There was an art gallery at one end featuring exquisite oil canvasses by great masters. Upstairs there were Japanese, Moorish, and Egyptian rooms each fitted with marble inlaid beds and mirrors on the ceiling. Nothing was overlooked to beguile the guests. String musicians stationed at strategic intervals softly played Mozart and Haydn quartets. A $15,000 gold piano stood ready to yield its dulcet tones at the wish of a patron, and Buddhist censers suffused the air with ravishing Oriental perfumes." After laying a wreath on Abraham Lincoln's monument in Springfield during his 1902 visit, Prince Henry of Prussia, the Kaiser's brother, spent an enchanted evening at the Everleigh Club. Girls decked in fauncolored tights danced on the tables and the prince, it was said, drank champagne from the slipper of one of the bacchanalian nymphs.

That the thirty-seven-year-old Marshall Field Junior might have been shot at the Everleigh Club was just too scabrously delectable for the press to pass up. At the *Daily News*, Augustus

Hirth, an enterprising reporter and gun enthusiast, squashed the accidental discharge hypothesis. To prove that dropping the pistol could not result in a discharge, Hirth took an identical gun, cocked it without loading it, and threw it several times on the floor. Marshall II must have *held* the gun, Hirth reported. It was almost impossible for a man as familiar with firearms as the younger Field was to have shot himself accidentally. Frank Carson of the Chicago *Inter-Ocean* and Tom Bourke of the City Press Association received a tip that Marshall II had spent Tuesday afternoon at the Everleigh Club, that he had been shot either by a prostitute or a gambler and his body smuggled out to be found at home in his room. The Everleigh sisters, who claimed they paid $150,000 a year in protection money to police and city officials, denied knowledge of anything, and Carson and Bourke learned nothing that was safe to print.

Arthur Meeker said he and his sister Mary were playing in front of 1905 Prairie Avenue when Marshall II "stopped to speak to our nurse before going off to get himself shot at the Everleigh Club—if it *was* the Everleigh Club." "It's impossible to say now what happened," Meeker would write, "all we can be sure of is that the version the family gave out and forced the papers to print—that the accident occurred while he was cleaning a gun at home in preparation for a hunting trip—had no truth to it. That, again, is something that couldn't be put over today; the power of the press would prevent it."

Junior's condition deteriorated. On the fifth day Dr. Frank Billings, the family physician, told Albertine her husband was near death. He was given the last rites of the Roman Catholic Church, which he had joined in marrying Albertine. Conscious until the end, he died in the late afternoon.

The coroner decided no autopsy was necessary. Two days

later, Marshall II was laid to rest next to his mother at Graceland Cemetery. His widow made a statement indicating that she understood the tragedy of her husband's life. "American wealth is too often a curse," Albertine said. "I want it to be the means of the greatest blessing to my sons, the means of fulfillment of the highest patriotic ambitions. I should like to see them grow up into politicians, for then they would, it seems to me, employ their wealth to the greatest good for their countrymen." What was behind this outburst? The patriotism was short-lived, as she would return to Britain and bring up the boys English. The curse might not have been her father-in-law's money that had allowed Junior and her to lead a privileged, self-effacing existence at a remove, but the strings attached, the slow burn of cumulative dependency ending in a tragedy that no doubt she saw as an indictment of a social system.

The death shattered Field. He tried to carry on, but never recovered. Friends noted a sagging of his figure and a look of inescapable sadness in his face as he sought distractions, plunged into work, and, it was said, was never seen smiling in public. Like the elder John Rockefeller, he had discovered a passion for golf and played eighteen holes or more three times a week. On New Year's Day 1906, he played a game with his nephew Stanley; James Simpson, his personal secretary; and his old friend Robert Todd Lincoln at the Chicago Golf Club in Wheaton, west of the city. It was bitterly cold. To see their game's progress in the snow, they used red balls. On their way back to Chicago after the game, Marshall was unusually cheerful, and teased the two younger men. The next day he had a sore throat. He and Delia were scheduled to go to New York. John Shedd came to the house the day before their departure and, seeing Field's pained appearance, tried to persuade him to postpone the trip. Field wouldn't hear of it. He was still trying to shake the cold when he, Delia, and his valet boarded the Broadway Limited. Doctors met the train at Pittsburgh and diagnosed pneumonia, but Field wouldn't hear of interrupting the trip. When he checked them in at the desk of Manhattan's Holland House, he was almost too sick to hold the pen.

Specialists examined the prostrate millionaire. Dr. Billings was summoned from Chicago. With one lung affected, his temperature shot up. His stamina astounded the physicians. Family members and presidents of railways and industry visited the suite. Delia stayed at his bedside, as did his nephew Stanley and daughter-in-law Albertine. For nearly a week he held on. Death came on January 16, from sheer exhaustion, Dr. Billings said.

The *New York Times* set the tone of newspaper obituaries the next morning. It saw Field's career as proof that the opportunity to do what he did is open to "every beginner of native or foreign birth in this great and happy land. What is the use of talking about proletariats and classes in the face of such an object lesson that the hopes of American life are still as open as they ever were?" The *New York Evening Post* said Field "accumulated his immense fortune by methods which the considered judgment pronounced legitimate." *Everybody's Magazine* came closest to analyzing Field's powers as a trendsetter. At the end of a generally flattering article in the magazine's March 1906 issue, the anonymous author wrote that by giving his customers "beauty, order, harmony and artistic perception," he both prevented and created demand.

A private New York Central train brought his body home. On the day of the funeral, not only the store on State Street but also his competitors closed their doors for an hour. Altogether nine hundred Chicago businesses also paid tribute. There were three funeral services: one from the Prairie Avenue home, another an hour later in the First Presbyterian Church, and the final one in Graceland Cemetery. During the noon hour flags were lowered to half-staff, not only in Chicago but also in New York, St. Louis, Milwaukee, Kansas City, and Philadelphia.

15

THE WILL

MARSHALL FIELD'S WILL WAS FILED IN PROBATE COURT TEN DAYS after his death. William Beale, a corporate lawyer who had a number of rich clients for whom he wrote airtight testaments, had drawn up the 20,000-word document that Field had signed on February 25, 1904. Beale died with the conviction that the Field will and last testament was his masterpiece. Time proved him right. There would be nine attempts to break it, but Beale had done so well that federal and state inheritance tax laws had to be rewritten.

It listed the following assets:

Business, wholesale and retail	$30 million
Real estate, downtown	35 million
" " outlying	6 million

" " New York City	5 million
Pullman holdings	7.5 million
North Western Railroad	5 million
Rock Island Railway	2 million
United States Steel	1 million
Chicago Edison	1 million
Chicago City Railway Company	1.5 million
Merchants Loan & Trust Co.	1 million
Illinois Trust & Savings Bank	600,000
Other Chicago bank holdings	400,000
Mining and farming lands	2 million
Other stocks and bonds	20 million

Total $118 million ($2.1 billion in today's money)

At the time of his death his descendants numbered only six—daughter Ethel and her two sons, Arthur Ronald Tree and new-born David Field Beatty, grandsons Marshall III and Henry, and granddaughter, Gwendolyn—but nearly forty relatives were provided for. There were twenty-three basic points, some of them showing that Marshall Field had not taken time during the weeks after his son's death to make changes in his will. Because of his ill health, it said, Marshall Junior should be spared the burden of caring for property. Ethel inherited $6 million ($108 million in today's money) and shared in the income of the estate. A codicil provided that she in turn could will her trust fund to her son Arthur Ronald by her first marriage. In case of Marshall II's death, Albertine was to have his share of the estate plus $500,000. Three-year-old granddaughter Gwendolyn was also given a $1 million trust fund, to be "reinvested for accumulation" until she was eighteen. Albertine did not want the house where her husband had shot himself. Nor did Ethel, who lived in England, the wife of Captain David Beatty. The mansion on Prairie Avenue therefore went to Delia, along with $1 million. Delia lived there for a few years with her niece, but in 1912 left the house in charge of a caretaker and moved permanently to Washington, D.C. Marshall's sisters, Laura Field Dibblee and Helen Field James, were given $500,000 each; there were numerous bequests to nephews and nieces, and $100,000 to distribute among employees who had worked in the store for twenty-five years. Nannie's spinster sister, Nora Scott, was given $200,000, and $5,000 was set aside for the selectmen of Conway, Massachusetts, for the maintenance of his parents' graves. There was $20,000 for the two daughters of Deacon Davis, his first employer back in Pittsfield. There were donations to the University of Chicago. As Edward Ayer had told Field back in 1893, "Your story will be lost, but the museum named after you will last through the generations." The legacy to the Field Museum of Natural History came to $8 million. In all, the bequests totaled $17 million.

The bulk of the estate went to the male-line grandsons, Marshall III and Henry. The money was set aside until the boys turned fifty, that is, until 1943 in Marshall III's case, and 1945 for Henry. While providing ample means for them in the meantime, Field expressed the hope that, unlike their father, they would work: "Earnestly hoping that they will each seasonably adopt some regular occupation in life, inasmuch as such an occupation will, in my judgment, greatly promote their usefulness and happiness."

Just what was Field's purpose in seeking to perpetuate for so long his wishes through trustees? Various conjectures were advanced. Some said he sought to found a great house of merchant princes, like the Medicis and the Rothschilds. Others thought the will indicated nothing more than a wish to provide for his children and children's children. Still others saw in it Field's passionate desire to project his personality beyond his own lifetime and to be identified with succeeding generations.

Fortunes passing from fathers to firstborn sons in patrilineal lines had existed since the Middle Age, but, as one scholar put it, had never before been equaled in old England or New England. In his 1839 book *Democracy in America*, Alexis de Tocqueville had noted with approval the tendency in the United States to disperse and distribute wealth. Was Field trying to establish a dynasty in the manner of a medieval lord? Would it be in the public interest if his grandsons in turn rolled over the estate until it exceeded billions of dollars? The trustees showed that under the income tax laws in force in 1920, 72 percent of the gross income of the estate would go to the government. The Illinois Supreme Court agreed. It ruled that holding the residuary estate in trust until the grandsons reached fifty did not violate regulations governing perpetuities and was not contrary to public policy. Was there a second reason behind piling the fortune forward? Postponing payout delayed Illinois death taxes—federal estate taxes were not adopted until 1916. A realist, however, would probably bet that politicians, always in search for revenues, were more likely to increase than lower estate taxes in the future.*

National magazines analyzed and assessed the life. The *Outlook* weekly, for which Theodore Roosevelt wrote reform arti-

---

*Settling the Marshall Field fortune was a charm compared to resolving the Levi Leiter inheritance. To share out the Leiter trust among some twenty descendants took sixty-five years and the death of Leiter's last surviving great-grandchild.

Daniel Chester French's Field memorial at Graceland Cemetery.

cles, applauded Field for not having been a speculator, for having "abstained from those gigantic schemes of foisting upon the public great blocks of inflated securities which have made the phrase 'high finance' a byword, and from using trust funds for secret and personal ends." *World's Work* saw a "scientific" method to buying and selling. The muckraking *Everybody's Magazine* thought his winning trait was his foresight and concentration on making money. His fault was his poor politics. As Chicago's leading citizen, it said, he sided with the despoilers in the Yerkes case. As the city's richest man, his philanthropies were tremendous and admirable, but did not exceed those of some other citizens, and never represented sacrifice.

After much discussion, the executors of the estate approached

Daniel Chester French about creating a monument to Field at Graceland Cemetery. French, the most famous American sculptor, worked in the Renaissance idiom of Augustus Saint-Gaudens. He had won the competition for the *Minute Man*, a monument commemorating the rising of the citizens of Concord, Massachusetts, and was the sculptor of *The Republic*, a sixty-four-foot personification for the 1893 Columbian Exposition, the largest figure ever constructed in the United States. His inspiration for the Marshall Field cenotaph was Mary Lawton, a tall, red-headed actress. In 1908, she became his house guest at his Stockbridge, Massachusetts, studio and posed for him as a seated figure swathed in folds of drapery pinned at the shoulder, her arms resting on large boxes placed on each side like the armrests of a throne, a motif he repeated six years later when he began work on the seated marble figure of Abraham Lincoln for the Lincoln Memorial in Washington, D.C. For the Field memorial, entitled *Memory*, he adjusted the head of the life-size female figure to give her a sense of self-absorbed reverie. To enhance the feeling of meditation, a reflecting pool stretched horizontally at her feet.

After the day of mourning, the store reopened with John Shedd as president. After Junior's untimely death, Field had transferred his hopes to his twenty-six-year-old nephew, and the trustees duly elected Stanley first vice-president. Before the fatal New Year's trip to New York, Field had told Stanley he planned to modify his will, that among the changes he wanted to make were bigger donations to charitable institutions and a doubling of his bequest to the museum. Shedd, James Simpson, and Stanley Field were now the only close associates of the founder still active.

Shedd had obtained Field's approval for tearing down the State and Washington store and building a new, larger complex.

When the trustees refused, Shedd took them to court and won the right to proceed. Covering a city block and encompassing 2.9 million square feet, the new store opened on September 30, 1907 with eight thousand persons—nearly all of them women—lining the sidewalks for the 8:00 A.M. opening. Once the doors were unlocked, they brushed past Shedd in wing collar and cravat with a pearl stickpin to gaze at the Tiffany dome before rushing toward the seventy-six elevators. The "cathedral of stores" featured an entire floor dedicated to restaurants. A new shipping department was located deep underground, two stories below the bargain basement, with access to the city's new tunnel railroad. Shedd enhanced the foreign buying staff to seek out unique merchandise, which allowed him to say: "If you cannot find it at Field's you won't find it anywhere."

Albertine fled Chicago, fled the humiliating rumors that her husband had been shot in a whorehouse, fled the American wealth she called a curse, but not its dividends. Taking Marshall III, Henry, and little Gwendolyn with her, she escaped to London. She bought a house at 2 Carleton Terrace and entered Marshall and Henry—Gwendolyn was only four—in English schools. Two years later, she surprised her Chicago friends by marrying British army captain Maldwin A. Drummond, the son of the scion of an old banking firm that for generations had handled the accounts of royalty and members of the peerage. Albertine was received at court, and her parties were social events of the London season. She was a frequent visitor to Chicago, and hit the headlines in 1911 when her stateroom onboard the Hamburg-American liner *Amerika* was broken into and she was robbed of $130,000 worth of jewelry. Not in the best of health, she sold the London house and retired to Cadland, her husband's ancestral home near Southampton Waters in southern England. Cadland was vast and Georgian, with an enchanting view of the English Channel. Albertine's money allowed her husband to support the expense of the estate and its modernization. The boys had friends down for weekends of shooting, fishing, sailing, and riding. Marshall Field III loved his stepfather and Cadland. Later in life he would say the pre–World War I years were the last period in history when being rich was pure, careless fun.

16

GRANDSONS

MARSHALL III WAS OLD ENOUGH TO UNDERSTAND THE TRAGEDY
and as an adult came to believe his father had committed suicide.
However, the mystery of Marshall II's death would not go away.
In the weeks that followed Junior's death, Marshall Senior had Dr.
Robert H. Harvey, a highly regarded physician, say that in the
absence of family physician Frank Billings, he had been called to
Prairie Avenue. Here, the thirty-seven-year-old heir had told him,
"I do not know how this happened. I can account for it in no way.
It was an accident. What are the chances of my recovery,
Doctor?" It seemed no one had witnessed the shooting, acciden-
tal or self-inflicted, and it was painfully apparent that the family
was hiding something. Marshall III was twelve and his recollec-
tion, perhaps encouraged by his mother and grandfather, of hear-
ing a shot clashed not only with the accounts of a sensationalist

Marshall III, Albertine and Henry.

press, but with the research of the historian Ferdinand Lundberg. In *America's Sixty Families*, Lundberg would write: "Marshall Field II was fatally shot or stabbed by a Spanish girl in the Everleigh Club." And there was Pony Moore's story. This black gambler and owner of the Turf Exchange Saloon was involved in a scheme by brothelkeepers to frame the Everleigh sisters in Marshall's death. Moore and his associates offered one of their girls $20,000 to testify that she had seen Minna Everleigh shoot the Field heir. Overhearing the plot on the telephone—the first use of the phone to make a dramatic plot point—Minna had police haul Moore in and, two days later, revoke his saloon license. The only Chicago newspaper that alluded to this misadventure of one of the city's newsworthy personages was the *Chicago Daily Socialist*. The Associated Press was silent, and the newspapers of the nation were therefore not advised of the episode. Eighteen years later, however, the *Chicago Daily News* incidentally mentioned the affair in another connection, creating a nine-day sensation among Chicago newspaper people. The connection was the arrest of Vera Scott in Los Angeles in 1924. Questioned as a suspect in a series of frauds, Scott presented herself as a former chorus girl who had danced in such New York shows as *Hanky Panky* and *Hoity Toity*. She told police she had shot Marshall Junior by accident during a party at the Everleigh Club, and that he had insisted on going home alone in a taxi. Marshall Field had been dead for eighteen years in 1924, and it was safe for her to claim the old man had paid her $20,000 to skip town. A spokesman for Marshall Field & Company dismissed her assertions as "the ravings of a drug-mad unfortunate," adding that police and coroner's reports had concluded Marshall Junior had shot himself with his own pistol while packing for a camping trip.

Marshall III was, like his father, delicate. As a youngster, he had suffered from rheumatic fever, the then ill-understood condition caused by a streptococcal infection and marked by acute inflammation and pain of the joints. He enjoyed Cambridge because the university exposed him to new ideas and to people who were completely different. With Oliver Lyttleton, a classmate, Marshall borrowed his stepfather's yacht and crossed the Channel to carouse in Deauville. His mother had made it clear that he owed it to himself and to his fortune to do something responsible with his mind, and Trinity College made him aware of the world and its problems. His closest friend was Rudolph de Trafford, the respectable son of one of Albertine's acquaintances, and Rudolph was often a guest at Cadland. "I found Cambridge utterly delightful," Marshall would write later. He took private lodging outside Trinity College and with his tutor mapped out a program. "He proved to be conscientious enough, but not at all a hard worker," his biographer Stephen Becker would write in

1964. "Much more is left to the individual in English universities than in America, and there was no nonsense about Field's being a freshman; a Trinity man was a Trinity man from his first moment, with all the rights, privileges, and obligations implied, and he could be brilliant in his first week or a damned fool for three years. Field was neither. He was a well-turned-out young gentleman, more interested in recreation than in study, but aware that he was expected to become, somehow, moderately well educated."

Henry, two years Marshall's junior, hated his boarding schools. Although he had lived and gone to school in Britain since he was ten, he showed a studied dislike for things British. These sentiments echoed the misgivings of the Field trustees back in Chicago. When Albertine asked the estate for more money for her children's education, one of the trustees asserted that the amount asked for was too much and reminded the former Mrs. Field, now Mrs. Drummond, that her father-in-law had wanted the boys, and eventually little Gwendolyn, to have an American education. The trustees relented, however, and Mrs. Drummond got the money she wanted.

Marshall's good looks and pleasant manner as well as his wealth made him popular. He spent the summer 1914 at Cadland. Albertine had cancer, and the summer's social rounds were curtailed. Guests dropped in quietly. One houseguest who made an impression on Marshall was Evelyn Marshall, the daughter of the late Charles Marshall, who at age fifty had married a daughter of the colonial Lenox family half his age. In 1912, the Marshalls had been on their way to Europe on board the *Carpathia* when their ship interrupted its voyage to steam to the rescue of the survivors of the *Titanic*. Fearful of icebergs, they started out again from New York on a southern route. Evelyn's mother went ashore at Gibraltar and caught pneumonia. She began a difficult recovery in

Naples, and the couple and their daughter continued to Paris, where Charles died of heart failure.

Albertine's deteriorating health and the widowed Mrs. Marshall's convalescence subdued Marshall and Evelyn—Bunny to her friends—during the month of July that Mrs. Marshall and her daughter spent at Cadland. Evelyn was twenty-five, four years older than Marshall. The young people liked what they saw in each other.

Marshall was a few weeks short of his twenty-first birthday when the Guns of August catapulted Europe into the most brutal conflict humanity had ever seen. The United States expected to remain indefinitely at peace, and President Woodrow Wilson immediately issued a proclamation of neutrality. Evelyn left for Paris, where her mother wanted to volunteer for hospital work.

Nineteen-year-old Henry considered himself American, which didn't prevent him from being swept up in the patriotic fever that motivated Great Britain during the first months of the war. He signed up as a civilian volunteer on an ambulance team, and left for the front in France. The first battle of the Marne was fought in the early weeks of September. The casualties were horrendous—more French and British soldiers were killed in a few months than Americans lost in the four-year Civil War. Marshall, meanwhile, headed in the opposite direction. In order for him to take his seat as a trustee at his maturity, his presence in Chicago was required. From Paris, Evelyn wrote that she was booking passage aboard the British passenger liner *Lusitania*. Marshall made arrangements to cross on the same ship. The indiscriminate sinking of Allied ships by German U-boats was several months away and the crossing was uneventful, except for the time he and Evelyn spent together. Their summer together at Cadland and shipboard reunion blossomed into romance. The Hearst *American*

Weekly reported the story under the title: A SENSIBLE ROMANCE OF MARSHALL FIELD III, THE RICHEST BOY IN THE WORLD.

To see New York's large German population cheer the kaiser was a shock for someone arriving from wartime England. Recent German immigrants, many of them still reservists in the German army, paraded down Fifth Avenue with German flags and brawled with New Yorkers of British and French descent who displayed the Union Jack and the *Tricolore*. William Randolph Hearst, owner of *Deutches Journal*, a New York German-language period- ical, opposed any help to the Allies. Federal officials scanned Hearst's papers for sedition, and a Secret Service agent infiltrated the news tycoon's home disguised as a butler.

Albertine's failing health brought Henry back from the front. London had its attractions for young men heading to war or, like ambulance driver Henry Field, coming back from the trenches. He met Peggy Marsh, a fellow American and member of the *Palace Theatre Follies* cast, and promptly fell in love. Née Annabelle Greenough, a descendant of forebears who had arrived in the American colonies in 1650, she had taken the stage name Peggy Marsh when she became a chorus girl in New York's *Palace Theatre Follies* and was sent on tour to London. The outbreak of war demanded entertainment for the armed forces, and the troupe stayed in Britain. Stage-door Johnnies were a dime a dozen, and Peggy was discerning enough to realize her admirer was the mil- lionaire grandson of Marshall Field and the nephew of Royal Navy Commander Beatty. When Marshall telegraphed that he was marrying Evelyn Marshall and asked Henry to be his best man, Henry told Peggy he would send for her, and sailed to New York.

NEW YORK

17

SECRETS AND SPIES

A WEEK BEFORE MARSHALL AND EVELYN'S PLANNED WEDDING, they both came down with influenza—so-called because it was believed to be caused by the influence (*influenza* in Italian) of some mysterious agent. Some people believed the flu amounted to German biological warfare. New York's health commission pronounced the city in no danger of an epidemic, only to be proven wrong as more New Yorkers fell ill and died. Incoming ships were fumigated. Too late. In twenty-four hours the death toll in the city climbed to more than eight hundred. Overcrowded hospitals turned away patients, and doctors urged everybody to stay home. Marshall and Evelyn followed this advice and opted to be married at her parents' home at 6 East 77th Street. To please his mother, the February 8, 1915, wedding was Catholic, although neither Evelyn nor Marshall was Catholic. The honeymoon took the newlyweds to Florida, but news of his mother's worsening health made them embark for England. They were halfway across the Atlantic when a shore-to-ship telegram advised them that Albertine Field Drummond had died. The death was hardest on thirteen-year-old Gwendolyn. She went to live with Aunt Ethel, whose husband, now Admiral David Beatty, was at sea on active duty commanding a Royal Navy battle cruiser.

Marshall and Evelyn sailed back to New York shortly after the May 7, 1915, sinking by a German submarine of the *Lusitania* off the coast of Ireland. The loss of 188 American lives radically changed the mood in America. Politicians who the year earlier had applauded Wilson for keeping the country neutral, asked when he would declare war on Germany. What also riled public opinion was the Allied interception of a German Foreign Ministery note to the Mexican government, offering Mexico the return of Texas, New Mexico, and Arizona after an American defeat, if Mexico would ally itself with Germany. Still, the president hesitated and appealed to the warring powers to come to an understanding and achieve "peace without victory." At the same time, he ordered stepped-up shipments of war matériel to the Allies. A mile-long peninsula jutting into the Hudson River from Jersey City behind the State of Liberty was the transfer point of munitions to Allied ships. When two million pounds of explosives erupted in a series of blasts during the night of July 30, 1916, windows shattered as far north as Manhattan's 42nd Street. German saboteurs were suspected, and a giant ring of German spies was uncovered. Financed by Count Johann von Bernstorff, the kaiser's ambassador to the United States, the spies' nest was an old-fashioned house at 123 West 15th Street rented by Martha Held, who called herself Martha Gordon.

*   *   *

Henry was twenty-two, single, and rich, and despite influenza and ammunitions blowups, peacetime Manhattan was far from the trenches of the Marne. His brother and new sister-in-law took him everywhere. At a lawn party he met and fell in love with Nancy Keene Perkins. She was a Virginia debutante and the daughter of the eldest of the legendary Langhorne sisters. Her mother, Lizzie, was the first of the five daughters of Chillie and Nanaire Langhorne. The Civil War had ruined the Langhornes, but railway speculation revived the family fortune. Lizzie had married Moncure Perkins, a fellow Virginian, and over the years became jealous of her four flamboyant sisters. Irene was the wife of painter Charles Dana Gibson and the "Gibson Girl" star model. The remaining sisters, Nancy, Phyllis, and Nora, married Englishmen. Nora became the wife the London architect Paul Phipps, and Phyllis married the City banker Robert Brand, later Sir Bob, vice president of the League of Nations financial conference. The most spectacular catch was Nancy's. After divorcing an alcoholic millionaire polo player she had met at Newport, Rhode Island, she married Viscount William Waldorf Astor, the son of the richest man in the world. In a by-election to fill her husband's House of Commons seat in 1919, Nancy became the first woman elected to Parliament. Over the next decade, Lady Astor, as she was universally known, displayed such a flair for politics that she remained a Conservative MP until 1945, concentrating on issues affecting women and children. She acted in the forefront of events and was loved and hated, admired and deplored. It was she who told Winston Churchill that if she were his wife she'd poison his tea, to which he famously replied, "My dear Nancy, if I were your husband, I'd drink it."

Nancy Perkins was a vivacious girl with a flair for decorating. She was with several girlfriends when she saw two men walk across the lawn and said she was sure the tall handsome one was married, and the other one not. She was wrong on both accounts, and was soon introduced to the tall and handsome Henry Field. When he proposed, she said yes.

He suggested a quiet wedding—and no wonder. Peggy had arrived in Chicago with a baby boy she claimed was Henry's and was bargaining with Marshall and the family attorneys. On February 6, 1917, Henry and Nancy's wedding day, Peggy signed a financial agreement filed with Chicago's probate court. Henry agreed to pay her $1,000 a year in monthly installments to support her child born "on or about July 11, 1916." The annual remittance would increase to $2,500 when little Henry reached five and again by that amount at age ten, and big Henry would either designate little Henry the beneficiary of a $100,000 insurance policy or set up an irrevocable trust paying the boy a minimum of $20,000 annually for life. On signing Peggy received a $5,000 bonus for accepting three conditions: that she renounce all future claims against big Henry, never communicate with him except through his attorney, and bring up the child "with care and diligence."

Two months to the day after Henry and Nancy's wedding, the United States declared war on the Central Powers of Germany, Austria-Hungary, Bulgaria, and the Ottoman Empire. The first act of war took place in New York Harbor when six hundred customs agents seized eighteen German ships in port and interned fifteen hundred German sailors and naval officers on Ellis Island. Before Henry could even think of enlisting, Marshall had already tried, only to be turned down because of his rheumatic fever. He found the rejection humiliating, all the more so since Aunt Ethel's husband was a British naval hero. The battle cruiser David Beatty commanded had drawn the heaviest fire during the 1916 Battle of

Jutland, the only major engagement between the British and German fleets. Marshall was at Evelyn's side on June 15, 1916, when Marshall Field IV was born in New York. The proud new father sent a cable to his Cambridge chum Rudolph de Trafford, now a lieutenant: WANT YOU TO BE GODFATHER TO YOUNG MARSHALL. HE WILL DO YOU CREDIT.

Passionate patriotism swept the country. Although the "selected draft" exempted fathers, Marshall couldn't wait to be one of the one million men enlisting. He decided to use Chicago family influence. With Evelyn and baby Marshall, he rushed to Chicago, where Colonel Milton J. Foreman, a family friend and commanding officer of the First Illinois Cavalry, chose to ignore Marshall's rheumatic fever and swear him in on the spot. The *Chicago Tribune* applauded:

> America's richest young man has taken the direct step dictated by unadulterated patriotism. Many will rise to say that Field has done only what everybody should do. They will be careful to ignore the fact that everybody isn't doing it.

"From now on I am just plain Private Field," he told reporters, "and I shall feel very uncomfortable if it is suggested that I be treated as anything but an ordinary private in Headquarters Troop. . . . My wife, after some reflection, agreed to my enlistment. Because I don't know enough about military matters to be an officer, I enlisted as a private. I chose the cavalry because I believed this organization was more likely than others to see service, and because I considered it the most distinguished of the Illinois organization. The fact that I like horseback riding and have done a great deal of riding may have had something to do with my enlisting in the cavalry."

Marshall Field III.

Until the First Illinois Cavalry—renamed Second Field Artillery, First National Guard—was up to full strength, army life was relaxed. Marshall learned the regulations and studied tactics and leadership. He was far from the gentlemen's code of Cambridge, and learned to live in barracks with working-class men. Several tried to borrow money from him, and he found himself compelled to offer small loans. "He subdued his suspicions," his biographer Stephen Becker would write, "and suffered quietly for the first time from a conflict that would be refought time and again in his life between his belief that men were naturally good and his knowledge that some of them would take what they could get."

In New York, meanwhile, former frontline ambulance driver Henry decided to have his tonsils out before enlisting. After a successful operation at the Presbyterian Hospital, he was released. He was back three months later with a raging infection. Empyema, a condition characterized by accumulation of pus in a body fissure, was found in the pericardial cavity. Doctors postponed a then life-threatening heart operation in the hope that the abscess would clear of itself. When it didn't, surgeons inserted a drain behind Henry's heart. Marshall was granted a compassionate leave and rushed to join his sister-in-law at Henry's bedside. A hospital spokesperson told inquiring reporters that Henry Field had been readmitted "for a slight operation" and that a speedy recovery was expected. On July 9, Chicago newspaper reported that the "slight operation" had failed and that Henry Field was dead. Reporters would write that Marshall left the Presbyterian Hospital morgue the wealthiest young man in the world—sole benefactor of his grandfather's trust. Although he would not come into possession of the estate until he turned fifty, the press estimated his wealth to be $200 million.*

It is not clear *who* decided to stop the child support payments to Peggy Marsh. The mother of Henry's illegitimate child would accuse Marshall, but the decision was more likely made by one of the Field estate lawyers, since Sergeant Marshall Field III was in the army.

---

* $2.6 billion in 2002 money. Starting with the inception of the Federal Reserve Bank in 1913, the Minneapolis Federal Reserve calculates the Consumer Price Index year by year at its web site, woodrow.mpls.frb. fed.us, under "What's a dollar worth?"

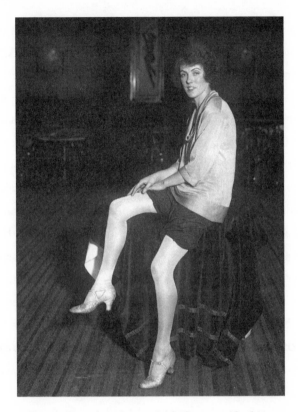

Peggy Marsh. *(Copyright © Bettman/Corbis)*

Peggy lived in a modest apartment in New York with her son and an often-absent lover named Antoine Jechalski. Jechalski had a scar on one cheek, which he claimed was a memento of a saber duel during his student days in Vienna. His origins and allegiances were a little hard to sort out. He had arrived in 1914, he said, to procure American steel for the Russian imperial army. While the United States was neutral, he openly espoused the cause of Russia's enemy and spoke enviously of his brother in the Austro-Hungarian cavalry. He claimed inside knowledge of German weapons. He said he knew about the *Grosse Bertha* before Kaiser Wilhelm's huge cannon was aimed at Paris from 100 kilometers away. Because he was a skillful polo player and a keen judge of horses, he had ingratiated himself with the Long Island equestrian set, and was a habitué of watering holes where German spies and American counterspies mingled with slumming debutantes and young society matrons with husbands "over there." His close associates were Russian immigrants who squandered questionable incomes on gambling. One was his friend Prince Paul Trubetskoy, the Russian sculptor whose brace of Russian wolfhounds and escapades with fast automobiles and fast women caused a sensation. Peggy had accompanied Jechalski in his private Pullman compartment to San Francisco. They had stopped along the way at various mining towns, where she spent nights alone in small hotels while he visited with miners.

A knock one morning made Peggy rush to the door in the hope that one of Field's lawyers was hand-delivering a check. Instead of a messenger, she confronted a man in uniform who identified himself as Chief Yeoman Macgregor Bond of naval intelligence. Could he ask a few questions?

Bond's report on the first of several interviews described Peggy Marsh as "a well-bred girl, with quiet manners and maternal instincts." In civilian life Bond was an investigative reporter for the *New York Herald*, and he phrased his questions without letting her know how intimate he was with the government's file on Jechalski. Possibly to scare her, he told her that Secret Service and Department of Justice investigators had already interrogated Jechalski. Their reports described him as having "a very slight German accent, rigid, erect, cold and formal carriage and manners."

Peggy spilled all she knew. She had met Antoine through another free-spending Russian immigrant, Alexander Weinstein, a stage-door Johnny she had known during her chorus girl days in London. Weinstein had given each girl at the Palace Theatre a handbag with her initials in diamonds. Peggy still had her hand-bag and showed it to Bond. When Bond commented on the good behavior of the toddler clinging to Peggy's chair, she told the sad story of her romance with Henry Field, of his promise to marry her and make little Henry his legitimate son and heir, and how Marshall Field III had reneged on the settlement. "Miss Marsh believes it is the intention of the family to cut it off entirely," Bond noted.

Bond was not unsympathetic to the unwed mother. He was there to find out whether Jechalski was a German spy or a Bolshevik provocateur. A month after the October Revolution brought Lenin to power, the new Russian leader made a separate peace with Germany. When Peggy told Bond how Jechalski had left her alone in hotels in western mining towns, the suspicion that he was a Bolshevik provocateur seemed to fall into place. Copper, lead, and zinc miners' strikes had followed the stopovers at mining towns. She also remembered that Antoine traveled with a camera, and from the moving train had snapped photos of military installations, hydroelectric dams, and transmission towers.

Bond saw signs of alcohol abuse in Peggy's face and shaky hands. In his report he noted that despite her misfortunes and her rather doubtful friends—British intelligence had shadowed Weinstein during his 1914 stay in London—"she is a pure American, intensely loyal and shows every desire to help this office in its investigation." However, she was not candid enough to tell him Jechalski had found her a couple of lawyers and staked them to the retainer they required to file suit against the Fields.

Peggy knew she shared Antoine's affection with other women—Bond could have told her who. He had interrogated two of them. One was Clara Kimball Young, a movie queen of regal beauty and yearning eyes famous for her portrayal of Anne Boleyn. The actress had taken up with Jechalski on the rebound after an affair with Lewis Selznick, who had made her a star in *Trilby* and *Camille*. She, too, had cooperated with Bond, and so did Nita Naldi, a screen vamp who would star with Rudolph Valentino in *Blood and Sand*. "She said she always suspected he was a German spy," Bond reported, "she even accused him to his face, but he always laughed and shrugged his shoulders and said he was used to being called a spy." Jechalski was playing polo at a cavalry station in Texas when he was arrested on spy charges, jailed at Fort Sam Houston, and isolated in solitary confinement.

Ironically, Marshall Field III was also in Houston. As a sergeant in the 58th Artillery Brigade, he spent six months at Camp Logan waiting to be shipped to France. Evelyn came down for a visit. The 58th was still there in January 1918 when Evelyn gave birth to their first daughter, Barbara.

In May, Field's unit moved to Camp Merritt, New Jersey. At Hoboken, they boarded the *Kashmir* and, after a cramped if uneventful crossing, arrived at Liverpool June 8 and were ordered to Southampton. Cadland was nearby, but there was no time to visit his stepfather. A day later, the 58th doughboys, now part of the 33rd Division's 122nd Field Artillery, crossed the Channel and found themselves on French soil at Le Havre. For five nights they marched north and finally reached the front on the Meuse River. On September 12 they were thrown into the battle for Saint-Mihiel. In September 1914, the Germans had captured the town to isolate and capture Verdun, thirty miles to the north. From February to December 1916, Verdun had been the center of the bloodiest fighting of the war, with French forces resisting relentless German offensives. But September 1918 was not September 1914. Bulgaria surrendered, and the Ottoman Empire collapsed under its own weight. In the Verdun sector there were seven hundred thousand Americans. Marshall's unit was in the thick of mopping up. The Americans took seventeen thousand prisoners as they gradually dislodged the enemy from Saint-Mihiel. Revolution and mutinies swept Germany. The kaiser abdicated. A weapons standstill ended the war on November 11. Marshall was now a captain.

War's end changed the mood in the United States. The armistice had come a few days after state and congressional elections. Little attention had been paid to politics in the civilian administration of the war, but peace revived partisanship. Prominent Republicans attacked President Wilson, resulting in the election of a slim Republican majority in both the House and Senate. Peace translated into roaring inflation and indifference toward wartime intrigues. As Captain Marshall Field went on furlough to Rome, Antoine Jechalski walked out of prison in Texas.

All that the government's massive investigation added up to was that Jechalski had been a war profiteer who had raked in a fortune by wedging himself between the Russian Supply Committee in New York and its American arms suppliers of rifles, munitions, locomotives, and boxcars. After he left Fort Sam Houston a free man, he caught a train to New York. Here he cleaned out his financial accounts and left for Poland, again a sovereign nation under the Versailles Treaty. He became a Polish government official, but whenever he applied for a U.S. visa, the State Department denied him entry on the grounds that he remained under suspicion as a communist spy.

In Rome, Captain Field spent a few weeks with U.S. Ambassador and Mrs. Thomas Nelson Page. The envoy's wife was almost family. Her first husband had been Marshall's great-uncle Henry Field, who had died in 1890 and left her an estate of $2 million. Still in uniform, Marshall was attached to the embassy staff and given diplomatic privileges. His biographer, Stephen Becker, would write that the trip gave rise to false rumors that Marshall somehow played a backstage part in preparing the Allied negotiations that resulted in the 1919 Versailles peace treaty. Before President Wilson joined British Prime Minister David Lloyd George, French President Georges Clemenceau, and Italian Premier Vittorio Orlando to negotiate and impose the Allies' terms on Germany at Versailles in June, Captain Field sailed home. He was ready to assume the mantle as America's richest twenty-five-year-old.

The death of his brother—and demands on behalf of Henry's illegitimate son—required Marshall's attention. The trustees of his grandfather's will were not sure whether Nancy Perkins Field had dower rights to her late husband's estate or whether Henry's inheritance should go to Marshall. To solve the question, Marshall met with the trustees in Chicago and, with their consent, sued the estate. The case involved some $40 million, and the complicated lawsuit had him appear as both complainant and defendant. The litigation took the better part of two years to resolve. The court case Peggy Marsh brought on behalf of two-year-old Henry involved $2 million, but with appeals took the same amount of time.

The attorneys Antoine Jechalski had retained for Peggy were no ambulance chasers, but a father-and-son team calculated to strike fear in Marshall Field III. Former Illinois governor Edward Dunne represented little Henry Anthony Field Marsh, while Dunne's son, Edward Junior, served as the boy's legal guardian. Both Dunnes were prominent Chicago Democrats. "We feel that Mrs. Marsh has a perfectly legitimate claim," Dunne Senior told the press on the courthouse steps in January 1920, "as is further shown by the fact that it is recognized by young Field's family."

With that he handed reporters copies of the 1917 agreement signed on Henry Field's wedding day.

Peggy and little Henry suffered a setback on March 13, 1920. Attorneys for Marshall III had petitioned the Illinois Supreme Court to "construe" the definition of "issue" in the late Marshall Field's will to exclude offspring born out of wedlock. The court sided with the Field family. Peggy persevered, filed suit in circuit court, and on June 11, 1920, suffered a second defeat when the court ruled that her son had "no right, title or interest of any kind in or to any of the property" in big Henry's estate.

Seven months later, Peggy married Albert "Buddie" Johnson, a flying ace war veteran with some money of his own. Days before the probate court was ready to approve distribution of Henry Field's personal estate, Marshall III offered her $100,000 in exchange for dropping all claims against the Field family on her son's behalf. She quickly accepted, and held a press conference to announce that she and Buddie would hit the vaudeville circuit as a song-and-dance act. They were in a private island resort in the Adirondack Mountains one stormy night eight months later when Peggy brought Buddie to a hospital in Plattsburgh, New York, with a bullet in his abdomen. Fellow vacationers told police of nightly shouting in the Johnsons' quarters and of hearing a shot ring out. Peggy explained that she had heard the shot, too, rushed to her room, and found Buddie lying in a pool of blood. She had dragged him to the dock, loaded him into a dinghy, and through torrential rain rowed to the mainland. Her husband told police it was an accident. He had been fooling with a pistol he had found in the resort owner's cabinet and the weapon had discharged. No charges were filed.

Two months later Peggy called another news conference to announce she and Buddie were splitting because "he is so tempera-mental and high-strung that I decided we had better part for six months to see how things develop." She returned to the London of her chorus girl days and opened a dance club. When Buddie died of pneumonia four months later, she went back to New York, shed a tear for reporters greeting her White Star liner, and announced that she had expected Buddie to join her. She returned to London a rich widow, and celebrated the arrival of 1925 by marrying Captain Keld Robert Fenwick of the Royal Horse Guards. Three years later she told a news conference she was divorcing Captain Fenwick and was "fed up" with British men. She and her son vanished into what Karl Marx once called "the dustbin of history."

After months of submissions—records of the proceedings, printed and typed, filled several thousand pages—and a week of hearings in May 1920, the probate court handed down its ruling on Henry's estate on June 20. The decree cut both ways. The late Henry Field's share in all trusts and interests was to be transferred to Marshall, and Nancy Perkins Field was entitled to dower rights. Marshall would receive the sums specified in his grandfather's will, plus the amount specified for Henry, and, if he lived to be fifty, would receive the entire residuary estate. In the meantime, he was free to work out a settlement with Nancy Perkins Field. In regard to Henry's former mistress and her son, he was free of all obligations.

Nancy settled for an undisclosed sum. Like her famous aunts, she moved to England, and in 1920 married Ethel's son, Ronald Tree. The marriage didn't last, and her third husband was Juby Lancaster. In old age, she flew the Confederate flag from the pediment of her Haseley mansion and from a window once threatened an official trying to serve legal papers with a shotgun. Her aunt Nancy Astor spent time at Haseley, and told male visitors either to court her niece because she adored men or not to pay attention to Nancy because "she lies for pleasure."

18

HOW TO SPEND IT

MARSHALL FIELD III BEGAN A FABULOUS LIFE IN THE FABULOUS ERA after he and Evelyn moved to New York. The signposts of the Roaring Twenties were the speakeasy and the bull market, and Marshall patronized both. When reporters asked if he was the richest young man in America, he said, "I can't answer that. I won't come into the bulk of my fortune until I'm fifty years old, if I live that long." To follow-up questions about his role in administering the estate, he said, "I'm not going to run anything. There are four trustees, and I'm one of them. Another is the bank, and the other two are getting old. I'm just going to help. I have no title, no official situation."

The first Chicagoan to know the Fields were planning to live in New York was George Richardson. We do not know who recommended this trainee at the Northern Trust Company, but one afternoon in the spring of 1921 the young man received a phone call from Field asking if they could meet. When they did, Marshall told him he was planning to move to New York and wondered whether, in his absence, Richardson would like to represent him as a trustee of his grandfather's estate. The offer was an unheard-of opportunity. The other trustees resented Richardson in the beginning, but he took pains to familiarize himself with the estate and with tax laws, and remained a trustee for thirty-five years.

Americans were cheerful and optimistic, and a short-lived postwar recession blew over in an avalanche of consumer goods, from radios and refrigerators and shiny bathroom fixtures to that new craze, automobiles. Women threw away tassels and trains, laces and hoops, cut their hair, and went for an all-new look. Gabrielle "Coco" Chanel typified womanhood in a decade in which a woman might earn her own living, choose whom to love, and live according to her own precepts. Serpentine slimness replaced Rubenesque fullness, and the new feminine ideal was "flexible and tubular, like a section of boa constrictor," as Aldous Huxley described the New Woman in his 1923 novel *Antic Hay*. Forty thousand shoppers thronged the Marshall Field & Company store every day. Two hundred thousand shoppers filled the store daily during the Christmas rush, when tradition demanded that parents take their children to the Walnut Room for its trademark Frango-mint chocolate ice cream pie, and a look at the forty-five-foot tree and the State Street windows. The man in charge was Hughston McBain, who had joined the company shortly after leaving the University of Michigan, and while still in his thirties, became a director and first vice-president. While lagging behind R. H. Macy & Company in sales—$116 million to $95 million by 1940—Marshall Field & Company's net was twice that of Macy's.

In business, McBain was another Harry Selfridge. He closed the wholesale division and concentrated on upgrading the department store. With grand openings that became breathless social events, he launched twenty-eight swank in-store shops. After one year, the shops' profits were $150,000. Shoppers lunched in five restaurants where the perambulating chef Duncan Hines of the future cake fame made on-the-hour appearances. A bookstore was added on the third floor next to an enlarged toy department. The management of the new division found it unwise to attempt to censor books, but what it called "radical" books were not featured. The store's maxim was all-encompassing: Just as Marshall Field's took care of a customer when her means were modest, it would fulfill her wishes when she became rich. To appeal to middle- and lower-income consumers, McBain improved the lower-end "budget floor." The proof of his régime's success was to be found on the balance sheet. By 1938, the corporate debt was $14 million, as compared with $32 million eight years earlier. In a move that would have scandalized the founder, McBain allowed 20 percent of the workforce to unionize.

The 1920s were prodigal years for Harry Selfridge. Rose had died in 1918, and the widowed Harry found solace in a May-September affair with the extraordinary Gaby Deslys. The two had met during the war when the French actress appeared at the Palace Theater and shocked London not only with her ooh-lá-lá naughtiness, but also with her no-nonsense attitude toward young officers who invited her to late-night suppers after the show. She had a cut-and-dried tariff for stage-door Johnnies who requested the pleasure of her company, however innocent, in public. She had refused to marry the Duc de Crussol, stating that no man was rich enough to buy her. Harry was in his sixties when he set her up in Kensington Gore, where her bed lay on a dais beneath an arch of black marble supported by marble pillars. He gave her the run of his office and the store and spent tens of thousands of pounds on jewelry and gems. She died in 1920. Harry lived another twenty-seven years, dying in 1947 a few weeks short of his ninetieth birthday.

Marshall Field III was neither McBain nor Mile-a-Minute Harry. Nothing in Marshall's upbringing had prepared him for merchandising, and he knew it. He possessed an English gentleman's education and had been tempered by war. People called him "a damned nice fellow." He was a solid conservative, a sportsman, a father of two, and, first and inescapably, a multimillionaire. Wisely, he declined any role in the department store, yet sought to make himself useful. Many of his classmates from Cambridge were among Great Britain's 900,000 war dead—Germany suffered 1.8 million casualties, France 1.4 million, and the U.S. 116,000. For four years of trench warfare, Europe's youth had been sacrificed to advance, surrender, and regain once more a few hundred meters of muddy no man's land. Rudolph de Trafford was one of the survivors, and Marshall invited him to join Evelyn, the children, and himself on a California vacation. Marshall talked of having done his duty, but like his grandfather's experience during the Civil War, he believed war was bad for business. What the world needed was the League of Nations, a forum to settle its disputes. If peace could be maintained, even the new Soviet Union might moderate its revolutionary politics. He was appalled by the internal Republican Party squabbles that led to the nomination of Warren G. Harding of Ohio as the Republican Party's presidential hopeful in the 1920 election, the first election in which women could vote. The Democrats' candidate was Ohio

Governor James Cox. Harding won handily, although he had little experience in national politics and in foreign affairs wanted to keep the country out of the League of Nations.

The Fields and Rudy de Trafford went to Santa Barbara after spending time in Los Angeles and on Catalina Island, the tony weekend retreat for the new movie people. Marshall's cousin Arthur Ronald Tree joined them. After a stint as an economics professor at the University of Chicago, Ethel's eldest son spent most of his time in Britain, where he owned a country estate. Ronald was both imaginative and practical, and for a while was the managing editor of *Forum* magazine. After divorcing Nancy, he married Marietta Endicott Fitzgerald, the future U.S. representative to the United Nations' Human Rights Commission.

The subject of discussion in California was: What could a rich man like Marshall, passably optimistic, enlightened, and aware, do? Perhaps because he was born to it, Marshall didn't think wealth was its own justification. In the enforced discipline and camaraderie of the trenches, he had found a way to make himself effective. How could he make himself useful to peacetime society? They pursued the subject and found international finance and investment banking suitable avenues. De Trafford was also in search of a job, and the two friends chose an Anglo-American bond and brokerage house. Marshall went to work at the Wall Street firm of Lee, Higginson and Company, Rudy in London at Higginson and Company.

We do not know whether economist Ronnie Tree came up with the idea, but the choice was a smart one. The United States had lent money to its Allies, and after Lenin reneged on the czarist régime's debt and other countries sought to have their war debt lowered, if not forgiven, public opinion was aroused. You borrowed the money, you pay it back, was the American answer.

Reflecting the public mood, President Harding forcefully opposed any forgiveness of debt. Bankers saw opportunities here. Rescheduling and refinancing debt meant floating huge foreign bond issues. Marshall started as a bond salesman. The times were good, the economy booming, and Marshall had a lot of rich friends. He and Evelyn leased an investment banker's house and soon decided to build their own home on 69th Street and 5th Avenue. The townhouse, designed by David Adler and Robert Works and erected on four city lots across from the Frick mansion, was spacious and lavish.

The stock market was tricky, but there were exciting opportunities in the new industries: automobiles, radio, telephone, electric refrigerators, and phonographs. Women were taking up smoking, and cigarette production was doubling. Marshall learned the ropes and the jargon. "The law of averages is the keynote of the selling game," he told a *Literary Digest* reporter who asked him if selling bonds was a career for a young man with a good education. "The more calls you make, the bigger the results. Dress neatly. People always like to do business with a young man who looks very much a success. Always talk to a man about *his* business, not about yours. Show him how he can make some money, and he is interested. A good sound bond issue needs no flowery arguments. A handful of facts is sufficient." Not that he worked very hard himself. He soon left Lee, Higginson, ostensibly to devote time to his grandfather's estate, in reality because he and Evelyn had found a new infatuation.

Their passion was 1,900 acres of marshland on Long Island's North Shore, less than forty miles from midtown Manhattan. Here, above Huntington in the Lloyd Neck district, the Fields created the country place to end all country places, an imitation English country estate they called by its original Indian name, Caumsett.

The property had been neglected for thirty years, but the potential was truly manorial. East of Oyster Bay and Sands Point, the estate had woodlands sloping down to handsome beaches that echoed the Drummonds' parkland at Cadland. A structure dating from the Revolutionary period and several nondescript cottages and sheds stood on the harbor side. The land was partly covered with woods, second-growth timber. Marshall set to work.

Marshall ordered landscaping, draining, gardening, road grading, and the construction of docks, garages, kennels, and barns. Under the overall supervision of architect John Russell Pope of New York, a hundred engineers and workers labored for five years. When it was finished, Caumsett was ready for golf, tennis, riding, pheasant shooting, polo, and trout fishing. It offered swimming on the private beach along the Sound and motoring along twenty-five miles of private roads. A staff of eighty-five ran the domain, which had its own electricity and water supply, fire-fighting equipment, special seaplane and boat landings, private guest apartments, and twenty tenant houses to accommodate the servants. At the disposal of host and guests were eight automobiles and a steam yacht named *Corisande*. The master's chief preoccupations were horses and cattle. Besides the Caumsett stables, Marshall had horses in Kentucky and Ireland. Cream and milk came fresh to the table from a herd of registered Guernseys. He also acquired a 13,000-acre South Carolina property that he referred to as the "quail lodge."

"It required a sense of position and family, a confidence, an appetite for life on the grand scale," Stephen Becker would write in *Marshall Field III*. "It required a strong ego: building Caumsett

Evelyn with Marshall IV, 1917.

was a massive investment in time, taste, and personality, and it takes a certain Alexandrian recklessness to build a manor every lintel and post of which will bear the mark of its owner. Field was accomplishing several things at once. He was expressing himself in a traditional way—constructing something vast yet personal. He was asserting a notion of fitness appropriate to his station and attitudes: not simply the estate, but the working part of it. The farm and herds and dairy and greenhouses. He was restoring to his life some of the grandeur of his English youth; not recreating a corner of England—he was never prey to such affected strokes of sentimentality—but drawing from his memory and experience all the best that England could offer a man of his class, and adding to it the technology and amenities of a prosperous America." Horse breeding cost him money, but he had three Futurity winners in his stable and sold one yearling that went on to win the

Preakness. He was a formidable polo player at the mount of his own horses. It was Harry Payne Whitney who had made Long Island the mecca of polo, and Marshall succeeded Whitney as a director of the Saratoga Racing Association in 1928. Weekend sporting guests at Caumsett included Tommy Hitchcock, a war hero who was considered the world's greatest polo player; W. Averell Harriman; Ralph Pulitzer; and Devereux Millburn, usually the captain of the U.S. team in matches against British polo players coming over to compete for the Westchester Cup.

Evelyn was now the mother of three—Marshall IV, Barbara, and Bettine. In 1923, when young Marshall was seven, Barbara five, and Bettine four months old, the family attended Gwendolyn's wedding to Captain Archibald Edmonstone in London. Since their mother's death, Marshall's sister had been brought up by Ethel and now-Admiral David Beatty, First Sea Lord, Earl of Brooksby and of the North Sea. Gwendolyn was twenty-one. Edmonstone was twenty-six. After the war he had served as aide-de-camp to Lord Willingdon, Viceroy of India. The wedding was held at Admiralty House in Trafalgar Square.

Ethel was not doing well. Her illness took the form of severe depression. She had David sell Hanover Lodge because she found it too noisy. They moved to 17 Grosvenor Square, but for the better part of the year Ethel traveled in search of a cure. She became a patient of such famous psychiatrists as Emile Coué in Paris and Frank Dengler in Baden-Baden. Sessions with Coué, she wrote home, brought some relief.

The stepgrandmother Marshall and Gwendolyn had barely known was also there. Now in her early eighties, Delia Field had lived in Washington, D.C., for a while and traveled a lot. She adored the Jazz Age, and dancing the Charleston earned herself the nickname "Shaky," as David Beatty noted in 1925 in a letter to Ethel: "'Shaky' Marshall had a terrific party last night, 48 to dinner. Princess Mary was very charming. The dinner was followed by a Cotillion. I haven't seen one for years. I was lucky getting hold of Violet Mar [Countess of Mar and Kelly] as my partner, and so we sat through it all. It was over by 12." While David was attending dinner dances in Mayfair, his wife was suffering an accelerated decline. The summer of 1931 was the last year the Beattys spent together as a family. Late in the year Ethel began to fail. In the spring of 1932 she fell into what was diagnosed as a state of acute melancholia. She died the following July, aged fifty-nine.

Marshall III had a distracted rapport with his children and left the discipline to Evelyn and a series of nannies. He cared for their future and taught them how to ride, shoot, and fish, how to play bridge and chess. Barbara loved fox hunting with her father in the fall because for a couple of hours she had him to herself. Servants had them up before dawn. After breakfast the two of them mounted already saddled horses and, with the hounds yelping, rode into the frosty morning. Later in life, she said her father had given them too much freedom.

A secure, considerate, though essentially unproductive existence was not for the grandson of the dry goods entrepreneur. Marshall the First had made a fortune that, nurtured by expert hands, continued to grow. Since Marshall III wouldn't control his inheritance until his fiftieth birthday, he didn't even have the option of ruining himself. Gambling and wild women, the traditional despoilers of inherited wealth, were not among his vices. Caumsett was no doubt an extravagance, but not to the extent that he had to appeal to the trustees to advance him money. The vice of the decade was booze, which Prohibition made so much more exciting. Playwrights and screenwriters wrote smart-set characters getting out of wet raincoats and into dry martinis. Weekend parties on Long Island spilled into Monday mornings, and Marshall and Evelyn began to worry about their alcohol intake.

Looking for something meaningful to do, Marshall got into investment banking again. The incentive came from meetings with Charles Glore, a thirty-two-year-old Chicagoan who had already been a bank vice-president and accumulated capital of his own. Field knew something about recycling foreign debt; Glore had experience in investment opportunities in expanding Midwestern industries. He had become a partner of Pierce C. Ward and two other bankers in 1920 and formed Glore, Ward and Company. Marshall and Charles hit it off and together formed an investment firm. Marshall had hoped to call it Marshall Field & Company, but the board of the department store vetoed the name. He had no right to the commercial use of his own name—in 1917 the trustees of the estate had sold 90 percent of the stock in the store to its officers and managers, who, for an extra $10 million, acquired the name and goodwill. When banker Ward joined Field and Glore, the investment bank became Field, Glore, Ward & Company, address, 38 Wall Street.

Marshall *cruised* to work. Boarding a speedboat at Caumsett, he tore down the Sound past Great Neck and Kings Point into the East River down past the Williamsburg, Manhattan, and Brooklyn bridges to tie up at the River Club at Pier 13 and walk to his office. The company, which became Field, Glore and Company after Ward retired in 1928, was enormously successful. Marshall knew money and he knew Europe. Field, Glore and Company floated $20 million of Italian bonds, participated in $10 million for French rails, Rhine Ruhr East Road, $4 million for

Hamburg municipal power and light, and $30 million for the city of Milan. His partner was an expert on the industrial heartland. They floated $100 million for the Illinois Power and Light, and even handled a $17 million debt issue for Marshall Field & Company. To be perfectly impartial, they also handled $6 million in preferred stock for Fair Stores. Robert Fair had been an executive at Marshall Field's wholesale division who set up his own chain.

The hectic pace Marshall set for himself took its toll on the marriage. Because of his investment firm and his responsibilities as director of a dozen corporations, his time at Caumsett was as

The Fields of Caumsett: (left to right) Barbara,
Evelyn with Bettine on her knees, Marshall III,
and Marshall IV. *(Chicago Historical Society)*

planned as his business appointments. While others relaxed on his yacht, he would board his speedboat and zip down to Manhattan for nothing more than a casual luncheon date. By 1925, Evelyn felt that she was no more than another engagement in her husband's activities. He, in turn, was becoming dissatisfied with her bridge parties and preferred a younger and more pleasure-hungry crowd. Women liked him, and although no stories of infidelity surfaced, scandal sheets liked to call him a playboy.

There is no evidence that F. Scott Fitzgerald knew Marshall Field III, but Scott and Zelda lived at Great Neck during 1922–23. In *The Great Gatsby*, Great Neck became West Egg, and another peninsula across the bay became East Egg, where Daisy and Tom Buchanan and the old-money families lived. Biographers acknowledge that Long Island provided material for Fitzgerald's characters. Jay Gatsby was modeled on Max von Gerlach, a car dealer in Flushing who owned a yacht and was suspected of being a bootlegger. But who was Tom Buchanan? In *Marshall Field III*, Stephen Becker imagines Gatsby meeting Marshall and commenting on his lifestyle:

> Very handsome. Well-dressed. *Always* the proper tie, accessories, etc. Always considerate, if anything overpolite. Shy, quiet voice, noticeable but not offensive British accent, natural result of life abroad. Drinks; partial to martinis and Scotch; never drunk. Sign of responsibility. Tipsy once; sat down and stopped drinking. Talk to the crew of his boat: they have never seen him drunk or really angry. (Possibly just being loyal; they like him; but I decline to believe them.) Generous, prefers to be host, but will accept invitations. Brings small gifts, always the best. Women very fond of him. Daisy says it's not his money but his calm, plus a remarkably attractive and hearty laugh. Some gossip now and then, but I suppose

Barbara and Bettine Field. (*Field Foundation*)

that's natural; they gossip about me, too. Newspapers call him a playboy, but I'm not sure he's happy. Moody now and then, in the middle of a party at that. Friends call him a good banker. Average polo player; has a practice field on his place Caumsett; his children learning the game . . . Likes to talk about his grandfather; terrific respect for the old man.

Fitzgerald and Field moved in different circles. Just as freeloaders crashed Gatsby's parties, so "it became a habit with many world-weary New Yorkers," Fitzgerald wrote in the *Saturday Evening Post*, "to pass their weekends at the Fitzgerald house in the country house." Edmund Wilson, the critic, poet, novelist, and friend of the Fitzgeralds, listed the visitors to whom Scott promised to introduce the critic and biographer Van Wyck Brooks if the latter accepted an invitation to Great Neck: Gloria Swanson, Sherwood Anderson, John Dos Passos, Marc Connelly, Dorothy Parker, Rube Goldberg, and Ring Lardner. It would be another decade before the master of Caumsett would move in intellectual circles and Parker would write for publisher Marshall Field III.

Marshall and Evelyn separated. To give himself space and occasion to reflect on his ten-year marriage, he moved out of their Manhattan townhouse, got an apartment of his own, and spent time in England. The separation embittered Evelyn, and she took out a good deal of her resentment on their son, now a very bright nine-year-old. Marshall IV in turn begrudged his father for leaving him and his sisters, seven-year-old Barbara and two-year-old Bettine. All three felt traumatized. When Evelyn was on her way to Reno, Nevada, for a divorce, she told reporters that she and her husband were "as far apart as the sun and the moon."

The divorce, granted on August 4, 1930, made friends gasp, startled the readers of tabloids, and gave Marshall's lawyers heartburn. He kept Caumsett, but insisted that Evelyn get $3 million ($25 million in today's money), the Manhattan townhouse, and a $1 million a year settlement. After Caumsett, Barbara and Bettine found the Manhattan townhouse dark and depressing. Their mother bought an estate at Syosset, a few miles inland from Oyster Bay and close enough to Caumsett so that the children could divide their time between their parents. Late in life, Barbara would write:

> I was brought up in enormous and isolated places, and in what seemed to me dark, cold, and somewhat frightening houses. I was taken care of by a string of nurses, governess, and innumerable servants. My parents were remote, not only because they carried on a very busy social life and were frequently away on trips. My older brother was sent to boarding school at the age of eight. My younger sister had an English nurse who wasn't on speaking terms with my French governess, and in the summers my brother had

Evelyn Marshall, the divorcee.

tutors who loathed them both, so life wasn't precisely what you would call congenial. I think too much was expected of us by too many people. We felt we had to at least appear perfect. So many people told me that I would be like someone else, I ended by not knowing who I was.

Two weeks after the divorce was final, Marshall married one of London's "Bright Young Things."

19

AUDREY

THE FIELD FORTUNE WAS NOT ONE OF THOSE FINANCIAL CON-
structs honeycombed with speculative credit that came crashing
down on Tuesday, October 29, 1929. Marshall sustained losses
and so did the estate, but the damage was limited. The portfolio
was shrewdly diversified into real estate holdings and blue-chip
stocks. His former employers were less lucky. Lee, Higginson was
one of the first investment banks to collapse. By New Year's 1930,
Wall Street seemed to collect itself. Stock trading reached the
previous summer's fever pitch in the spring, with leading stocks
regaining more than half the ground they had lost. But in April
commodity prices began to slide, followed by declining factory
output, followed by another stock market tumble.

Marshall was in England wooing, and on August 18, 1930, marrying Audrey James Coates. She was a cousin of Gwendolyn's hus-

band, Archibald, goddaughter of King Edward VII, the onetime fiancée of Lord Louis Mountbatten, and a former girlfriend of Edward, Prince of Wales. In Los Angeles, she had gone nightclub hopping with Rudolph Valentino and pronounced him a divine dancer. In London, she danced at the endless revelries hosted by Loelia Ponsonby, later the Duchess of Westminster, and Tina, the marchioness of Blandford, and dined at Sir Philip Sassoon's parties in his sumptuous apartments at 25 Park Lane, where Venetian candelabra illuminated dinners for thirty and each place setting came with Venetian crystal bowls brimming with white chrysanthemums. These get-togethers, Evelyn Waugh wrote in *Vile Bodies*, were "masked parties, savage parties, Victorian parties, Greek parties, Wild West parties, Russian parties, Circus parties, parties where one had to dress as someone else and almost naked parties in St John's Wood, parties in flats and studios and houses and ships and hotels and nightclubs, in windmills and swimming baths." Audrey started the craze for Victorian games like musical chairs, blind man's buff, and staged scavenger parties that Elsa Maxwell immediately copied. When Marshall had first met her a year after her American tour, she had been the twenty-three-year-old widow of British textile tycoon Captain Dudley Coates, who had been badly gassed during the war. She was everything Evelyn was not—carefree, glamorous, and above all eager to match him in sports.

The honeymoon of the thirty-seven-year-old groom and twenty-eight-year-old bride set the pace of the marriage. After the London wedding, Audrey and Marshall embarked on a big game hunt in Kenya, and had several thrilling brushes with death. Their bush pilot and safari leader was Denys Finch Hatton, the onetime lover of Isak Dinesen, played by Robert Redford in *Out of Africa*. As Marshall told his business partners in a letter dated Nairobi, October 13, 1930:

We landed here last night, after quite a series of misfortunes, providentially not worse.

The moth plane turned over in a sandstorm on the ground at Wadi Halfa, and the Loening crashed the landing gear again at a place called Nimule, a day's flight from here. Nimule is very inaccessible and it took two days to get out, on our feet, bicycles and a passing lorry. As we'd practically no food and little water it wasn't so comfortable. Luckily we found an air survey machine to fly us here.

I'm afraid the plane is finished, so that means a boat back, and there isn't a chance in the world now of making it by Xmas. I hope everything is arranged so you can get on with firm matters without me. If so, I shan't be back till the end of March. If absolutely necessary I can probably get back some time in January—so cable me.

I wouldn't have missed the experience for the world and have seen a marvelous country. What one doesn't realize is the enormous distances and little means of communications. We crossed a great many miles of country that would have been pretty nasty to get out of. Saw lots of game, including a real good herd of elephants.

The plane really hadn't enough radius. We had a forced landing on the Nile as it was, through lack of enough gasoline, and only just made our destination when we met a very heavy storm, which we could make little progress against.

We have a safari arranged in a fascinating part of Tanganyika, which has been very little shot over. You'll be amused at some of our pictures when we get back.

Please have this letter go the rounds, out to Chicago, George Richardson, Buddie Marshall, etc.

Yours ever

The list of trophies forwarded to Caumsett after they left Africa included two whole lion skins, the hides of two leopards, a gerenuk (a long-necked antelope), a rhino, a waterbuck, a water buffalo, a pair of rhino horns, and 140 pounds of elephant ivory tusk. In a followup letter, P. W. Whetham of Safariland Limited in Nairobi informed the Fields that their friend Lady Tina had returned the amateur movies they had wanted her to have, and that because of the plane mishaps, Finch Hatton agreed to the 10 percent markdown on the rental of his camp equipment. Finch Hatton was killed a month later when his two-seater crashed after takeoff in Voi, southeast of Nairobi.

Audrey proved to be as restless as her husband. She was a crack shot and vied with Marshall in flying airplanes and racing speedboats. The pleasures of Caumsett were not enough. The Fields went hunting in England, yachting on the Mediterranean. They rehabilitated an ancient Virginia plantation to antebellum splendor, and leased a ranch in Wyoming for a party. We do not know what Audrey thought of her husband's children, but they were devastated by his absence. Barbara especially missed her father and in later life would attribute much of her and her brother's harrowing descent into mental illness to the sense of abandonment they felt as teenagers.

As the Depression deepened and thirteen million Americans were out of work, society columnists distracted the Depression's victims with reports on Audrey's redecoration of the Fields' dining room, on how she had taken her cue from Sir Philip Sassoon's music room to install mirrored walls. Her husband's directorship in Continental Insurance, Continental Illinois National Bank, Westinghouse Electric, and Marshall Field & Co. made him acutely aware of the deepening crisis, and how offensive Audrey and their lifestyle were to a majority of Americans. Audrey was tone-deaf to economics and within a year out of tune, even with London's Mayfair set. The effects of the Wall Street crash took twelve months to cross the Atlantic, but when it did it was considered bad taste to even *look* rich. Women who were still wealthy wore plain dresses, furless wool coats, sweaters, and slacks. Economic and washable fabrics were popular, and Coco Chanel was persuaded to come to London to help promote cotton as a fashion fabric. Throwing caution to the wind, Mile-a-Minute Harry marked the jubilee celebration of King George V in 1935 by decorating the Oxford Street store inside and out. A golden Britannia, eighty feet high and flanked by huge golden lions, covered the facade. After the new king, Edward VIII, abdicated so he could marry Wallis Simpson, Selfridge surpassed himself by spending £50,000 in decorations to celebrate the coronation of George VI. He chose the occasion to announce that after twenty-eight years in England he was applying for naturalization papers as a British subject.

20

EVOLUTIONS

MARSHALL VOTED FOR HERBERT HOOVER AND THE RETURN TO normalcy that Republicans promised in the 1932 election. However, he was soon drawn to Franklin D. Roosevelt and his heady crew of New Dealers. He repeated Joseph Kennedy's line that the country's rich should go down on their knees and thank FDR for saving their fortunes. Eighteen months into the Roosevelt administration, he admitted he was rather disgusted with the Republican Party and that he was interested in what FDR was trying to do. On other occasions when people asked why he was a Democrat, he arched an aristocratic eyebrow and said, "Because I can afford it." Such talk made him a traitor to his class.

The economic downdraft caught the Marshall Field trust, Marshall Field & Company, and several banks with a half-finished forty-three-story office building. The site was half a block from the Chicago Loop, north of Adams and bounded by LaSalle and Clark streets. Although office buildings were hanging "to let" signs on every other floor, Marshall convinced the trustees and bankers not to get cold feet. He saw the three-year construction as a quasi-civic duty giving the city a psychological lift and buried himself in architectural plans. The gamble paid off. The relative opulence of the Field Building pleased upscale tenants, who by 1934 leased entire floors.

Marshall Field & Company adjusted to the vanishing purchase power. The department store earned $1.6 million in 1931, but the wholesale and manufacturing divisions lost so much money that the company closed its books for the year $5 million in the red. The following year the deficit reached $8 million and the company stopped paying dividends for the first time since its incorporation thirty years earlier. Marshall controlled over 60 percent of the preferred stock and almost 10 percent of the common shares. Store manager John McKinley, who had started as a cash boy in 1888, told employees to be upbeat. To show he meant it, he asked engineers of Westinghouse Company to design escalators. Two flights of escalators costing half a million dollars were installed in the State Street building, saluting Chicago's 1933 Century of Progress Exposition. Wholesale and manufacturing continued to slip. And there was an even bigger black hole—the Merchandise Mart. The idea for the world's largest building dated from better times. James Simpson, who had played golf with Marshall Field in the snow on New Year's Day 1906 and was remembered in the will with a $50,000 legacy, was the company's CEO. In 1927, he had turned the first spade of sod at the gigantic construction site on the Chicago River. The building, he believed, would do for wholesale what the State Street department store had done for retail. The architects were Graham

Anderson, Probst and White, who had designed the Civic Opera.

The wholesale and manufacturing divisions would occupy half the five-million-square-foot building, estimated to cost $15 million, while the rest of the Mart would be leased to some two thousand jobbers and manufacturers' representatives. The building would have the world's biggest restaurant and the world's biggest broadcast studios. The Depression turned the Mart into a losing proposition. The wholesale and manufacturing divisions were in the red, and tenants were hard to find. The fate of the Mart first divided Simpson and McKinley, then caused them to clash head-on. Simpson, who had a $3.3 million investment in Marshall Field & Company stock, fought for the status quo. McKinley knew something had to give. He convinced John Shedd to come out of retirement. "Some departments must be killed," Shedd told McKinley after a quick survey. "They are gone and gone forever, and they can't come back. The oldtime country merchant who used to sustain wholesale has dried up, or he's buying cheaper goods. Another thing—if wholesale paid its fair rent for space in the Mart, the figures would look worse than they do."

The liquidation was brutal. Still, the wholesale division lost $13 million in 1934, and there was the $18 million loan that had financed the Mart. Simpson thought he had an ally in the founder's grandson. But Marshall Field III forced the board to accept outside corporate management. Several board members resented the imposition of an outsider, but Marshall won the day and brought in James O. McKinsey, a management consultant he knew. After McKinsey and his team of experts went through the company's finances, most of the textile manufacturing was sold off. Simpson resigned, and McKinsey was named CEO. It was the first time in the company's history that an outsider had become boss.

*   *   *

Marshall was wealthy enough not to have to let the shrinking economy crimp his lifestyle. At Caumsett, he nevertheless cut back the staff's work hours without laying anybody off. Audrey continued to enjoy glamour and the sporting scene. Despite Marshall's sensitivity to the country's darkening reality, she insisted on continuing their social agenda, going wherever they pleased and inviting whoever they fancied to Caumsett. She insisted on wearing the ruby-and-diamond necklace he had given her as a wedding gift to the opera. She wanted to see South Carolina's old Charleston, and he booked overnight sleeper accommodations. When they rolled up the compartment shades the next morning, they discovered they were in Charleston, West Virginia. No matter. Marshall was a director of the Libbey-Owens-Ford Glass Company, and a tour of the plant was hastily arranged. After that the Fields retired to the Greenbrier resort at White Sulphur Springs.

He turned forty on September 38, 1933. Six months later, Audrey and he divorced, perhaps not so much victims of divergent lifestyles as of different outlooks. Before Audrey fled to Paris where Cecil Beaton, the gay celebrity photographer, made her his fashion model for a season, she had Marshall pay dearly for their four-year marriage. In the divorce agreement he signed on September 29, 1934, he agreed to pay her $400,000 in sixteen equal installments of $25,000, due on the first day of each January, April, July, and October every year until 1938. The settlement further specified that should he live to be forty-five, another $2 million was due. In the meantime, he made her the beneficiary of a £250,000 life insurance policy, and agreed to amend his will so that Audrey would inherit one-fourth of his wealth. No wonder he said his second failed marriage made him introspective.

He was more than ever *the* Field. The Depression was grinding on and he was quoted as saying that if he couldn't make himself worth three square meals a day, he didn't deserve them. Though tolerant of the faults of others, he hated brutality and double dealing. He was in good health. He was honest, generous, and a good friend to his friends, but he felt diminished by his two failed marriages. While Audrey was in Reno waiting for the divorce, he turned to psychoanalysis to get some answers.

His psychiatrist was Dr. Gregory Zilboorg. A Russian-Jewish intellectual three years older than Marshall, Zilboorg had embraced the Revolution in 1917, joined the Socialist Revolutionary Party, and served as the secretary to the labor minister in the short-lived government of Alexander Kerensky. He was less enthusiastic when Lenin's Bolsheviks overthrew the Kerensky government. Via Austria, Germany, and Holland, he made his way to the United States in 1919 to become the psychiatrist to Manhattan's liberal rich and famous and a minor figure in avant-garde New York. People would remember him as a heavily mustachioed, walrus-looking personage holding forth like an egomaniac.

Zilboorg was a Freudian of progressive views. He considered it his mission to counteract the oversimplifications of Sigmund Freud's ideas popularized by magazines and Hollywood. He later converted to Catholicism, worked vigorously to reconcile psychoanalysis and the Church, and in the early 1950s would attack L. Ron Hubbard's "dianetics" cures of psychosomatic and other ills as dangerous. He believed humans cannot face the whole truth of their nature and that their denial of truth about themselves is built in. He was writing a book on Renaissance medicine and witchcraft when Marshall became his patient—George Gershwin, Moss Hart, Lillian Hellman, and Broadway producer Herman Shumlin were among his other analysands. As a time when the average fee for psychoanalysis was $4 an hour, Zilboorg charged $75, which didn't deter his celebrity patients. That he was a gossip, however, disturbed some of them. Kay Swift, George Gershwin's lady friend who recommended that the composer see Zilboorg, was shocked when the psychiatrist discussed Gershwin's sessions with her. A trip Gershwin, Swift, and Zilboorg made to Mexico City in 1935 was a fiasco. The psychiatrist overwhelmed and embarrassed Gershwin at a party given in the composer's honor and attended by Diego Rivera and Miguel Covarrubias. As a reformed Bolshevik, Zilboorg loudly condemned the left-leaning artists. Hellman, with whom Marshall became friends, sought out Zilboorg to help her with her alcoholism. She found his analysis helpful and dedicated the play *Another Part of the Forest* to him. Her longtime lover, Dashiell Hammett, claimed that he had learned more about himself from Zilboorg's treatment of her than Lillian learned about herself.

Audrey was in Reno when Marshall began five-days-a-week analysis. We do not know whether she was the origin of the tittle-tattle, but the New York *News*'s London correspondent reported her friends saying she wouldn't be seeking a divorce "if the fabulously wealthy merchant prince hadn't met a psychiatrist who told him his second wife would be unlucky for him." Marshall's own take on his two years of Zilboorgian analysis was positive. He came away feeling a better man and believing his failed marriages were the result of the psychic circumstances of his childhood and that wealth in itself was not creative.

Zilboorg delved into his millionaire patient's motives, needs, and wishes and, in accordance with the professional credo, refrained from giving advice. He helped Marshall dig deep into his childhood and his father's death. While his grandfather and mother had insisted that Marshall Junior shot himself by accident that November afternoon in 1905, Marshall III was convinced, or became convinced through Zilboorg's analysis, that his father had indeed committed suicide. In gratitude for the insights Zilboorg helped him discover, Marshall funded his analyst's research into suicide. In a paper presented to the American Orthopsychiatric Association in 1937, Zilboorg suggested that the will to die was latent in most people, that the act was not impulsive, but the result of unconscious desires rooted in biology.

Analyst and patient also explored the present and Marshall's less than sterling opinion of himself. Zilboorg made him understand that his need to be "of service" didn't mean kissing lepers, weaving Christmas baskets, or attending weekly charity functions. It could simply mean getting involved, offering help, influence, perhaps leadership. The world had given Marshall wealth, health, and a good mind. Perhaps it was his turn to give back.

Zilboorg succeeded in giving his millionaire patient new self-confidence. Two years was not long as psychoanalysis goes, but Marshall came to see himself as a person with a healthier outlook on life. The first significant step he took was to withdraw from the banking business and the Field, Glore Company. The United States went off the gold standard and Congress granted the Roosevelt administration power to regulate the value of the dollar. Cynics said Marshall's retreat from Wall Street had less to do with philosophical perspectives than with Roosevelt's new tax code.

In May 1936, Marshall lent his grandparents' big house on Chicago's Prairie Avenue to a group of young socialites for an 1885 ball. The "the street of the stately few" had fallen on hard times. Smoke from the trains killed the elms faster than they could be replaced, and during the 1920s, the exodus to the North Side became a stampede. "People sold their houses if they could," Arthur Meeker would write. "If they couldn't, they simply tore them down to save taxes, leaving unsightly heaps of rubble. Here and there a small factory dared to show its dingy brick face. Business moved into some of the few dwellings that were left; others were turned into ramshackle boarding houses." The residence of Marshall Field II at 1919 Prairie Avenue was converted into an alcoholic rehabilitation center and later abandoned. When the city dredged up new land in order to build a boulevard to the far South Side, Prairie Avenue lost its one remaining beauty, a view of Lake Michigan.

But for one night in May 1936, 1905 Prairie Avenue glittered as guests in period costumes posed on the grand circular staircase and danced under the chandeliers. A year later, Marshall deeded the decaying mansion to the Association of Arts and Industries, with the understanding that it be used as an industrial school. Laszlo Moholy-Nagy, the Hungarian painter, sculptor, photographer, and writer, and his German architect friend Walter Gropius turned the mansion into the "New Bauhaus." Moholy-Nagy taught industrial designers and advertising students all he had taught Bauhaus students in Germany about new modes of graphic expression. It didn't take, and in 1939, he started his own school of design, prospered, and exercised an important influence in introducing American designers to constructivist techniques. The house at 1905 Prairie Avenue was torn down in 1955.

After withdrawing from banking, Marshall's second step was to marry a friend's ex-wife. She was Ruth Pruyn Phipps, the former wife of Marshall's sporting friend Ogden Phipps. Ruth was no liberal. Her family background was Hudson Valley Dutch, well-to-do, traditional, and aware of its responsibilities—her great-grandfather had served Abraham Lincoln. Ruth was the mother of two young boys and, fearing a custody battle, was reluctant to proceed with a divorce. Marshall persuaded her to meet with his lawyer Louis S. Weiss.

A senior partner in Paul, Weiss, Wharton and Garrison, Weiss was an intense, outgoing, talkative, chain-smoking lawyer with a talent for working out compromises. He had saved Marshall a lot of money in tax matters that had less to do with suspicions of tax evasion than with interpreting tax law. His sister, Carol Weiss King, also a lawyer, was destined to be more famous than he as defense counsel for communists and radicals and a specialist in immigration law. Louis Weiss's knack for finding common ground and building on it helped Ruth obtain a civilized divorce and custody of her two sons, seven-year-old Harry and five-year-old Bobby. Her January 15, 1936, wedding to Marshall took place in her parents' elegant apartment at River House in Manhattan. Harry and Bobby called their stepfather "Marshie," and came to live at Caumsett. Their new stepbrother and stepsisters were older than they. Marshall IV was twenty and away at Harvard, Barbara was eighteen and president of the graduating class at Brearley School for Girls on Manhattan's Upper East Side. Bettine was thirteen and still at home. Eight months after the wedding Ruth gave birth to a daughter, Phyllis. A second daughter, Fiona, was born to Marshall and Ruth on Christmas Day 1938.

Marshall's relationship with his son was distant and their communications epistolary. Since attending St. Paul's School in Concord, New Hampshire, Marshall IV had communicated with his father by telegram (CAMBRIDGE MASS 1020A. MARSHALL FIELD=250 PARK AVE=HAVE BEEN ELECTED TO HASTY PUDDING IN FIRST GROUP. LOVE=MARSH," read an October 5, 1935 cable).

Marshall Field IV: "To the best Dad in
the world." *(Field Foundation)*

After graduating *magna cum laude* with a Bachelor of Arts degree
in 1938, he further distanced himself from the family by enrolling
at the University of Virginia Law School. His three years at
Charlottesville were a happy time for him. He fell in love with
Joanne Bass, the daughter of a former New Hampshire governor,
and got to exercise his full intellect, winning four of the school's
highest honors: presidency of the graduating class of 1941; edi-
torship of the Law School Review periodical; the Woods award,
granted by vote of the faculty to the outstanding member of the
graduating class; and selection to clerk for Judge Armistead Dobie
of the federal Circuit Court of Appeals. He sometimes spent as
much as eighteen consecutive hours researching and writing an

opinion. Judge Dobie considered one of these opinions so good that he submitted it from the bench almost verbatim.

Marshall III was now the head of the clan. His grandfather's second wife, Delia, had died in 1937, the same year nineteen-year-old Barbara married Anthony A. Bliss. The June wedding of Marshall IV and Joanne Bass was the social event at Caumsett in 1938. Barbara made Marshall III a grandfather in September 1939 when she gave birth to a girl she and Tony Bliss named Barbara. The outbreak of World War II that same month distanced Marshall III from his sister Gwendolyn, Lady Edmondstone, the mother of six children. Marshall's cousin Ronald Tree had become a Member of Parliament for Harborough in Leicestershire in 1933 and at the outbreak of World War II served as an undersecretary in the Churchill government's Ministry of Information, advising on American policy. Because the Prime Minister's estate, Chequers, was considered a prime target for night bombings during the Blitz, Ron extended to Churchill the hospitality of his own great Ditchley house in Enstone.

21

ROOSEVELT RADICALS

MARSHALL FIELD III DISCONCERTED PEOPLE. HE WAS EXQUISITELY polite, but had the unfortunate habit of yawning. We do not know whether the yawns were due to a lack of oxygen or a peculiar aftereffect of his rheumatic fever condition, but friends and acquaintances were often taken aback by his yawning. Ralph Ingersoll, the editor of *Fortune* magazine and Henry Luce's bright light at Time Inc., found Field to be gentle and a bit shy when they met in 1937. Full of talent and flair, Ingersoll had lost his capital in the Wall Street crash, but not his sense of independence. He was soliciting seed money to launch a daily newspaper, and as he delivered his pitch and showed a dummy of the future paper, he saw Marshall yawn politely a couple of times. Recalling the meeting at the Field apartment, Ingersoll got the impression Marshall was not interested. "I could not remember a single individual whose reaction was as negative as Marshall's. His glance at the dummy was perfunctory. Clearly he was thinking about something else—and I was wasting my time. But Field didn't waste much of his. He gave the dummy back to me, shook hands, backed nervously through the lobby to the elevator where his man waited with his hat and coat. 'Ingersoll,' he said in that shy, gentle voice as the elevator door opened. 'I can't really take this on you know. And I'd hate for you to be under some kind of misapprehension, two hundred thousand dollars is absolutely all I can put into it.' Then, the coat was on, Field was in the elevator and the door closed." A baffled Ingersoll had $200,000 ($2.4 million in today's money) toward the $1.5 million he needed to start the newspaper, and, unlike other rich men's pledges, Field's assurance stayed firm. Louis Weiss was responsible for bringing the editor to Marshall's Park Avenue office, but Gregory Zilboorg later claimed he engineered the meeting on the theory that the psychic ills of both men could be cured with the founding of a progressive newspaper.

Luce, who had cut his journalistic teeth as a legman for the Chicago *Daily News*'s inventive reporter-turned-playwright-turned-screenwriter Ben Hecht, wanted to keep Ingersoll in the Time stable. He had made Ingersoll vice-president and general manager, and given him the new *Fortune* magazine to run, and now offered him a cool million in stock options. But Marshall's pledge set the ball rolling. Zilboorg had advised Marshall to be "of service," and helping to bankroll a newspaper was one way of giving back to society. The psychiatrist was careful not to suggest possible goals for his millionaire patient, but to let Marshall find his own directions and purposes. Besides funding Zilboorg's suicide research—the doctor's enemies implied that he milked his wealthy client—Marshall found gratification and purpose in organizing a committee on child welfare. Despite Roosevelt's 1936 reelection, the Depression was far from over. Child welfare led him to funding new buildings, equipment, and personnel for ten children's societies, and to organizing the Field Foundation.

To guide him through the labyrinth of child welfare, Weiss introduced him to Justine Wise Polier, a rabbi's daughter, widow of a young professor of law and a lawyer herself. The choice was perfect. Her passionate advocacy on behalf of children, the under-privileged, and minorities made her an authority on welfare and big-city politics. In 1936 Mayor Fiorello La Guardia had offered her a judgeship on the Court of Domestic Relations. She was more interested in social problems and individual cases, but accepted a ten-year term as judge of the Children's Court. Sitdown strikes paralyzed General Motors, and FDR refused to call out troops in Detroit. Al Capone fed the homeless in Chicago, and New York had its own soup kitchens. Marshall sat in Polier's court and heard horror stories of children living close to starva-tion. Some of them survived by stealing food. Polier told him to go out and see for himself.

Besides visiting New York shelters for the orphaned and the "wayward," Marshall went to Chicago, Boston, and Buffalo. What he saw made him look into the socialist ideas that had frightened his grandfather. These Dickensian shelters, run by religious char-ities, gave children food, a place to sleep, and little else. The best were Roman Catholic and Protestant facilities, but they took in only white children. He believed these shelters were beyond reform, that they should be abolished since they offered neither education nor hope. Also, he wanted to set up an experimental program to find foster homes for black children. With Polier, he toured Wiltwyck, a Protestant Episcopal Missionary Society insti-tution near the Roosevelts' Hyde Park residence. He thought

Wiltwyck's progressive ideas were at least in the twentieth century and offered money for renovation, casework, and psychiatric services. Faith-based child welfare—and wealthy "do-gooders" like him—were archaic and unworthy of a modern society. Social services should be a public responsibility and should be funded by local, state, and federal governments. Such views were not accepted in Marshall's Upper East Side and Long Island milieu. The scorn and outright hostility he faced amplified when he became the publisher of New York's brilliantly innovative newspaper.

In Ralph Ingersoll's view, New York's eight dailies—the *Times*, *News*, *Mirror*, *Telegram*, William Randolph Hearst's *Journal*, the *Tribune*, the *Sun*, and the *Post*—were either stodgy and authoritative or trashy and, with the exception of the *Post*, illiberal. He believed there was no need to be stuffy or pretentious or to run sex murders on Page Two. Why not cover strikes, riots, wars, scandals, profiteering, and, even under La Guardia, municipal graft? If the truth were to be served, a news story needed perspective so the reader could place an event in its appropriate context. *Why* should be as important as the traditional journalistic *who, where, when, what*, and *how*. The Washington press corps and foreign correspondents of major news outlets were already doing this. And who said difficult subjects like science and economics could not be made interesting? Instead of "entertainment," the paper Ingersoll had in mind would report on the world of Hitler, air travel, Social Security, technology, and psychiatry. Interpretive reporting, intelligent writing, and excellent photos making the point were what an informed public wanted and deserved. Instead of asking readers to respond to appeals for charities, a paper would ask readers for political input. Yes, the paper Ingersoll wanted to publish would express a liberal point of view. To raise capital for the venture he had formed Publications Research, and taken offices in the old Time-Life Building. By the time Field pledged his $200,000, Ingersoll had trimmed the projected $6 million startup costs to $3 million, and cut that amount in half to an unrealistic $1.5 million.

Marshall's decision to take a flyer on *PM*, as the first new daily newspaper in New York in fifteen years would be called, brought other investors in. The two biggest stockholders were Field and John Hay Whitney, who was also shifting the family wealth from Standard Oil to *Newsweek* and Hollywood (*Gone With The Wind*). The book trade was interested, too. Lincoln Schuster, president of Simon and Schuster, joined the board, and Harry Scherman, head of Book-of-the-Month Club, became a shareholder. Other investors included Broadway producer Dwight Deere Wiman, grandson of John Deere of agricultural machinery; Philip Wrigley, of the chewing gum Wrigleys; writer and commentator Dorothy Thompson; and Elinor S. Gimbel, of the department store family.

Ingersoll was difficult to please and inclined to arbitrary decisions, yet he was someone people instinctively liked. Writers didn't ask themselves how they should write a story, but how Ralph would write it. He believed good writers should be paid well, and appointed Dashiell Hammett to do the hiring. Nearly every writer wanted to work for *PM*, at any salary. Hammett and Lillian Hellman, Ingersoll's former mistress, had joined those who rejected capitalism, and "Dash" sought to hire as many Marxists as he could. At least three were Party members; others were so-called dues cheaters, Stalinists who remained formally outside the Party but accepted its discipline. Bea Bakrow Kaufman, the wife of the wit, playwright, stage director, and ladies' man George S. Kaufman, was an often less-than-focused editor. An all-star cast of friends put the dummy issue together: Heywood Broun wrote about sports, Erskine Caldwell national news, Dorothy Parker drama reviews, Louis Fischer and Leland Stowe foreign news, Oscar Levant music, Hammett a book review, and Hellman a movie review.

It was at a stockholders' meeting that Marshall first met the playwright—*The Little Foxes* opened on Broadway on February 25, 1939, starring Tallulah Bankhead as the icy incarnation of ambition, treachery, and greed. Hellman had a small financial stake in the paper, and pronounced the prepublication mockup "a mess, badly written, no stance, cute and unprofessional," but liked the elegant financier. As her biographer, Carl Rollyson, would note, "Field would have a special appeal for Hellman, who was always so well turned out herself and so good at being a high-society radical." Louis Kronenberger, a writer Ingersoll had lured from *Time*, also noted Field's "great elegance as well as good looks."

Virginia Schoales was the only woman of consequence in the nearly all-male newsroom. "Ginny" to everybody, she was Ralph's assistant and, if not his bodyguard, his guard dog. She found that writers looking for assignments could too easily hoodwink him. "He was fooled and tricked, and incredibly stupid about judging people," Schoales would remember. "He indiscriminately chose people to give him advice."

The international situation degenerated quickly during the summer of 1939. France and Britain had wasted time coaching the Soviet Union into an Allied coalition, and Adolf Hitler made quick overtures to Joseph Stalin and on August 23 was rewarded by the German-Soviet Nonaggression Pact. A week later, Hitler invaded Poland, and Britain and France declared war on

Germany. As autumn slipped into winter, Europe settled into the "phony war." After Poland's fall, German and French forces merely stood and glowered at each other across the Rhine River. The Soviet Union's invasion of Finland in November brought Hammett and Hellman into the absurd situation of signing an open letter to President Roosevelt demanding a U.S. declaration of war against Finland. FDR obtained a revision of the Neutrality Act as a first step to reverse the country's isolationism. In January, when all New York theaters were asked to offer a night's box office receipts to a benefit for Finland, Hellman refused to allow *The Little Foxes* to join the fund-raiser. The star of her play, Tallulah Bankhead, protested. Hitler's Blitzkrieg, a new style of warfare heavily reliant on armor and aircraft, began in the spring of 1940. After invading Denmark and Norway, Germany launched a gigantic offensive against Holland, Belgium, and France.

At 10:00 P.M. on Tuesday, June 18, 1940, New York's newest daily arrived with all the modesty of a Barnum & Bailey circus. The prepublication buildup was such that the first delivery trucks to go out were mobbed, and some news dealers charged a quarter for the five-cents-a-copy tabloid. Its headline HITLER ARRIVES IN MUNICH TO MEET MUSSOLINI shouted the defeat of France as Marshal Pétain asked Hitler and Mussolini for a truce. The subheadline read: "Dictators to Confer Today on Price They Propose to Exact for Stopping Destruction of France . . . Unconditional Surrender Reported Only Basis for Negotiations . . . Fighting Continues." Over 400,000 copies were sold.

Ten days later *PM* still sold over 200,000 copies a day. The paper ran more photographs than other tabloids, and its news stories carried built-in analysis. But it couldn't live up to its advance notices, and the hype backfired. In retrospect, Ingersoll admitted as much: "The cocky inference had been clear enough. The editors of *PM* were going to knock 'em dead. They were going to show the rest of the newspaper staffs in New York how good a paper could be when its reporters, photographers and editors were given their heads. Out of the phrases as 'a new kind of newspaper' and 'a daily picture magazine' the public conjured up something superlative and when they didn't get it they were disgusted." FDR's open support, the paper's pro-labor stand, and its lobbying for U.S. intervention in the war in Europe showed its political coloring. "*PM* is a verbose tabloid in two colors, every story staff-written and signed, news highly departmentalized, pictures modeled on *Life* and supplemented with arty drawings, style more or less modeled on *Time* with hangovers of *New Masses*, accent on radio, labor, youth, cosmopolis and stunt features," Eugene Lyons wrote in the *American Mercury*, the iconoclastic magazine that had turned conservative after its founder, H. L. Mencken, retired, and by 1940 was a rightist organ owned by millionaire J. Russell Maguire. The common denominator of *PM* staffers, Lyons wrote, was their connection "with endless Communist organizations and enterprises." In Congress, Mississippi Democrat John Rankin called *PM* the uptown edition of the Communist *Daily Worker*, financed by the tax-escaping fortune of Marshall Field III. Native Chicagoan journalist turned playwright-screenwriter-wit Ben Hecht quipped that at *PM* "Man bites underdog" was the rule.

PM was up front about its goals and principles. "We are against people who push other people around," became a catchphrase printed several times a week. The full text of the paper's objective read:

We are against people who push other people around, just for the fun of pushing whether they flourish in this country or abroad. We are against fraud and deceit and greed and cruelty and we seek to expose their practitioners. We are for people who are kindly and courageous and honest. We respect intelligence, and accomplishment, open-mindedess, religious tolerance. We do not believe all mankind's problems are soluble in any exciting social order, certainly not our own, and we propose to applaud those who seek constructively to improve the way men live together. We are American and we prefer democracy to any other form of government.

In the paper's second month, Ingersoll redesigned it to try to attract enough readers to reach the 300,000 breakeven point. After the initial spurt the daily circulation never exceeded 122,353, and *Business Week* reported that *PM* needed a fresh infusion of cash.

Investors were ready to bail out, however, and in desperation Ingersoll appealed to Field. Marshall offered to buy out the other stockholders for 20 cents on the dollar. Investors happily accepted. To help him administer the paper, he brought in Charles Cushing, a Caumsett neighbor and conservative financial expert with little love for the crusading, impulsive *PM*. As the owner, Field was blamed for the paper's politics and found himself denounced as a communist. Marshall's friends were irritated by his open-ended support of the aggressive, individualistic Ingersoll. Marshall had promised his editor that he wouldn't interfere, and he kept his word. Friends, however, took his hands-off approach to mean he endorsed the paper's politics. *Life's* profile on Field recalls that when he attended editorial conferences he sat in a corner, and if a writer or reporter asked his opinion he would reply: 'I really couldn't say. I'll just let Mac [sic] Ingersoll decide that for me.'"

The attacks were vicious. Field was either a naïve good guy

mixed up with odd people or a brainwashed victim of Comrade Gregory Zilboorg. *Life* wrote that Marshall "tries to atone for his many millions by good works and profitless journalism," and his life was "a magnificent Horatio Alger story in reverse." The fiercest assault came in the February 15, 1941, issue of the *Saturday Evening Post*, which was anti-New Deal, anti-labor, and traditionally a great advertising medium. In "Muddled Millions," Field and his money were vilified, and he and Ingersoll described as "brother alumni of the Zilboorg office." The extreme left showed matching aggression. Stalin's nonaggression pact with Hitler humiliated Marxists. Fear of war ran through the national conscience. After the fall of France, England was Hitler's only adversary still standing. By mid-summer, however, the defeat of Great Britain seemed entirely possible, and Americans were debating whether to rush war supplies to England or stay out of the conflict. Henry L. Stimson, Roosevelt's Secretary of War, told the Senate Military Affairs Committee, "France has been conquered and the sea power of Great Britain seems to be trembling in the balance. We may be next." In September, Roosevelt transferred fifty destroyers to Great Britain in exchange for naval bases.

Ingersoll asked Hellman to cover the Republican convention in Philadelphia. The playwright wrote two paragraphs on the wheeling and dealing among supporters of Robert Taft of Ohio, Arthur Vandenberg of Michigan, and Thomas Dewey of New York—Wendell Willkie won the nomination—and seven paragraphs on the city that she said was afraid to speak its mind. In November, Roosevelt won with a five-million-vote margin over Willkie. American communists denounced the President as an imperialist warmonger and *PM* for supporting Congress's lend-lease program to Great Britain. That changed on June 22, 1941, when Germany invaded the Soviet Union. The next day, *PM* came out with a special edition. "This is the time to keep as cool as the news and the temperature permits, to watch what happens and to remember that your President foresaw it many months ago when he warned you that this was a *total* war," wrote Ingersoll in an editorial. "The sudden scrapping of the world's most momentous pact is one of the things total war means. What it might do to the U.S.A. before it is over could be just as dramatic—if we ever let anything happen to Great Britain or we take our eye—for one single moment—off our enemy, Hitler. It will not end until he is destroyed." Hitler's scrapping of the nonaggression pact by invading the USSR had American comrades execute a sharp U-turn. They declared Roosevelt a hero and rediscovered their sympathy for *PM*. The *New York Daily News* had backed Roosevelt in 1936 and again in 1940, but the drift toward war made publisher Joseph Patterson—a cousin of Colonel Robert Rutherford ("Bertie") McCormick, the controversial publisher of the *Chicago Tribune*—break with Roosevelt.

McCormick's father was a diplomat, his mother a daughter of Joseph Medill, editor and owner of the *Tribune* and one-time Chicago mayor. As a young boy visiting the *Tribune*, Bertie had met Marshall Field I and Joseph Leiter, who had tried to monopolize the wheat market and lost $10 million of his father's money. Bert had never forgotten Field's comment on Joe Leiter's failed attempt at cornering the wheat market: "It pays to have a good cash balance in the bank." Since 1925, when Bertie had become the *Tribune*'s sole editor and publisher, he had built the enterprise to include forests, paper mills, hydroelectric power plants, and shipping interests. By 1940, when he turned sixty, he was among the most powerful figures in newspaper publishing.

The *New York Daily News* came out for appeasing Hitler. At a big Manhattan rally of the America First Committee, Charles Lindbergh asserted that the United States could not win the war for England and that Britain should follow his advice and negotiate peace with the Third Reich. In Chicago, the *Tribune* opened its editorial columns to Nazi officials, slandered England, and praised Japan as its forces sacked Nanking.* On October 27, 1941, the paper wrote: "What vital interests of the United States can Japan threaten? She cannot attack us. That is a military impossibility. Even our base at Hawaii is beyond the striking power of her fleet." The press echoed popular sentiments. News polls during the summer of 1941 showed that seven out of ten Americans opposed going to war.

Everything changed on December 7.

---

* McCormick's anti-British mindset was inherited. His paternal grandfather, Joseph Medill, hated the British for a minor intervention on the side of the Confederacy in the Civil War.

22

PATRIOT GAMES

AS THE UNITED STATES WENT TO WAR AND THE RIGHT-WING PRESS
scrambled to align itself with the popular anger over the Pearl
Harbor "day of infamy," a Chicago North Side dowager was said to
have said, "Nothing is left any more, except, thank God, Marshall
Field's." Marshall Field III took the lessons he had learned at *PM*
and applied them to a new daily newspaper. Bankrolling *PM* had
turned him into a controversial figure, even though he had allowed
Ingersoll to make all the decisions. Sitting in on editorial meetings
and, above all, taking over the finances had taught him enough
about the newspaper business to launch a full-sized newspaper of
his own. The newspaper he had in mind would be experimental
only in its liberal policies. To thrive, its bottom line would have to
be healthy. The city he chose for the newspaper venture was
Chicago.

His choice was judicious. His name carried weight in Chicago, and his desire for an alternative voice found a ready echo in many Chicagoans' disgust with the *Tribune*. McCormick saw "Chicago-land"—a term he coined—as a bedrock alternative to the excesses of liberal Republicans, Democrats, labor unionists, internationalists, New Dealers, Prohibitionists, socialists, and all inhabitants of the Eastern seaboard. Especially rancorous attacks were mounted on Roosevelt and such Republican stalwarts as Henry Luce, and the Colonel lent his paper to the most strident voices of conservatism (he was once described as one of the greatest minds of the fourteenth century). No paper roused as much animosity against itself, in high places and low, as the *Tribune*. On election night 1936, crowds angered by the bitter attacks on FDR made *Tribune* bonfires in State Street and threw rotten eggs at the Tribune Tower. In the spring of 1941, McCormick agitated to have President Roosevelt impeached after a code clerk at the U.S. Embassy in London was caught passing embassy documents to a German agent and arrested by British intelligence. At a public meeting at the Opera House, three thousand people met to denounce the *Tribune*. Out of the meeting grew a list of 100,000 Chicagoans pledging support for the proposed new paper, under the slogan, "Billions for defense, but not two cents for the *Tribune*."

Getting deep into publishing had started during the winter of 1940–41 when Charles Cushing joined Marshall in finding outlets for feature stories that *PM*'s dynamic staff churned out but for which the paper had no room. Not all newspapers could afford the new "must have," a Sunday supplement. The Hearst and Scripps-Howard chains had their own Sunday supplements, but so-called secondary newspapers didn't. So why not print the overstock of *PM* features without local mastheads and logotypes for insertion in Sunday papers? Field and Cushing decided to name the supplement

Parade, and after sorting out claims by Time, Inc. and *This Week* for the title, a thirty-two-page *Parade* was printed and distributed to towns in New Jersey. Except for its connection with *PM*, the Sunday supplement was well received. Encouraged, Cushing made his first sale to a 100,000-plus circulation paper by convincing his army buddy Silliman Evans, owner and publisher of the Nashville *Tennesseean*, to buy the *Parade* service. Evans came to New York. For years, Marshall told Evans over lunch, people in Chicago had urged him to back a morning paper. The *Examiner*, the Hearst chain's Chicago daily, had recently folded, but Marshall didn't want to revive a ghost. Nor did he want to buy either the *Chicago Times*, a liberal, tersely written tabloid founded in 1929, or the respected *Chicago Daily News*, in existence since 1887. The *Daily News* staff included Leland Stowe, the standout among war correspondents who reported the Nazi invasion of Norway and was the first American to reach the German-Soviet front lines after Hitler's invasion of Russia. As Field found out later, it wasn't his liberal ideas but a chance to duel with McCormick that intrigued Evans.

After a business survey and other spadework in Chicago, Evans agreed to take a leave of absence from the *Tennessean* and come in as publisher. There was almost as much excitement about the new Chicago paper as there had been the year before at the birth of *PM*. The newspaper needed a name, and Marshall approved a $10,000 prize contest. Over 220,000 entries came in, subscriptions accompanying most of them. The winner was one Russell Trenholme, who suggested *The Sun* because "when morning comes you look for two things to make your world right, you look for the sun and sunlight, and you look for your morning paper for the truth of what's going on in the world." (Marshall liked a prankster's suggestion that the new paper be called *The McCormick Reaper*.)

Evans was the son of a circuit-riding Methodist preacher, a

rotund, energetic, and respectable southern liberal (he had led a two-fisted campaign against Tennessee's poll tax). He set up shop in the Field Building on La Salle Street, where the Field estate was administered. He began by screening job applicants, who formed long lines in the corridors and inundated the office with mail. Unable to reach an agreement with Cuneo Press, the only non-newspaper printing plant capable of huge press runs, Field and Evans made a proposition to Chicago's other publishing colonel, Frank Knox of the *Daily News.* Knox was happy to both make money and hurt the *Tribune.* The new paper could have the presses when the afternoon *News* was silent. Knox told FDR's secretary of the interior (and former newsman) that Harold Ickes he was sure the new paper would start with over 200,000 paid subscribers.

On November 12, the White House wrote:

Dear Marshall:

I congratulate you on the opportunity for constructive service to the public which is yours in launching a new newspaper in Chicago.

I am sure you will win the confidence and patronage of an ever-increasing clientele. I think it is particularly fortunate that you have my old friend Silliman Evans as publisher. And I know your paper will have all the success which an honest newspaper deserves.

The very simplicity of your motto: "An honest newspaper" is appealing. In living up to that high ideal you will, in Mark Twain's phrase, "gratify some people and astonish the rest."

Very sincerely yours,
Franklin D. Roosevelt

Field and Evans felt they had to hurry. Founding a newspaper was never easy; if the country went to war, it might be impossible. And it looked increasingly unlikely that the United States could stay out of the conflict that now raged from the frozen ruins of Stalingrad to the sands of North Africa. In Asia, the Japanese had overrun the British and French colonies of Malaysia, Indochina, and Burma and were just across the Torres Strait from Australia. Evans and staff worked feverishly to launch the *Sun* before a declaration of war would ration newsprint and curb advertising. Jack Stenbuck, a Hearst veteran who served as the *Sun's* first circulation manager, later described the startup as "the greatest thing since the Lord made the Earth in six days."

Shortly after midnight on December 4, 1941, the new paper hit the streets, to cheers from crowds gathered around downtown stands. By 9:00 A.M., 900,000 papers had been sold. The *Tribune* answered its new competitor with a front page banner screaming FDR'S WAR PLANS. The shock of Pearl Harbor came three days later. The *Tribune* printed the American flag in color on December 8, but its patriotic rallying lasted only one month. In its January 11, 1942, edition, it asserted that "the nation would have been spared much of the bitter news of recent days if the isolationists' advice had only been heeded."

Selling 200,000 copies turned out to be overoptimistic, and over the next months, the *Sun's* circulation fell by 75 percent. The battle with the *Tribune* was just beginning.

There was still *PM*. After the German attack on Russia, Ingersoll had flown off to report the war from Moscow, where Stalin granted him an interview but denied him permission to report from the front. Ralph was back in October 1941. After Pearl Harbor, he wondered aloud in the newsroom whether there was any reason for the paper to continue, since it had accomplished its mission. The nation was at war. He quickly found a new *raison d'être*. To help the country win the war, the paper should flush out right-wing conspirators and fascist saboteurs while at the same time goading industry to set aside the business-as-usual approach.

Two years of watching war in Europe and Asia had prepared Americans for conflict. News from the many fronts pushed the circulation up from an all-time low of 31,000 in August 1940 to over 90,000 by the end of 1941, but *PM* was still losing $25,000 a day. Ingersoll and Field met, and Marshall agreed to give Ralph a last chance to raise circulation while at the same time trim costs. By the end of the sixty days Marshall had imposed, it looked as if *PM* had turned the corner. By May 1942 unit costs had been slashed, and 77,000 in new circulation added.

A new blow came from an unsuspected corner. In June 1942, forty-one-year-old Ralph Ingersoll received notice to report to Draft Board 44 in New York, that he had been classified I-A and faced induction. He was convinced his draft board was biased against him. Most New York draft boards were made up of a Protestant, a Jew, and a Catholic. Number 44, however, had one Protestant and two Catholics, and both, he had heard, were followers of Reverend Charles Coughlin, the Roman Catholic priest who had cofounded, with Gerald L. K. Smith, the National Union for Social Justice, denounced Roosevelt as "a great liar and betrayer," and preached Coughlin's political gospel in radio broadcasts that reached more than thirty-two million people. At the launch of *PM*, Father Coughlin had attacked the paper from his pulpit and told Ingersoll to his face that he was setting up headquarters for an atheistic, pro-British, Moscow-inspired propaganda mill. Next, Coughlin had circulated an unsigned handbill to the city's other newspapers charging that card-carrying Marxists controlled some vital desks at *PM*. Twenty-four names followed. Ingersoll was outraged and, without consulting anyone except Dashiell Hammett, planned to publish photos of the twenty-four staffers, a copy of the handbill, and a signed editorial condemning the charges and welcoming an FBI investigation. Hammett talked Ralph out of dignifying the anonymous attack with a response. Ralph lost his nerve and sent a note to the author of *The Maltese Falcon*: "Incidentally, Dash, things are pretty hot down here right now on this Red issue. Maybe you'd better stay away from the shop for a month or so until it cools off."

Pearl Harbor had shifted the ground under both men. Ingersoll argued that Coughlin was supporting the enemy in a shooting war, and printed Abraham Lincoln's 1863 message to Erastus Corning, in which the President asked: "Must I shoot a simpleminded solider who deserts while I must not touch the hair of a wily agitator who induces him to desert?" The Catholic hierarchy found Coughlin to be an embarrassment, forced him off the air, and removed him from his magazine, *Social Justice*.

Ingersoll—and Field—could perhaps be forgiven for believing that Ralph was more important to the nation's defense at *PM* than in boot camp. A few months short of his fiftieth birthday, Marshall was himself beyond call-up age. We do not know whether Marshall consulted Ingersoll—Ralph would deny it—when he appealed to his friend General Lewis B. Hershey, head of the Selective Service System, to exempt the *PM* editor from the draft. The appeal must have been something of a concerted effort, since four hundred *PM* staffers signed a letter to President Roosevelt asking for Ingersoll's exemption from military service.

The will-he-won't-he suspense of Ralph Ingersoll's conscription became a gossip item and inspired a Columbia Pictures comedy, *Over 21*, in which Alexander Knox plays an editor who joins the army when he does not have to so that people will write about him after the war, and Irene Dunne plays his screenwriter wife coping with wartime domestic problems. In the *Chicago Tribune*, Colonel McCormick called Ingersoll a coward and a disgrace to journalism. McCormick's cousin Cissy Patterson, owner of the *Washington Herald*, and Mississippi Congressman John Rankin and others joined the attack, while the *New York Herald-Tribune*; the author Philip Wylie, best known for his attack on "momism"; and others argued that the editor of *PM* was worth a division of home guards.

We do not know whether Ingersoll saw himself as a battlefield hero, or felt that the appeals could backfire and ruin his macho reputation, because he shot off a telegram to the White House: PLEASE BELIEVE ME I SPECIFICALLY WAIVED MY RIGHT TO APPEAL AND ASKED ALL CONCERNED THAT MY DECISION BE RESPECTED. I BELIEVE IN DEMOCRATIC PROCESS OF SELECTIVE SERVICE AND WOULD FIGHT TO DEFEND IT. He accused Draft Board 44 of bias and in a *PM* piece wrote that he would waive his right to claim his two dependents and would serve in the army, that he was not asking for a deferral, only that his case be heard by another draft board. Draft Board 44 denied the request. One morning a few days later, he took a cab to the induction center on Whitehall Street and enlisted. The radio station that got the news first blared, "Ingersoll has enlisted."

If anybody had a gift for challenging superiors and alienating colleagues, it was Ralph. Everybody expected his army life to be a series of blowups ending in his court-martial. His rapid rise from private to lieutenant colonel went smoothly, however, and in his unpublished memoirs, he would credit Gregory Zilboorg.

Had I followed my preanalysis pattern, just as soon as this change in my status brought me into conflict with my first solid father image—and an army multiplies father images as in a mirror maze—I would have turned on him and surely have ended my war court-martialed for insubordination. Instead, for the first time in my life I found myself able to master a relationship with authority. Instead of making my superiors enemies, I made them into friends.

From boot camp, Ralph pleaded with Marshall to come to work on *PM*. Marshall declined, telling Ruth: "Ralph *thinks* he'd like me there, but after a week or two he'd resent me." The interim editor was John P. Lewis, who shared Ingersoll's politics but was a more easygoing personality. He thought Field wanted to do things but was diffident about saying how they should be done. Later Lewis wrote of Field:

He was not a man of controversy, yet he backed the most controversial newspaper enterprise of his time, and stood up under a good many personal calumnies as a result. I think Marshall had courage and patience and a stronger sense of historical perspective than most, and these were the things, not the seeming contradictions, which really were reflected in his personality. Marshall was willing to stand behind his editors, but he wished a way could be found to make the point without riling the others concerned. Looking backward, I think if we'd had more of his feelings for getting along with people—been less contentious on little points while standing firm on big ones—our wearing qualities would have been better.

Although Marshall was quite chummy with Roosevelt, he was not invited to Washington to be munitions czar, price administrator, or strategic planner. He was not sent abroad to create goodwill, although the President toyed with the idea of making him ambassador to London in 1940 after Joe Kennedy disgraced himself in the post with defeatist remarks on the British government and Congress. It seemed that Field was too controversial for diplomatic service, and he apparently turned down an offer for the ambassadorship to Mexico. Stephen Becker, his biographer, would suggest that FDR thought Marshall could best serve the administration's goals at the helm of the *Chicago Sun*. "As its publisher he could exhort, criticize, review, suggest; he could provide support and publicity for Roosevelt's decisions, and he could remind his readers that the war would end someday, that the problems dwarfed by it would resume their ancient importance."

Going from isolationist to hawk was not a stretch for McCormick. In *Tribune* editorials published on July 26, 1942, he called the owner of the *Sun* a slacker. "No one would suggest that he is indispensable to *PM* or to anything else. The term to fit him and to all the herd of hysterical effeminates is coward." Two days later, Field responded with a six-word editorial: "You are getting rattled, Colonel McCormick."

Marshall received support from an unexpected corner. With copies sent to every newspaper in Chicago and printed in the *Daily News*, the American Legion, 122nd Field Artillery Post #236, voted unanimously to condemn McCormick's editorial. "In 1917," it said, "although Marshall Field was married and the father of two children, he did not attempt to evade service, and although he was well qualified, he did not seek a commission in the armed forces nor did he seek a soft berth of any kind, but instead enlisted as a private in the First Illinois Cavalry Regiment." The letter cited his "courage, ability and leadership at the Argonne front in 1918."

On August 29, McCormick was back calling the *Sun* an illegitimate newspaper, "part of an alien and radical conspiracy against our republican form of government. It is subsidized by the government to the extent that its losses, running into millions of dollars a year, are deducted from the owner's income tax." Marshall took three months to reply. "If spending your own money in a new business can be construed as a government subsidy—Mr. McCormick forgets that *The Tribune* has often employed similar 'subsidies,'" Field wrote in the November 25 edition of the *Sun*. "The *New York News*, started by the *Chicago Tribune* in 1918, enabled the *Tribune* to deduct from its contemporary income taxes the amount due on more than a million dollars. *Liberty Magazine*, a *Chicago Tribune* project, is reported to have lost $14 million between 1923 and 1931, when the *Tribune* got out from under. *Liberty*'s losses drew loud complaints from minority *Tribune* stockholders who apparently did not realize they were being 'subsidized' by the government. The *Detroit Mirror*, sponsored by the *Tribune*, is reported to have lost $2 million in the seventeen months of its existence in 1931 and 1932—years when the government needed income taxes badly." The editorial ended with a zinger. "Does the devastating difference (in Mr. Cormick's mind) lie in the fact that Marshall Field spends his money in Chicago? And that the new newspaper may be 'subsidized' by some of the revenues that would have otherwise come to the *Tribune*?"

McCormick's response, when it came in a January 6, 1943, *Tribune* editorial entitled "The Pantywaist Press," was feeble and factually inaccurate. It mentioned "the cockroach newspapers conducted by Marshall Field to ingratiate himself with the family of his brother-in-law, the late John Hubert Ward, K.C.V.O." Marshall's only brother-in-law was Gwendolyn's husband, Archibald Edmonstone. The editorial was followed by a series on the New Deal's relations with the American press. The point of the piece, written by William Fulton, was that practically every-body in government was biased again the country's only true newspaper, the *Tribune*. Field ignored it.

Mudslinging and wild allegations were only part of the *Tribune's* offensive against the thriving, if not yet in the black, rival. The bylaws of the Associated Press stipulated that a member newspaper could veto applications from a local competitor. The nonprofit cooperative news and photo wire service, started in 1900, served over 90 percent of U.S. and Canadian newspapers and radio stations. The service was a two-way arrangement. A paper subscribing to the AP could print—radio stations could "rip and read"—any wire story from anywhere in the world. In return, it gave the wire service the exclusive right to "lift" its local stories—no big deal for a paper, since it was the sole AP affiliate in its own territory—and carry them on its wires to the rest of its national and international subscribers. The front page coverage of an earthquake in the *Los Angeles Times* might appear as a three-paragraph item in the *Toronto Star,* the *Philadelphia Bulletin,* and the *Miami Herald.* The arrangement allowed the AP to boast that on any given day its 7,200 correspondents and writers were multiplied by the staffs of member newspapers and affiliated news services in other countries for a total of almost 100,000 news-people. When the *Sun* applied for AP membership in 1941, McCormick used the local exclusivity clause to veto the new competitor. There were other, much smaller news services, of course, but the *Sun* was also denied access to the International News Service because as a Hearst organization its franchise belonged to the Hearst *Herald-American.* That left Marshall's paper as a subscriber to the United Press, Transradio Press Service, and Reuters.

Field had Louis Weiss take a look at the Sherman Antitrust

Act, which in 1915 had exempted the wire service. Much had changed since, and Weiss prepared a formal complaint to the Department of Justice. The federal government brought suit under the Sherman Antitrust Act against the AP, accusing it of restraint and monopoly of interstate commerce, and both the AP and the *Chicago Tribune* of conspiring in such restraint and monopoly. The move was by no means welcome. Newspapers widely condemned Field for upsetting the applecart. The Cincinnati *Enquirer* editorialized that the government's action against the AP was a threat to the freedom of the press. The *New York Times*, the *New York Herald Tribune*, and the *Washington Post* all refused to publish a letter to the editor from Zechariah Chafee, a Harvard Law School professor and authority on the freedom of the press. Chafee's letter was finally published in the April 18, 1943, issue of the *Providence Journal*. It read, in part:

Liberty of the press is commonly said to be endangered by the pending Sherman Act suit against the Associated Press. Innumerable editorials in member newspapers have denounced the suit as a senseless and malicious attack on this cherished constitutional right and as an effort to undermine the efficiency of this great organization. As a longtime advocate of free speech, I have tried to learn what all the shouting is about. I have no opinion whether the AP is violating the Sherman Act or not. That question can safely be left to the able Federal judges in New York and eventually to the Supreme Court. The purpose of this article is to show the unsoundness of the prevailing opinion that liberty of the press will be promoted by retention of the present barriers against the admission of new members to the AP. On the contrary, it is these bylaws which abridge the liberty of the press.

After Marshall told the Ontario-Quebec Circulation Managers' convention in Peterborough, Ontario, in October 1942 that a government victory against the AP "would be one of the most important moves ever made toward real freedom of the press," Colonel McCormick issued an inflamed statement: "Marshall Field is an authority on horse racing, yacht racing and grouse shooting but he knows little about newspapers and nothing about the great constitutional subject of freedom of the press." The District Court for the southern district of New York ruled in favor of the government. The AP appealed. The American Newspaper Publishers Association filed *amicus* briefs on its behalf. In its October 1944 term, the Supreme Court upheld the decision, 5–3.*

Field expressed his satisfaction: "When organizations get to be overwhelmingly large and self-protective—whether they be news-gathering combines, medical associations, steel companies, trade unions, or any others—they gravely threaten democratic liberties in areas of our national life and, when large and powerful enough, the whole democratic framework."

The country was fighting the costliest war in its history. Three months after the United States District Court ruling against the AP, Congress amended the tax code to give the Treasury Department the means to crack down on taxpayers with large incomes who wrote off bogus businesses. The tax code amendment was introduced by Senator John A. Danaher (R, Connecticut), but instead of being called the Danaher amend-

---

* Justice Black delivered the majority opinion, and was joined by Justices Douglas, Frankfurter, Reed, and Rutledge. Justices Roberts and Murphy and Chief Justice Stone dissented. Justice Jackon did not take part in the case.

ment, it got labeled the Marshall Field amendment. McCormick, Hearst, and the conservative press loved the brouhaha. Wasn't Marshall Field throwing millions at subversive newspapers and deducting the losses from his income tax? The amendment, timed to embarrass Roosevelt and rich liberals who supported the President, passed. Prudently, Field reorganized his corporate finances by setting up and folding his various undertakings into Field Enterprises Inc.

The Field Foundation was also busy. It was giving grants to such causes as Open Road, Inc., something of a travel agent for academics; People's Institute of Applied Religion; and the Southern Conference for Human Welfare. Another recipient was the Institute of Pacific Relations. One of the Institute's enthusiastic members was Owen Lattimore, the brother of the poet Richard Lattimore. Like Marshall, Owen had been educated in England; after graduate research at Harvard he had spent years in China and Mongolia and written books on Mongolia, Manchuria, and China's outer provinces, and in 1943, *America and Asia*. He was director of the Page School of International Relations at Johns Hopkins University and, in the words of Pacific Fleet commander Admiral Harry E. Yarnell, "the greatest authority in America on China and Manchuria." Lattimore believed that if the Chinese had more confidence in themselves they would "start winning for themselves the victory they want in the East." Chiang Kaishek felt isolated and apprehensive watching Roosevelt, Churchill, and Stalin concentrating on the war in Europe and asked Washington for an adviser. FDR recommended Lattimore, who became the Kuomintang leader's political adviser. When he left China, Chiang Kaishek wrote to Roosevelt, "Mr. Lattimore has fully measured up to our expectations and has entirely justified your choice."

Wartime censorship rules were issued on January 15, 1942. They spelled out what constituted improper handling of news about troops, plane, and ship movements and war production. The Office of War Information accredited war correspondents. *PM* fielded a woman correspondent, Leah Burdette, who lost her life in Iran. Without Ingersoll, the paper was subdued and many staffers breathed easier when, after interim editor Lewis was called up, Field appointed Max Lerner. Ralph could trace his family to one John Ingersoll, born in Bedforshire, England, in 1615, but Lerner was happy to have escaped the *shtetl* in Belarus where he was born in 1902. He was a fervent intellectual who, after Yale had studied at the London School of Economics, where he was a protégé of socialist Harold Laski. While teaching at Sarah Lawrence College and Harvard during the 1930s, he wrote articles applauding France's *front populaire* government in the *New Republic* and *The Nation*. His numerous books included the 1938 critical social analysis *It is Later than You Think*. Ingersoll had found Lerner's prose long-winded and rambling and told him, "You'll never be a newspaperman."

Juicy sex scandals sold newspapers. Compared to the rest of the New York press, *PM*'s coverage of Errol Flynn's statutory rape trial was modest. A grand jury acquitted the movie star of raping two underage girls: Peggy Satterlee, who was known around Hollywood as a pro, and Betty Hansen, who had been picked up by the police for vagrancy. In a rarely used procedure, the Los Angeles District Attorney's office overrode the acquittal and prosecuted Flynn. Women found the dashing thirty-three-year-old Australian-born star irresistible, and his defense attorney, Jerry Geisler, considered Hollywood's sharpest lawyer, made sure nine of the twelve jurors were women. The New York tabloids reported breathlessly how Geisler got Hansen to admit that she had not objected when Flynn took her clothes off, how he picked apart Satterlee's version of a night aboard Flynn's yacht, and how she had the jurors in stitches when she quoted Flynn whispering in her ear, "The moon would be more beautiful through a porthole." Flynn was found not guilty. Lerner, however, managed to offend the liberal Catholic publication *Commonweal* when he wrote of Flynn's acquittal, "The case is over—and it ends well." *Commonweal* clobbered *PM*. "The verdict is fantastically wrong. But the case for the kind of radicalism which ignores or denies humanity's right to be protected against the disruptive press must soon come into the court of public opinion." Ten years earlier, *Commonweal* would have been right. Even acquittal would have meant cancelled contracts and a star's ruin. The war had loosened morality. GIs began using "in like Flynn" as jargon for getting away with fornication.

Ernest Hemingway reported from the Pacific theater for *PM*. Lieutenant Ingersoll, on the other hand, was back from service with the First Army's Engineer Corps on the North African front and ensconced in Marshall's Park Avenue library dictating a quick book into existence. He wasn't sure he'd even want to return to *PM* after the war. With permission from army public relations, he composed *The Battle Is the Payoff* in one hundred hours of dictation and was ordered to report to the American military headquarters in London before the Harcourt Brace book came out. The *New York Times* reviewer called it the number-one book of the war. The Book-of-the-Month Club picked it up as its November 1943 selection, and it was the war's first big bestseller.

Field's refusal to give up hope that *PM* could exist on the basis of its intelligent writing, excellent pictures, and interpretive appeal slowly faded. The paper shrank to twenty-eight pages in 1943 as newsprint and ink were being rationed. The second color on the color page was abandoned. "The News for Living section was considerably abridged," Paul Milkman would write in *PM: A New Deal in Journalism*. "In a time of war, this was an understandable editorial judgment, but the character of the paper was narrower, more exclusively political than it had been. By 1944 consumer news sometimes vanished entirely; more rarely, sports news suffered the same fate." On some days *PM* printed as few as sixteen pages. That over 100,000 New Yorkers continued to spend their nickels to buy it showed the unflinching loyalty of its core readers. Others, including Lewis Weiss, saw the mathematics differently. The paper needed another 100,000 readers to break even. To appeal to these new readers it would have to transform itself, which probably meant losing a portion of the first 100,000.

Field took on new responsibilities. With Weiss, he plunged deeper into the paper's management. Apparently uncomfortable in the newsroom, he usually arrived with Ruth and Weiss. Marshall and his lawyer met privately while Ruth stayed with the newsmen.

23

COMING OF AGE

ON SEPTEMBER 28, 1943, MARSHALL FIELD III CELEBRATED HIS fiftieth birthday in the city of his birth. After breakfast with Ruth and leafing through the newspapers—his own, Colonel McCormick's, and the *New York Times*—he joined Louis Weiss downstairs for a ride to the Field Building. It was a fine, brisk fall day, and as they alighted two men on the tailgate of a *Tribune* delivery truck looked up, recognized Marshall, and in unison shouted, "Happy birthday, Mr. Field." At the conference room upstairs, George Richardson and Carl Weitzel, lawyers for the estate, joined them.

Weitzel laid out Marshall Field's famous 1905 will with its ardent wish that his grandsons "will each seasonably adopt some regular occupation in life, inasmuch as such an occupation will, in my judgment, greatly promote their usefulness and happiness."

Henry had been dead for twenty-seven years, but Marshall, sitting at the end of the table with an unlit pipe between his teeth, could be said to have adopted a useful and happy occupation. He picked up his fountain pen and signed papers that abolished the estate of Marshall Field and gave him sole control of $75 million. He already had $93 million and, with a total of $1.6 billion in today's money, was now one of the world's wealthiest men. He had been the beneficiary of wealth, tradition, and position. Now he was the lone custodian of all three. "I came of age today," he smiled at a dinner party that evening.

The family was not all there. Marshall IV was fighting in the Pacific. His law clerking had been cut short by the declaration of war. He had received a new appointment to become law clerk to Supreme Court Justice Stanley Reed and was planning to move Joanne and himself to Washington, D.C., when Pearl Harbor canceled, forever as it were, his career in law. Like his father in World War I, Junior, as he liked to be called, enlisted. His choice was the navy. After midshipman's school, he emerged as an ensign, and immediately became a gunnery officer aboard the aircraft carrier U.S.S. *Enterprise*. The *Enterprise* was the only operational carrier during the early months of the war in the Pacific. The *Enterprise* carried out what amounted almost to a private war with such success that the Japanese claimed to have sunk her seven different times.

His sisters, Barbara and Bettine, were at their father's birthday party. Twenty-five-year-old Barbara had divorced Anthony Bliss and married Robert Boggs, a physician. Twenty-year-old Bettine was also a doctor's wife. Her husband was Dr. McChesney Goodall Jr., a research doctor who would contribute to the discovery of levodopa, or L-dopa, for the treatment Parkinson's disease.

Field III had put on weight. His hair, combed straight back, was nearly white, but his eyes sparkled and his smile was winning. He had gone from Great Gatsby idle wealth at Caumsett, to patron of public services in New York's raunchier neighborhoods, to patron of information. His benefactions were many. He was a director of the Metropolitan Opera Association of New York as well as the Metropolitan Museum of Art, the University of Chicago, and his grandfather's Field Museum. At the beginning of the war he had founded the United States Committee for the Care of European Children. To administer his philanthropic interests, he organized the Field Foundation in 1940, which by 1944 had given away $4.5 million, mostly in the field of race relations and child welfare. He was a New York state delegate to the Democratic Party conventions in 1944 and opposed the nomination of Harry Truman as the vice-presidential candidate. Truman had none of FDR's vision and courage to direct the national mood and resources, and Marshall would have preferred Henry A. Wallace or Justice William O. Douglas.

The big store on State and Washington, meanwhile, was no longer his responsibility, although he was still on the board. A month before Pearl Harbor, the store had opened the 28 Shop, a upscale fashion store-within-the-store, named for the traditional entrance of the carriage trade, 28 East Washington, and for its twenty-eight dressing rooms. Joseph Platt, an assistant to *Gone With The Wind* art director Lyle Wheeler, designed the interior. Forty-year-old Hughston McBain was now the president, and to compensate for the near-total wartime shutoff of imports, he found inventory by expanding the company factories. The company temporarily gave up advertising its Fieldcrest sheets and pillowcases, and concentrated on turning out parachute fabric, camouflage netting, wool blankets, mosquito netting, army uniforms and overcoats, and hosiery for WACS. By the end of 1944, Field's earned $20 million before taxes.

With the consent of Field, McBain sold the Merchandise Mart. Low-paying government agencies occupied more than a third of the space, and although the giant building was bringing in $3.5 million a year in rent, it was still not paying its 1930 mortgage. After extended negotiations, the Mart, which had cost $35 million, was sold for $12.9 million. Former Wall Street speculator and former ambassador to Britain Joseph P. Kennedy bought the Mart and within a few years turned it into a huge asset bringing an annual income of $20 million that would help finance his son John F. Kennedy's winning presidential campaign in 1960.

The publishing world was a cheerier story. The *Sun* paper celebrated its second on birthday December 4, 1943, with a dinner honoring publisher Field. "It is a pleasure to extend congratulations to you and your associates on the occasion," FDR wrote in a book of testimonials. And in New York, *PM* reached break-even if not profitability even though it was still in search of the second 100,000 readers. Pessimists told Field that *PM*'s solvency was due to wartime price controls. Peace would mean the lifting of price controls and a plunge back into red ink.

24

BEARING WITNESS

HIROSHIMA WAS BOMBED ON AUGUST 6, 1945, NAGASAKI ON THE 9th. On the warm, still afternoon of August 14, a crowd of one hundred thousand Chicagoans stood within sight of Marshall Field's waiting for the famous clock to strike 6:00, the time of Japan's announced surrender. When the clock hands stood straight up and down, Chicago knew the empire of Japan had capitulated. Employees stood in the display windows and at the moment World War II was over waved flags and streamers.

Among the returning GI Joes who concerned Marshall were his son and Ralph Ingersoll. The war had taught the two men different lessons. Twenty-eight-year-old Marshall IV had survived twelve major engagements in the Pacific, and came back with a piece of shrapnel lodged in his head and an attitude of moralistic self-righteousness. In the armed forces, issues were clear-cut and one-sided. He had witnessed great sacrifices and resented the robust leftism that had been the credo of New Deal intellectuals and artists, but he was also offended by the corruption of the home front. A thousand bucks under the table was the formula for buying a new car, and when it came to buying a house, the real estate squeeze was on for servicemen. He and Joanne found readjusting to each other impossible. They divorced. Joanne kept custody of four-year-old Marshall V and their daughter, Joanne, born in 1942. Instead of resuming his law career, Marshall came to Chicago and asked his father for a job on the *Sun*. "The war made a lot of things look different," he later wrote. "My basic interests were unchanged, but it seemed to me that I could bring whatever interest I had in government and politics to bear better through journalism and the mass media than through the law." He might be the son of the owner of the *Sun* and *PM*, but his veteran's ethics told him to start at the bottom—on the tailgate of a delivery truck, even though he knew the distance between tailgate and driver's seat was shorter if your daddy owned the truck.

Ingersoll returned a celebrity and immediately popped out to Caumsett to tell Marshall III how he planned to revitalize *PM*. With the publication of *Top Secret*, Ralph was a swirl of controversial fame. Written at top speed in the emotional aftermath of the war, the book exposed jealousies and rivalries at the highest level of the British-American alliance. The author revealed that Churchill and Roosevelt had a serious falling out over the strategy for occupying Berlin, and that in dealings with Britain's top soldier, Field Marshal Sir Bernard Montgomery, Supreme Commander General Dwight Eisenhower had been weak and indecisive. History would prove Ingersoll close to the mark. In 1946 his revelations were explosive.

Field had reacted with shock to the April 12, 1945, news of

Franklin D. Roosevelt's death. Vice President Harry S. Truman was sworn in and immediately faced mounting economic problems. Inflation following the lifting of wartime controls led to heightened labor demands. Congress passed few of Truman's major recommendations, as a number of southern Democrats opposed to continuing New Deal politics joined Republicans to form an opposition bloc. When the Republicans took both houses of Congress in the 1946 elections—the last Republican Congress had been in 1928—Field panicked and asked Truman to resign. The voters had spoken, Marshall said in a signed frontpage editorial in the November 7 edition of the *Sun*. To give the electorate a clear-cut choice in 1948 and a chance to elect a liberal Congress and to continue Roosevelt's achievements, Truman should let the Republicans deal with the transition to a peacetime economy. "Therefore, Mr. President, we urge you to ask the Republican members of the new House and Senate to suggest to you a man whom you will name Secretary of State, in whose favor you can resign your high office." Robert Lasch, the chief editorial writer, tried to dissuade his boss from publishing the alarming editorial.

Field had little prescience of the looming Cold War. Americans were shocked when they heard that the Soviet Union had detonated an atom bomb, that Mao Zedong's communists were winning in China, and, at home, that *Time* editor Whittaker Chambers, a former communist himself, accused former State Department official Alger Hiss of espionage. All too soon, a majority of citizens in America—and in the Soviet Union— believed that a nuclear World War III was inevitable. The fierce ideological issues of the Cold War favored right-wing sentiments, and even the liberal voice of Adlai Stevenson warned that the country's enemies planned total conquest of the human mind.

Marshall could have read in the September 13, 1946, issue of

PM that a State Department official had named Dashiell Hammett a communist. But Marshall spoke out against labor secretary Lewis Schwellenbach's proposal to outlaw the Communist Party, and against Truman's economic and military aid to Greece and Turkey. To the Truman White House, the two countries looked like the next dominos to fall to communism. To Field, giving weapons to a pair of reactionary governments was little more than bribery. Working this time with Lasch, Marshall came up with an editorial that said Schwellenbach was yielding to fear.

> Secretary of Labor Schwellenbach wants to "outlaw" the Communist party. His outburst on the subject last week was a timely illustration of the confusion with which many of us approach communism as well as foreign policy.
>
> Secretary Schwellenbach evidently hopes to suppress the idea of communism in this country by denying it legal political expression. But neither history nor common sense supports the notion that any idea, however unpalatable to the vast majority of us (as communism is), can be obliterated by force or legislation.
>
> Christianity was not killed by the might of ancient Rome. The ideas of Locke, Hume and Montesquieu were not killed by the British Tories who tried to "outlaw" the American Revolution. The ideas of Plato and Aristotle, which underlay the Renaissance, were not smothered by the weight of the Dark Ages.
>
> The only way to kill an idea is with a better idea.

To make his points, Marshall wrote a book. *Freedom Is More than A Word*, published by the University of Chicago Press in the spring of 1945, was the first book written by any member of the Marshall Field dynasty. A short book that pleaded for universal human rights and condemned the power of money in the news business, *Freedom Is More than A Word* was at first assumed to be ghostwritten. The author acknowledged the help of Alfred McClung Lee, a historian of the news business, Max Lerner, Louis Weiss, *Sun* executives, and others, but the ideas and the execution were his. Field applauded the creation of the Atlantic Charter, the appeal by Churchill and Roosevelt for self-determination for all people, and the formation of the United Nations. "Only in the faith of Jefferson and Lincoln can we find the spiritual drive that will keep America and the world on their course toward greater opportunities for greater numbers of people, greater free enterprise in the real sense of that expression." As for his own sphere of influence, he warned that newspaper chains and broadcast companies were all too often under the control of vested interests. "Wherever there is a striking issue between property rights and human rights upon which the people are permitted to pass judgment, the majority of the press has aligned itself on the side of property rights," he wrote. "Sometimes, when the issue is confused, the press has carried the people with it. But when the issue has been clearly enough defined between the partisans, and the facts have reached the public, the majority of America's voters have ignored the special-interest pleas of the publishers." Who owns information was a timeless subject. Forty years later Noam Chomsky and David Halberstam would debate the question more forcefully.

If Marshall IV had come home to shed a wife, Ralph Ingersoll had married the moment he got out of uniform. She was Elaine Cobb, a *Time-Life* researcher who was soon pregnant and had no intention of working at *PM*. Reclaiming his editor's chair at *PM* in January 1946, Ralph kept Max Lerner as editorial writer. Lerner, like young Marshall Field, turned sharply to the right during the McCarthy era and by the 1960s became an apologist for the Vietnam War. Besides returning *PM* to "old-fashioned crusading journalism," as Ralph told Field in the first weeks after his return, he wanted to hire a number of new writers, paying them at least $15,000 a year ($133,000 in 2002 money). To his surprise, the boss was no longer a pushover. Marshall told him *PM* was losing between $5,000 and $6,000 a week. If more money were to be poured into the endeavor, the paper would have to carry advertising. Ralph raised objections. Marshall stood firm: Either you accept advertising or you cut staff. Ralph tried to wriggle out of any such commitment, but in the end fired I. F. Stone and another Washington bureau staffer he didn't like. In an attempted end run around Marshall, Ralph decided the way to raise circulation and money was through an appeal to *PM*'s loyal readers. He wrote a self-glorifying "History of *PM*," a twelve-page insert scheduled to appear in the June 18 issue, the date *Top Secret* was to begin serialization in the paper. The text landed on Marshall's desk at the *Sun* with a note from Ralph saying he'd have come to Chicago if it weren't for the fact that his wife was expecting their baby any minute.

Marshall resented not having been consulted on the "History," and the two men's relationship deteriorated rapidly from there. The "History" solicitation did not add new readers and by October, the advertising question gave Ingersoll an excuse for resigning. As he put it, "I resigned one sentence before I would have been fired."

PM survived his departure and the introduction of advertising. John P. Lewis, who had been with the paper since the beginning and shared Ingersoll's politics but not his idiosyncrasies, became editor. He thought Field possessed more courage and patience and a stronger sense of historical perspective than any of them, and found it ironic that this noncontroversial man was funding the most controversial newspaper.

Advertising did not prove to be the rescue everybody had hoped for, because few advertisers wanted to put their ads in *PM*. Field threw in the towel when Bartley C. Crum, a prominent Democrat and lawyer whose partner had been William Hearst's personal attorney, proposed taking over *PM*, bringing in his own staff, and seeking out advertisers for a renamed paper. Originally from San Francisco, Crum had served on Roosevelt's first Fair Employment Practices Commission, and in 1946 had been a member of the Anglo-American commission recommending the partition of Palestine that led to the United Nations resolutions establishing the state of Israel. In June 1948, Crum became the publisher and renamed *PM* the *New York Star*. He and his backers put a lot of money into the tabloid, but advertisers stayed away. The *Star* backed Truman for reelection before suspending publication in 1949.

Field had his hands full in Chicago, a city with five daily newspapers. Mergers and consolidations were a constant in the newspaper business, and in 1947 he did what in 1943 he had said he wouldn't do: He purchased the *Chicago Times*. The *Sun*'s printing arrangements with the *Daily News*, now owned by John S. Knight, had become increasingly expensive, and the acquisition gave Field what he desperately needed: his own printing facility. In response to technical difficulties in the *Times* plant, the *Sun* abandoned its full-size broadsheet format. In response to a strike by typesetters and compositors against all five Chicago dailies two months later, he merged the two papers and produced the *Sun-Times* on a twenty-four-hour basis. Whether by foresight—television would slowly choke off afternoon papers—or because of the cost of around-the-clock editions, the *Sun-Times* gradually made itself into a morning paper. It was a ticklish undertaking, the *Sun-Times* admitted in a December 11, 1966, silver anniversary edition, "Because the canceling of each edition usually triggered a circulation drop. Each drop had to be met with promotions of the morning paper and an aggressive news policy, which would change people's reading habits." Like modern-day media barons, Field added radio stations and magazines, and purchased Simon & Schuster and Pocket Books. In 1945 he acquired the Quarrie Corporation, publisher of World Book Encyclopedia and Childcraft educational books. Quarrie was not large, but its profits were consistent.

He also joined a score of newspaper chiefs on an Around the World in Thirteen Days tour arranged by the State Department and Pan American Airways president Juan T. Trippe. The days when half the newspaper publishers denounced him for busting the Associated Press closed club were gone, and his planemates included Frank Gannett of the Gannett Newspapers, Roy Howard of the Scripps-Howard Newspapers, *New York Herald-Tribune* owner Helen Ogden Reid, a dozen other senior newsmen and women, and Trippe himself. The 22,297-mile tour of ten countries during the summer of 1947 was the opinion-makers' first glimpse of the postwar world, their first encounters with foreign leaders. Conscious of being a very privileged witness, Marshall took lots of notes.

In London, still plunged in wartime austerity, they met Prime Minister Clement Attlee ("very shy man given to understatement," Marshall wrote in his personal diary), who told them of Britain's energy crisis. Marshall and Reid dined privately with newspaper magnate Lord Beaverbrook. Marshall had time to drive out to Ditchley and spend a weekend with his cousin Ronald Tree and his wife, Marietta. U.S. Ambassador Lewis Douglas and his wife,

Peggy, were there, giving Marshall their take on Britain's slow recovery.

In Istanbul, local newsmen told of the Turkish government's press restrictions ("soldiers everywhere—60% national budget to army though local Communists practically nonexistent"). He marveled at the American Arabian Oil Company's air conditioning and plumbing in the middle of the Dhahrani desert. The British Raj was in its twilight zone, but the Americans were bidden to lunch with the Governor of Bengal and Lady Burrows in Calcutta. ("The contrast between the large and pompous house, servant behind every chair, etc., and the condition of the population of Calcutta, pretty depressing, however that will be over [with Independence] in August. One doesn't see how even a free India is going to do much for their standard of living—Calcutta has population of over 5,000,000 . . . many Hindus murdered every night if they wander into Moslem portions of city and vice versa.") In Bangkok, he noted, the people seemed happy, but the venereal disease rate was 90 percent. The ambassador told him the French in neighboring Vietnam would have a hard time putting down the Viet Cong insurrection. ("Convoys cut up all the time, etc. Soldiers mostly foreign legion. Ex-Nazi soldiers who sing Horst Wessel song more than Marseillaise.")

They landed in Manila in the middle of a typhoon. War had destroyed the old Spanish city center and all government buildings ("Manila hotel very well restored considering we fought the Japs in every room and hallway"). He found newly elected president Manuel Roxas a remarkable man, but heard that government efforts to settle farmers in Mindanao amounted to little more than furnishing local landowners with sharecroppers.

From Manila they flew to Shanghai. Mao Zedong's triumph over the Nationalists was still two years away, and in Nanjing the Americans paid their respects to Generalissimo and Madame

Chiang Kaishek. The nationalist leader talked off the record, but said little. In Shanghai, many people told him the communists were winning:

> It is openly stated that there is no chance of Chiang holding beyond the Yellow River . . . The correspondents who have been up in Manchuria and Yenan and Shantung can find no direct evidence of Russian participation. In fact the Chinese Commies are sore at Russia who have closed the border making it impossible to export from Manchuria, where food is plentiful, and manufactions are going strong. There is a tremendous propaganda campaign to make the U.S. believe that the Russians wish to control China and that the only thing to save the world is a large loan to the Nationalist Government. I should further guess that any loan, no matter how large, would be poured down a rat hole. It looks, very superficially of course, as though the days of the Nationalist Government were numbered and that China would go back to being split up with Communists in control of Manchuria and the North and possibly penetrating further and further to the South. You can hear terrible stories of atrocities and killings on both sides, which is the nature of a civil war.

What struck him as he was being driven around Tokyo by U.S. military personnel was the reconstruction. General and Mrs. Douglas MacArthur treated the globetrotting Americans to lunch. The general spoke until four in the afternoon, telling his guests he was anxious for a peace treaty. During the closing days of the war, the Russians had occupied the Kuril Islands, the northernmost specks of land of the Japanese Archipelago. MacArthur believed the Soviet Union would not be much of an obstacle, as this territorial question had already been decided in Russia's favor.

He said that whatever the Russians agreed to, they carried through. "For instance, in repatriation of Jap prisoners they had explained to him the difficulties of transport. The total, probably 1.2 million—agreement 10,000 per month—had extended this and in his opinion prisoners were in better condition than those repatriated by any country except our own. Much better than the British or Dutch." McArthur was anxious to kick-start the Japanese economy, as the occupation was costing American tax-payers $1 million a day. He approved of the continued purges of Japanese war criminals and profiteers, saying that if Japanese prosecutors were in charge of the eradication, the purges would be ferocious, as they were a people stunned by the betrayal of their ancient beliefs. Marshall came away believing the criticism of the purges back stateside was orchestrated by an ex-representative of National City Bank who was there before the war and obviously friendly to the big-money boys who had undoubtedly done him favors. After visits to the countryside, Marshall came away with little faith in a democratic Japan. "My guess: it would be meat for some gang of dissidents to take over and scrap constitution, which is excellent, but for which the Japs probably aren't prepared. It must be remembered that all my views are so superficial as not to be worth this paper they are written on."

After fuel stops in Guam and Wake Island, they arrived in Honolulu, swam and dined at the Royal Hawaiian Hotel, and flew to San Francisco. "The glimpses I had made me realize how far it is from the ideal of one world—India with its teaming population about to launch into an experiment the future of which is so uncertain—and China with its enormous numbers in such chaotic state. If they will accept it, I think our knowhow is more important to these people than wads of money or materials, which they are not in a position to use. We must create a dynamic democracy, which will be coupled with understanding, to fight revolutionary communism. We must practice it wherever we go—reaffirming the principles of the Atlantic Charter wherever possible."

He came back disheartened and discouraged by the suffering, fear, and panic he had observed. Inflation had wiped out the value of money everywhere, and financial crises confronted national governments. The United States, in his opinion, could provide know-how and encouragement but would be foolish to pour billions into Asian countries seeking aid. He felt certain the corrupt Chiang Kaishek regime would soon collapse, and that China and India, two countries containing half the world's population, might go communist. Disregarding his own observation that Japanese dissidents or organized crime elements would take over the country, he pronounced Japan the only bright spot, thanks to General MacArthur's benign rule.

Marshall was asked to run for governor of Illinois, as a possible stepping stone to the White House. The suggestion came from Samuel P. Gurman, a Chicago attorney, who wrote to him:

In a recent conversation with several people, I found that everyone seemed to be stumped as to who would be candidate for governor on the Democratic ticket, having in mind also that that would be a stepping stone to the Presidency. It has been suggested, and it was also my thought that you would make an excellent candidate. You would lift the campaign out of "gutter politics." People would expect the issues to be on the higher plane on which you are known to hold views beneficial to the common man.

Of course I don't know whether you have any political aspirations or ambitions, whether you're a liberal Republican or a New

Deal Democrat, but I think it may not be a bad idea at all for somebody to start the ball rolling, of course, with your consent.

President Truman was unpopular, and the upcoming 1948 election did not bode well for the Democrats. Marshall, however, shut down Gurman's trial balloon, saying he had no political aspirations. Publishing newspapers, he said, was incompatible with running for political office. Besides, the perfect Democratic candidate for governor was Adlai Stevenson.

The Republican and Democratic parties both chose Philadelphia for their 1948 conventions, and for the same reason—television. AT&T's coaxial cable could now feed programs to fourteen eastern cities, reaching an audience of over one million. Marshall was a Democratic delegate from New York, but thought that what the country needed was a progressive alternative. However, he could not bring himself to endorse Progressive candidate Henry Wallace, Roosevelt's former vice-president. Wallace was aloof and self-righteous, and his campaign for an expanded New Deal unwittingly defined the limits of postwar liberalism. Truman was detested and the Republican candidate, New York Governor Thomas E. Dewey, almost robotic. The *Sun-Times* supported Truman, but only after making energetic overtures to war hero Dwight D. Eisenhower in the hope that he would turn out to be a Democrat. Nobody knew where the general stood politically. He pronounced himself flattered when Field called on him, but nothing more than a swapping of political anecdotes came of their meeting. The *Tribune* endorsed Dewey for president. Marshall was as astonished as everybody else at Truman's "give 'em hell, Harry" come-from-behind election victory. Colonel McCormick suffered the famous embarrassment of rushing out an early edition of the *Tribune* with headlines proclaiming a Dewey victory.

25

COLD WAR

MARSHALL FIELD IV DIDN'T STAY LONG ON THE DELIVERY TRUCK. He climbed the rungs of publishing without the scorn usually heaped on the boss's son, and spent much of 1947 in London as one of the *Sun*'s European correspondents. Father and son shared a sense of family obligations. Marshall III was a confirmed liberal, his son a conservative, a Republican who nevertheless supported Democrat Adlai Stevenson in the Illinois gubernatorial race (Stevenson won). Marshall III turned over the newspapers to his then thirty-four-year-old son in 1950. Junior paid sufficient attention to the bottom line to run the newspaper in the black. Like his father, he was interested in education. Under his direction, the education division of Field Enterprises became Field Enterprises Educational Corporation, publishers of the *World Book Encyclopedia*, *Childcraft*, the *How and Why Library*, and related educational materials. Television also captured his imagination. The *Texaco Star Theater* with Milton Berle was a smash hit of 1950 for those who had television sets. Most cities had only one station—Austin, Texas; Little Rock, Arkansas; and Portland, Maine, had none at all. Junior had a hard time convincing the Field Enterprises board that establishing a Chicago TV station—he suggested the call letters be WFLD—would be a logical extension of publishing.

Father and son were separated by a reticence that neither could overcome. Junior and his sisters Barbara and Bettine were scarred by their parents' divorce, by the way their father had left the family for Audrey and, after her, for Ruth, who brought her own two sons to Caumsett. Marshall III had been too distracted to give much of himself to his children, and Evelyn's love had been reserved and often withheld. She was now remarried, the wife of the Colombian landscape architect Diego Suarez. Marshall V would remember his grandmother's husband as a charming, gracious man. Suavez spent his retirement years cataloguing and investigating the history of the Field family silver collection that his wife had inherited. Evelyn and Diego lived in New York City. Evelyn saw her children by appointment only.

Marshall IV was diagnosed a bipolar, and both he and Barbara were institutionalized for periods of time. Therapy in the 1940s and 50s was psychoanalytic, involving "talk" (for those who could afford it), isolation, and lengthy institutionalization. Today, depressive personalities and those suffering from bipolar disorders (formerly known as manic-depression) are believed to suffer neurochemical imbalances, and their treatment is most likely to be pharmacological. Still open for debate is the nature/nurture question of whether clinical depression is genetically inherited or is provoked by a patient's environment, childhood, gender, or misfortune.

Bettine tested everybody's tolerance when she divorced McChesney Goodall, the Virginia doctor with whom she had a daughter, and married a black man. He was Eldridge Bruce, a handsome college graduate she had come to know while working for Henry Wallace, the unsuccessful Progressive Party presidential candidate in 1948. Eldridge's mother had been a nurse for Bettine and McChesney's baby daughter. Without telling her father or the family, Bettine and Eldridge were married in a private home on Frederiksted in the U.S. Virgin Islands.

In a telling comment on the desertion she had felt as a six-year-old when her father married Audrey, Bettine told a friend she had hoped at least one generation of Fields would never have to know loneliness. In a troubling generational repeat, however, she now abandoned her baby daughter, Bettine. It was inconceivable in segregated Virginia of 1950 that a white woman marrying a black man could get custody of her white daughter, and despite the experiences of her own childhood, she didn't try. Little Bettine grew up with her father and married three times. With her first husband, Scott Weis, she had two children, Austin, who was severely retarded, and Evelyn. After a divorce, she married Robert D. Carroll. Their daughter, Bettine Field Carroll, came to believe that Stanley Kramer's 1967 movie *Guess Who's Coming to Dinner* was the story of her grandmother and black stepgrandfather. Her mother moved to rural Arkansas, where she settled on a large piece of land near Harrison and built a French-style villa. She was murdered one night by an unknown assailant who shot her through the window. A poacher with whom she had quarreled over hunting on her land was a suspect, but police could never prove he was the murderer.

It took Bettine and Eldridge six months to drum up enough courage to tell her family. Marshall III was appalled when he learned of Bettine's marriage, not so much because his new son-in-law was black, he said, but because of the prejudices that any mixed couple faced. Some family members severed all ties with Bettine, although her sister, Barbara, eventually came around. Bettine and Eldridge followed the example of her grandparents Marshall II and Albertine, her great-aunt Ethel, and her great-uncle Arthur Tree, and chose to live abroad after they had a baby girl they named Catherine. The Bruces moved to England and later settled in France, where a mixed-race couple was tolerated.

Marshall III found solace if not peace at Caumsett. Ronald Tree came over to spend a summer, and Edward M. Warburg, director of the American Ballet and a friend of Zilboorg, took a cottage. The summers were mellower than during Audrey's time. Marshall was in good health. He swam, played tennis, and rode to hounds. The drinking was limited, and the evenings' conversations more serious.

Marshall IV remarried in 1950. His new wife was twenty-two-year-old Katherine (Kay) Woodruff, the only child of a Joliet, Illinois, banker, and a recent graduate of Smith College. As the wife of a newspaper publisher and heir to a multimillion-dollar fortune, Kay was introduced to the world of journalism, but didn't think working in the field was an option: "I was closely associated with the effort behind the scenes, a once-removed education in all aspects of a metropolitan newspaper." Marshall brought home his newspaper acquaintances and, less congenially, his problems.

As was expected of her, Kay volunteered at various charities, and society columnists dubbed her the Grace Kelly of Chicago. A son, Frederick—Ted to everybody—was born in 1953. Two daughters, Katherine and Barbara, followed. Even though Marshall IV suffered bouts of depression and was scarred by his

mother's disciplinarian upbringing and his wartime experiences—
the shrapnel in his skull was still in his head when he died—he was
the brightest of all the Fields. He possessed an acute photographic memory, which at Harvard had brought accusations of cribbing
on exams. "He would open any two pages in Webster's, scan the
two pages very quickly and hand the dictionary to you and repeat
verbatim any of the definitions," his son Ted would remember.
"He didn't take very good care of himself, he had a drinking problem and took combinations of antidepressants."

Fellow publishers looked for devious reasons for Marshall III's
handing the reins of the *Sun-Times* to his fast-study son. Marshall
Field III was only fifty-seven. Why would he make his thirty-four-
year-old son editor and publisher? The consensus among newspaper owners was that the handover was Machiavellian, that politics
was behind the changing of the guard, that clamorous anticom-
munism was making left-of-center ideologies unpopular. Cousin
Ronald Tree had another theory. Gentlemanly codes of tolerance
and fair play were out of style as Senator Joseph McCarthy (R,
Wisconsin) warned of communists in every nook and cranny of
the U.S. government. The broadmindedness and acceptance of
radical and eccentric ideas that Marshall had learned at Oxford
clashed uncomfortably with smearing an ever-larger number of
Americans and their institutions as treacherous. Because he had
supported worthy causes that were now suspect, he, too, was
swept up in the anticommunist hysteria.

Junior had little taste for opinions that could be called controversial. The *Sun-Times* came out for Dwight Eisenhower in
1952. It was the first time in the history of both the *Sun* and the
Times that either had endorsed a Republican for major office.
Readers were confused and assumed that Marshall III had desert-
ed his liberal principles. To set the record straight, Marshall III

wrote a letter to his son, the editor, expressing his polite dissent. "I have always had a great admiration for the general, and was delighted to see him nominated at the Republican convention," he wrote to Junior:

Dear Marsh.

I had hoped he might lead the liberal element of the Republican Party into the ascendancy, and that whoever won the election; this country would look forward to furthering the social gains that have been made in the last 20 years. As the campaign proceeds, I develop stronger and stronger doubts that he will be able to accomplish this. On the other hand, Adlai Stevenson has made his position entirely clear, and I find myself in complete agreement with his aims, and more and more convinced that the country needs a statesman of his caliber . . .

The *Sun-Times* published the letter without the "Dear Marsh" salutation or the close ("With my best love, Dad"). The diffidence of Marshall III, still the head of Field Enterprises, which owned the *Sun-Times*, earned him kudos from editorial writers. "Marshall Field III was one of the few rich men I have ever met who did not think that his wealth gave his opinion a special value," Robert Lasch would remember. "In the daily editorial conferences at the Chicago *Sun*, my colleagues and I could never quite adjust ourselves to his genuine modesty. Here was a man who was paying for the enterprise, and paying in a handsome way, yet he deferred constantly to those around him and chose to solicit the judgment of others instead of imposing his own."

Ruth and Marshall campaigned for Stevenson. Eisenhower swept into office and soon fulfilled his campaign promise to end the Korean War. However, he didn't dare rein in the witch hunt that brought McCarthy fame and, eventually, infamy. Suspicion seeped through government, journalism, the arts, and the halls of academia as civil servants were tarred with the same brush as scholars and people in art and entertainment who were blacklisted. Marshall got into the crosshairs of the Senate Subcommittee on Internal Security because he became a trustee of Sarah Lawrence College. The House Select Committee to Investigate Tax-Exempt Foundations and Comparable Organizations hauled him to Washington to answer questions on whether the Field Foundation was using its resources for un-American and subversive activities or, as its mandate put it, whether foundations and organizations were used "for purposes not in the interests or tradition of the United States."

The day Field became a Sarah Lawrence College trustee, November 8, 1951, its board of trustees answered innuendos and accusations by the Hearst press, the *American Legion Magazine*, the Westchester County Legion, and the Bronxville post of the American Legion. The college incurred the wrath of conservatives and holier-than-thou patriots not only for being a liberal, integrated institution but because its faculty had the audacity to congratulate itself for not screening textbooks, for not barring speakers from its campus, and for not imposing loyalty oaths. With some trepidation, the board of trustees put together a forceful response and wanted to hear from its newest member. Marshall Field was a member of two Legion posts and, since World War I, had been a member of the American Legion's Society of Founders. Would he approve of a statement saying an educational institution must teach its students to think for themselves by giving them the knowledge on which to base judgments? He did, and suggested they get on with more important business.

Before the Senate Subcommittee on Internal Security got around to investigating Sarah Lawrence, Field was summoned before the House Select Committee to Investigate Tax-Exempt Foundations and Comparable Organizations. The committee was a lame duck, sitting in November and December 1952 after Eisenhower's election. Before Harold ("Cappy") Keele, the committee's general counsel, began his line of questions, Field read his own introduction to the first annual report of 1936 and gave the Field Foundation's assets as being between $11 and $12 million. Keele asked about Field Foundation grants to Open Road, the People's Institute of Applied Religion, the Southern Conference for Human Welfare, and the American Council of the Institute of Pacific Relations, before he got to Owen Lattimore.

Marshall had foreseen the collapse of the Chiang Kaishek's Kuomintang regime after meeting the generalissimo in 1947. When it happened two years later, Americans were baffled and troubled by Mao Zedong's armies chasing the nationalists from the mainland to Taiwan. To discredit the Truman administration, McCarthy almost casually chose the question "Who lost China to the communists?" Anyone who had anything to do with China before 1949 was particularly vulnerable. *Time*'s Henry Luce, born in Shan Xian, the son of American missionaries to China, agreed that there were American scapegoats in the "loss" of China. But who? Owen Lattimore. In reporting McCarthy's accusation, *Time* agreed that in speeches and books and in his influence at the State Department, Lattimore "undoubtedly contributed to Chiang's downfall and the triumph of Chairman Mao."

In questioning Marshall, Keele noted that in the mid-1940s Alfred Kohlberg, one of the board members of the Institute of Pacific Relations, had charged that the IPR was funding communist propaganda. Keele got to the crux of the matter when he asked Marshall if it wasn't true that in 1943 the Field Foundation had given a $1,250 grant to Owen Lattimore.

Chiang Kaishek might have praised Lattimore's integrity to President Roosevelt in 1943, writing: "Mr. Lattimore has fully measured up to our expectations and has entirely justified your choice. You unerringly detected the right man to select to act as a counselor at a time when decisions which will affect the whole world for generations to come are in the balance." But this was 1952, and McCarthy accused the Asian scholar from Johns Hopkins of being the top Soviet spy in the United States. The charge dumbfounded J. Edgar Hoover. Lattimore's name was on the FBI's list of subversives, but Hoover thought him unimportant, certainly not a spy. The FBI director, however, was no more anxious to take on McCarthy than anyone else, and kept his doubts about Lattimore to himself. McCarthy was sure he had unearthed the top Soviet agent. A few months before Marshall was called to testify, Lattimore had been indicted for perjury on seven counts by a federal grand jury on the charge that he had lied when he told a Senate internal security subcommittee that he had not promoted communism and communist interests.

Field's answer was a disappointment to the committee. No defense was necessary, he said, to justify a grant made nine years earlier, when Japan had been the enemy and China an ally. But what about the members of the Field Foundation? Wasn't the black leader Channing Tobias, a member of many dissident organizations, a director? Field said yes. Tobias was a valuable adviser who "shows the greatest wisdom and consideration and, furthermore, saved us from a lot of very foolish grants, I think, in race relations, which didn't really have any validity."

Keele moved on to Judge Polier. Wasn't she a member of the group challenging the American Bar Association—the National

Lawyers Guild, whose membership, in the subcommittee's mind, was a nest of radicals, free thinkers, and no doubt a few Marxists.

Marshall leaned into his microphone:

> Well, Judge Polier has been a judge on the Court of Domestic Relations in New York for over fifteen years. I have actually sat in on her court and listened to the way she handles children, and I really think that perhaps she is . . . among the greatest experts on children's courts in the country. I have found her the most charming person, the most understanding person about children, of anybody I knew. Furthermore, I have dined at her house and she has dined at mine, and I would never have had the slightest—I wouldn't have the slightest hesitation in saying that she has never by any intimation shown communistic leanings.

Without recommending legislation, the House Select Committee to Investigate Tax-Exempt Foundations and Comparable Organizations concluded in its final report that too few foundations supported pro-American projects. The committee was forgotten once Senator McCarthy was appointed chairman of the Senate's Permanent Subcommittee on Investigations and began conducting his famous televised Army–McCarthy hearings. Like Maximilien Robespierre, the instigator of the French Revolution's reign of terror, McCarthy spun out of control. He said Roosevelt and Truman amounted to "twenty years of treason." His innuendo that General George Marshall might be a subversive led Eisenhower to delete a defense of the general from a speech. In the end it was not the printed press but CBS's Edward R. Murrow who, in pointing out the difference between disloyalty and dissent, led to McCarthy's downfall in

Marshall Field III. *(Reprinted with special permission from the Chicago Sun-Times, Inc. © 2001)*

1954. A year later the Justice Department dropped all charges against Lattimore.

Marshall Field III celebrated his sixtieth birthday in 1953 by taking Ruth and the younger children to Europe. The family spent the summer catching up with relatives and friends in London and touring the Continent. In London, Marshall saw his sister Gwendolyn, her husband Archibald and their five children (a son, Ian Angus Marshall Edmonstone, had died before the war), and Rudolph de Trafford, his friend of forty years. On the continent the Fields traveled leisurely by car, visiting the Netherlands, Belgium, France, Austria, and Italy before swinging back through Germany.

The Cold War might be at its frostiest, but Marshall was at peace with himself. He was the head of one of the country's largest privately controlled corporations. The *Sun-Times* was in the black. *Parade* magazine, the Sunday supplement, was a winner, reaching 6.5 million circulation. Simon & Schuster and Pocket Books were making profits. The Quarrie Corporation, which remained a division of the Field Enterprises, expanded its *World Book Encyclopedia* sales force. Ruth and Marshall lived in New York. To show the family's attachment to Chicago, they attended the 1955 groundbreaking ceremony for a seven-story building to house the *Sun-Times*. Junior had been pushing for the construction on the northern side of the Chicago River and Wabash Avenue, and his father acknowledged as much at a luncheon at Palmer House before the groundbreaking: "As many of you know, my grandfather was a man of determined mind and unswerving purpose. So, I believe, is my son . . . I have only one injunction for Marshall and his associates, and that is to honor the original dream by always jealously keeping the paper's freedom and intellectual integrity. The Chicago *Sun-Times* was organized on the platform that it would stand up for and say what it believed, regardless of consequences."

Marshall and Ruth visited Ronald Tree in Barbados. Ronald and Marietta had divorced, but Ronnie was his bemused self and as gracious a host as he had been at Ditchley. He thought his cousin looked tired, and Marshall acknowledged that he suffered inordinate fatigue. He perked up during a long summer in Maine, but in the fall felt his energy sag again. In June 1956, he suffered a dizzy spell after delivering a commencement address at Sarah Lawrence. After losing consciousness during a subsequent episode, he saw a neurologist who could find nothing wrong. Another doctor suspected a minor stroke. Marshall and Ruth spent the summer at Caumsett.

His daughter Barbara, her husband, Robert Boggs, and their two teenage children were returning from Europe aboard the *Andrea Doria* on July 25 when the Italian luxury liner was rammed by the *Stockholm*, a Swedish cruise ship, off the coast of Nantucket. As the ship listed and the passageway to the lower decks was blocked with debris and sloshing water, Barbara panicked as she and her husband tried to reach her son Bobby. They found him asleep on the floor of the cabin. Together they reached the deck and saw that their daughter had sensibly gone to the assigned lifeboat station. The Boggs family were among the people in lifeboats rescued by the *Ile de France*. The *Andrea Doria* sank with a loss of fifty-two lives.

By October, Marshall III entered New York Hospital and was diagnosed with a malignant brain tumor. An operation was performed but failed to relieve pressure on his brain. The cancer had metastasized. Writing in *The Prison of My Mind* twelve years later, Barbara told of watching her father slip away. "This slow dying, watching him die with his little night cap on his poor shaven head, sitting in his room holding his hand, waiting for him to sometimes know me and sometimes not, tore me apart emotionally more than I can say. For his sake, I could not break down in front of him. We played records sometimes, whose melodies still pull at my heartstrings when I hear them today."

Ruth was at his side and for fear of frightening her husband discouraged her son Harry Phipps from flying in from Paris. During periods of lucidity Marshall wanted the electorate to deny Eisenhower a second term by voting for Adlai Stevenson. By Election Day he was in a coma. He died on November 8.

The public religious services were held at Episcopal churches in New York and Chicago. The mourners included politicians and friends who had been part of his public life. Ronald Tree was with

Ruth and the children at the St. James Episcopal Church in New York. Behind them sat Charles Cushing, James Warburg, and Carl Weitzel. Among the pallbearers in Chicago was Adlai Stevenson. Ruth received hundreds of telegrams, from Eleanor Roosevelt and Cole Porter, Averell Harriman and John D. Rockefeller Jr., the Boy Scouts of America and Anna Freud, Judge Justine Polier and Edward R. Murrow, Arthur Schlesinger and Rudolph de Trafford. Letters of condolence came from the British Solomon Islands Protectorate and the Chicago City Council, from hospitals, doctors, equestrian clubs, orchestras, the NAACP, and Adopt-A-Child ("An Interracial, Interfaith Program to find Permanent Homes for Negro and Puerto Rican Children").

26

SUCCESSIONS

THE DISPOSITION OF THE FOUNDING FATHER'S FORTUNE FIFTY years earlier had stirred public curiosity. Before Marshall Field had had a chance to change his will, his son had died in titillating, perhaps scabrous, circumstances, and the wealth was passed on to the underage grandsons. Marshall IV only survived his father by nine years, and when he died suddenly in 1965, the trust was divided between two sons who didn't know each other and barely knew their father.

No sensationalism accompanied the dynastic succession from the founder's grandson to his great-grandson. Marshall Field III's will, admitted to probate on December 10, 1956, was complex but nothing like his grandfather's twenty-thousand-word document. While Ruth and other dependents were provided for, Field Enterprises was passed on intact and in the manner envisioned by

Marshall Field I. There was one exception: Marshall III's preferred stock, which was left to the Field Foundation. During his lifetime Marshall IV was the sole beneficiary of the trust, after which Field Enterprises would, still intact, be left to his two sons. Marshall Field V was fifteen at the time and his half-brother Ted Woodruff Field, four.

The death was perhaps hardest on Barbara, who felt that her father had once more abandoned her. Her depression worsened to the point where she misinterpreted and distorted reality. Riding an elevator in the Boggs's New York apartment building was torture, and after a move to a house on Long Island failed to improve her condition, she was committed and told she could not communicate with her husband. She was treated by despotic doctors more interested in prolonging the stay of their wealthy patient than in her recovery. Under the strain of years of hospital stays, tentative home visits, and outpatient therapy, her marriage to Robert Boggs collapsed. In 1961, she married Peter Benziger. It was under the name Barbara Benziger that eight years later she published *The Prison of My Mind*, the story of her long, complicated, and shaky effort to regain a measure of mental health.

Marshall left both Caumsett and the South Carolina estate to Ruth, telling her to take all, some or none. Instead of giving Caumsett outright to the state of New York as she and her husband had discussed, she decided to make it a partial gift. She and Marshall had been supporters of the handsome parkways that Robert Moses, the crafty and powerful New York State administrator responsible for highways, parks, and bridges and head of the New York City parks commission, had slung around the suburbs. By making only part of Caumsett an outright gift, she upset Moses. He agreed that she could live in the so-called Winter

Cottage for the rest of her life. "So they made a deal," Marshall Field V would remember, "and Moses turned around a month later and tossed her out."*

Of Ruth's children, only Bobby Phipps, who was never considered to have any potential, got to lead a full life. His brother Harry was gay and died of an overdose of heroin in his boyfriend's apartment. Phyllis and Fiona Field, Ruth's two daughters with Marshall III, fared no better. Phyllis was also a bipolar who took her own life, while Fiona, as Marshall V put it, "was just crazy and, in 1999, killed herself."

In her widowhood, Ruth stayed in New York. She was a fringe member of the glitterati set, with Jackie Onassis and John Hersey at the book launch of Lillian Hellman's *An Unfinished Woman*, at dinners given by Marietta Tree, now U.S. representative to the United Nations Human Rights Commission. The one person she didn't get along with was her stepson. Marshall IV was a troubled man. Besides his continued bouts with depression, he drank heavily and developed a dependence on prescription drugs. Yet he was the brightest of them all, and his management of Field Enterprises was exemplary. He paid attention to audience and motivational research, readership studies, and design and layout, and was convinced that only a financially sound newspaper would also be an editorially powerful voice. The news desk found his editorial judgment wanting, but his critics admitted he possessed a knack for business. While his father was still alive, he started building a modern plant on the north bank of the Chicago River between Wabash Avenue and the Wrigley Building and installed faster presses with full color capability. For a city that

---

* Lillian Hellman remembered Ruth in her May 25, 1984, will and left her a small share of the playwright's estate.

prides itself on its skyline, the new *Sun-Times* home won few kudos. The squat, elongated building was called coffin-like and unattractive, but over the next forty years became something of a downtown landmark.

George B. Young, board chairman of Field Enterprises, called the new plant "a chancy, but wise, courageous decision." In 1959, Junior purchased the afternoon Chicago *Daily News* from John S. Knight for a then-record $24 million ($142 million in 2000 currency), and improved it beyond anything Knight had dreamed of. His father had merged the *Sun* and the *Times*, but Marshall IV insisted the *Sun-Times* and the *Daily News* remain separate entities and achieve stand-alone financial stability. The

Publisher Marshall Field IV. *(Reprinted with special permission from the Chicago* Sun-Times, *Inc. © 2001)*

same year he bought the Manistique Paper Company to supply part of the growing newspaper empire. The company pioneered recycling newsprint and built a plant in Alsip, Illinois, where it manufactured newsprint entirely from waste paper. His photographic memory amazed his children. He could read a book in half an hour, just turn the pages, and if challenged sum up the plot. His parlor trick was to read a page of the dictionary and dare family members to verify his memory. "He used to drive us crazy," his son Marshall would remember. "We'd say, Come on, you can't remember." 'Ask me anything.' So we did and he always got it."

Katherine divorced him in 1963. In search of a new beginning, she piled her three children into a Buick station wagon and drove to Alaska. Junior was forty-eight when he married twenty-three-year-old Lynne Templeton, who worked in the *Sun-Times* public service office. Their daughter, Corinne, was born in 1965.

Junior's ten-year reign at the *Sun-Times* was also devoted to expansion. Suburban newspapers were added, and in 1965 Marshall IV's dream of a television station was realized when Chicago's WFLD went on the air. It was followed by Detroit's WKBD and San Francisco's KBHK. The Fields' archrival, Robert McCormick, had died in 1955 without leaving descendants. Under professional management, the Tribune Corporation founded Chicago's WGN-TV, and acquired television stations across the country. It also bought the Hearst chain's faltering Chicago *American* and folded it into the *Tribune*, making the Second City a two-family newspaper town. At the *Sun-Times*, Junior promoted Emmett Dedmon, who had survived a German prison camp, to columnist and critic. When 335 editors, 311 publishers, and 125 journalism teachers ranked the country's leading newspapers in three different ballots in 1960, the

Chicago Daily News was among the top ten in two of the polls.*

Junior not only abused alcohol and drugs but food—he used to eat sticks of butter. He was taking a Saturday afternoon nap on September 18, 1965, and failed to wake up. When a medical report revealed high levels of alcohol and drugs in his bloodstream, the suspicion was planted, and never disproved, that, like his grandfather, he had taken his own life. He was forty-nine. Thirty-five years later, when Ted Field was himself in his late forties, he would remember his own curiosity about his father's possible suicide: "There has always been a rumor that my father committed suicide and I wanted to get to the bottom of that so I asked Jim Campbell, his attending physician, who swears not. And after Jim Campbell died, I asked his son who had been a friend of mine growing up, Douglas Campbell, whether he had ever heard anything. No, he didn't commit suicide. He had a drinking problem clearly, and he may have taken antidepressants or a combination. Everybody thought it wasn't a suicide. But who knows."

There was one dramatic sale. Marshall III had always been a board member of the department store, but in 1965 the family sold its remaining holdings in Marshall Field & Company. Back in 1917, the trustees of the founder's estate had sold 90 percent of the stock in the store to its officers and managers. The death of Marshall IV ended more than a century of bonds between the family and the store.

More seriously, the compact that had transferred the accumulated wealth from father to son for four generations unraveled. Twenty-four-year-old Marshall V, who had barely known his

---

* The *New York Times*, *Christian Science Monitor*, *St. Louis-Dispatch*, *Washington Post*, and *Milwaukee Journal* were rated in the top six dailies in all three polls.

father, and twelve-year-old Ted Field found themselves holding equal shares of 42.5 percent of the ownership of Field Enterprises, with their sisters holding the remaining 15 percent nonvoting interests. Marshall V and his sister, Joanne, did not know their half-brother and two half-sisters through his father, and a half-brother through his mother. And he himself was divorcing. His marriage to Joan (Bitsy) Connelly ended shortly after his father's death. Joan, the mother of Marshall VI, hated Chicago.

Divorces were not limited to the male line. Joanne married and divorced four times. When Herman Kogan, a longtime editor and writer for the *Daily News* and *Sun-Times*, interviewed Ruth in 1966 for a silver anniversary edition of the *Sun-Times* and asked how her twenty-seven-year old daughter was, the third Mrs. Marshall Field III, said, "Little Fiona is now twenty-five [sic], and she's getting divorced again. You know, Mr. Kogan, I don't know what it *is* about this family. We're all such nice people."

Marshall V was an easygoing fine arts graduate living in New York who barely knew Chicago. His parents had divorced when he was four, and Joanne had taken her son and daughter back to Peterborough, New Hampshire, where the children's maternal grandfather was the former governor and their uncle a congressman. "There was no dad in the picture and I was really too young to think about divorces," Marshall V would recall. "We stayed there for a little while, then moved to New York, and then my mother married my stepfather." Her new husband was John Bross, a lawyer who had worked in intelligence for John Foster Dulles during the war and was invited to Washington to help run the new Central Intelligence Agency. The family moved to McLean, Virginia, and when Marshall's stepfather was appointed the chief of the CIA in Germany, he and his sister were sent to boarding schools. "I never saw Chicago," he said when he was being groomed to take over the media empire. "I would come out and see my father maybe for a month in the summer on his farm." On occasion, Marshall IV took the boy to the *Sun-Times*. During one boardroom meeting, young Marshall was playing under the table and his father, deciding he was making too much noise, directed him to leave. Young Marshall complied, but flipped off the light switch as he left. The executives sat in darkness until Marshall Field IV announced: "Will the vice-president closest to retirement please go out and kick his ass."

Ted knew Chicago a little better, but neither brother met their half-sister Corinne. Cori, as she was known, was twenty-four years younger than Marshall V and thirteen years younger than Ted. She had been born three months before her father died in 1965, and was brought up by her mother. Ted and his sisters were growing up in Alaska, where his mother had reinvented herself. The *Anchorage Daily News*, an eight-page tabloid totally eclipsed by the *Anchorage Times*, had hired the divorcee to reorganize its library for $2 an hour. She quickly moved up through the ranks to become a reporter. In 1966 she married Larry Fanning, who had worked as editor at her first husband's *Chicago Sun-Times*. Against the advice of friends, Katherine and Larry bought the *Daily News*. When Fanning died at his desk of a heart attack in 1971, his widow became the sole editor and publisher. Like Ralph Ingersoll, she was fearless and courted controversy by taking up gun control, the environment, and the rights of Alaskan natives. She brought the *Daily News* from a circulation of 12,000 to 50,000 and made it Alaska's largest newspaper. Along the way, it won a Pulitzer Prize for public service for a fifteen-part series on the Teamsters in Alaska. Ted was brooding, self-conscious, and rebelling against his mother's conversion to the Christian Science church. "We were not overly close because we diverged very strongly on religion," he would remember. Her public comment when he produced his first movie was, "Growing up in Alaska, Ted had a lot of dreams about where his life would go." His mother's faith turned him and Barbara against her, and Kathy into an ardent believer in Christian Science. Their mother's religious belief aggravated Barbara's manic-depression because Katherine never did anything about her youngest daughter's illness.

George Young and his fellow trustees, Howard A. Seitz and Edward I Farley, appointed Emmett Dedmon editor of the *Sun-Times* and brought twenty-four-year-old Marshall V to Chicago to groom him for the mantle of publisher. "I was brought up in the East and when I came out here I couldn't have told you where State Street was," Marshall V would recall in 2001. "I was a big fan of my grandfather. I liked him very much. But he died when I was fifteen."

The whirlwind training mirrored his father's and began with heaving newspapers from delivery trucks. He apprenticed in every department and in 1969 took charge of the *Sun-Times* and the *Daily News*, becoming the youngest publisher of a major newspaper. "He knew enough not to pressure his editors," Daryle Feldmeir, a former editor, would recall. "I remember the mayoral campaign in which both the *Daily News* and *Sun-Times* endorsed whomever it was that year who ran against Richard Daley. A member of the Field Enterprises board came up to me at some function, ranting, 'You must be crazy.' And Marshall just took him gently by the arm and said, 'The fact that you're a member of the board doesn't mean that you have the right to tell our editors what to do.'" Traditionally, publishers shield their reporters from liability in lawsuits by accepting responsibility for what is printed. Marshall infuriated his staff by suggesting the opposite—that a reporter should suffer personal financial loss for negligence for sloppy research, "even if there is no malice." The *Sun-Times* star columnist Mike Rokyo called Marshall's idea "not, by any means, the most foolish speech I've ever heard. There are at least three or four others that I can recall being more foolish."

If the rise of Marshall Field V was fast, the advance of James Hoge was positively meteoric. This patrician son of a Park Avenue lawyer started at the *Sun-Times* as a night police reporter in 1959, and in less than ten years climbed to editor. The Black Panthers, the Democrats, the Yippies, hippies, and members of the American Nazi party came to Chicago to change the world. Baby boomers marched against the Vietnam War and dominated pop culture. Hoge tolerated long-haired male reporters and female journalists in miniskirts. He wanted younger readers and emphasized lifestyle stories and personality journalism, encouraged consumer-oriented investigations, and recruited, among others, future film critic Roger Ebert. The rival *Tribune* followed the Colonel's conviction that social and racial turmoil had to be met with a hard-nosed law-and-order stance. In December 1969, the *Tribune* reported that Chicago police had raided a West Side apartment and gunned down two leaders of the militant Black Panthers. It published photos, provided by the Cook County State's Attorney's office, headed by Edward Hanrahan, showing a doorframe with bullet holes allegendly from Black Panthers firing at police. Hoge and a *Sun-Times* reporter inspected the apartment and found no bullet holes in the doorframe. The report led to general public condemnation of the police raid and the dismissal of Hanrahan. Hoge spent several hundred thousand dollars on investigative reporting, sharing resources and manpower with CBS's *60 Minutes*. One such sting operation had the paper buy a neighborhood bar and, with *60 Minutes*'s cameras rolling behind two-way mirrors, catch city workers on the take. The result was dismissed city employees, dozens of indictments, and the reform of several government agencies. In Washington, the *Daily News*'s smart and quick Peter Lisagor kept the Vietnam War in perspective and, with *Time*'s Hugh Sidey, benefited from special attention from President Johnson.

Lisagor's personal authority in Washington was immense, but the *Daily News* was dying. Competition among the media after the rise of radio and television was intense, both for advertising revenues and for public attention. Economic pressures cut the number of newspapers everywhere. As head of the *Washington Post*, Katherine Graham miscalculated when she purchased the *Trenton Times*, the afternoon daily in the New Jersey capital (Ralph Ingersoll was the owner of the feisty morning tabloid *The Trentonian*). New York City suffered the worst loss of any metropolis, dropping from six owners and seven dailies in 1960 to three owners and three dailies seven years later. In December 1969, the *Sun-Times* outsold the *Tribune* on Sundays for the first time, but for its sister paper the writing was on the wall. Like many afternoon dailies competing with ever-earlier TV news hours, the *Daily News*'s circulation dropped from 550,000 in the late 1950s to 280,000 in its last month before it folded in 1978. After ninety-one years in existence, the final banner headline read: "So Long, Chicago."

In 1972, Marshall V married again. His new wife was Jamee Beckwith Jacobs, the daughter of a Chicago real estate broker. Three daughters, Jamee Christine, Stephanie Caroline, and Abigail Beckwith, were born, and the family moved to a sixteen-acre estate in Lake Forest, north of the city limits. The twenty-five-room English Georgian-style home is set back from the road in a section of big houses and tight security.

*   *   *

The department store was still giving the lady what she wanted, still living by the precepts of its founder. The 1960s and 1970s were the glorious decades of department stores before the Kmarts, Targets, and Wal-Marts and suburban malls eroded the glamour of downtown shopping. Marshall Field & Co. had been the first to buy another chain. After opening retail Marshall Field stores in Chicago suburbs—Evanston, Oak Park, Park Forest, and Lake Forest, and opening a Marshall Field in Milwaukee, it had bought Frederick & Nelson in Seattle, the leading department store in the Northwest. The postwar era had seen the Frederick & Nelson subsidiary follow the trend and open suburban stores in Bellevue and Tukwila, Washington. Other acquisitions followed, including the Crescent, a department store in Spokane, and the Halle Brothers with nine stores in Cleveland and Akron, Ohio, and Erie, Pennsylvania. In a last spurt of acquisitions and expansions, Marshall Field & Company acquired the John Breuner Company with fourteen furnishing stores in northern California, and in 1979 opened a Marshall Field store in the Louis Joliet Mall in Joliet, Illinois.

Ten years later, when junk-bond mergers, acquisitions, buyouts and sellouts reached their frenzy, Marshall Field itself became a takeover target. The biggest deal of 1989 was the completion of the $30.6 billion acquisition of RJR Nabisco by Kohlberg Kravis Roberts & Company, followed by the Time Inc. agreement to merge with Warner Communications to form the world's biggest publishing-entertainment company. Marshall Field was acquired by BATUS, the American subsidiary of London-based BAT Industries (formerly British American Tobacco). Eight years later, BATUS sold Marshall Field to Dayton Hudson Corporation, the Minneapolis-based retailer. In the late 1990s, Dayton Hudson sold its Marshall Field stores in

Texas and closed the downtown Marshall Field store in Milwaukee. Then Dayton Hudson closed or sold thirty-five Mervyn's in Georgia and Florida in a further retrenchment and, since the discount chains had become a darling on Wall Street, renamed itself the Target Corporation.

The arteriosclerosis of department stores continued as owners tried to fend off discount and specialty stores by merging. Montgomery Ward, born in Chicago in 1872, was on life support when its owner, General Electric, pulled the plug in 2001. With the explosion of malls, outlets, and superstores, Ward had become that most dangerous thing to retailing—irrelevant. Stronger upscale chains such as Federated, owner of Bloomingdale's and Macy's, and May, owner of Filene's and Lord & Taylor, were expected to cause a wave of consolidations that by 2005 might absorb the last family-owned company, Nordstrom of Seattle. Speculation about a spinoff of Marshall Field was constant as sales slumped slightly and Target tried to reinvent and reengineer its business model.

In the flagship store on State and Washington the clock is set, fastidiously and forever, on Marshall the First time. The century-old twelve-story atrium is still there. So are Daniel Burnham's massive columns on the State Street exterior and Louis Comfort Tiffany's mosaic glass dome, restored to its iridescent blue and gold splendor. Harry Selfridge's bargain basement is gone, but the store caters to everyone from career women to the jet set. Fashions change, but the lady is always right. Chicago families see to it that when native sons bring home an out-of-town bride she is issued a Marshall Field charge card. Births are registered at Marshall Field. The store means connectedness to the past, to Christmases and Easters and Mother's Days. Every Chicago child is taken to see the Marshall Field Christmas tree, ceremoniously cut from a Lake Superior forest every November, and five glittering stories tall. Year-round, out-of-town visitors reaching the seventh floor visitors' center are invited to sign their names and take home a bag of little goodies. Inquiring journalists are furnished with Xerox copies of a 1978 *Town and Country* photo essay of a Mrs. Coleman's shopping day and the founding father's exhortations ("Never misrepresent an article, or guarantee wear or colors," "Be polite and attentive to rich and poor alike, courteous and agreeable to all those around you") and aphorisms ("Give the lady what she wants" and "Never let a nickel loom so large that you fail to see the dollar behind it").

Field the First once said that if his building burned down and all his merchandise were destroyed he wouldn't worry so long as he could retain the goodwill of his customers. This sort of repute still sold 150 years after Field and Leiter took over Potter Palmer's emporium. In 2001, Target converted and renamed sixty department stores and four Dayton and Hudson stores Marshall Field. The move, said Linda Ahlers, president of Dayton's Marshall Field and Hudson's divisions, would increase the brand and strengthen its competitive position. The Marshall Field name had more recognition and represented the division's largest business. "One name gives us the opportunity to focus on a single brand at all levels of our business," she said. "This is particularly important for our Internet initiatives and the launch of our online gift registry that give us a presence beyond the markets where we have stores."

Consumer expectations, however, were changing faster than department stores could reinvent themselves. Marshall Field's quietly dropped the silversmith, the furrier, and many other special offerings that once made it the high end of retailing. Target's decision to no longer deliver such services saw it outpositioned by

Neiman Marcus and Bloomingdale's (in Chicago a dozen blocks north on Michigan Avenue). All art is a new way of saying old things, and the art of dressing is enriched by reinterpretation, but stores lost their fashion authority to designers who killed off store labels, once the pride of the industry. The aging population also changed consumer spending. The very young and the very hip follow fashion, but such stalwarts as DKNY flirted with bankruptcy as Americans spent more on their homes than on the designer and private-label clothes that department stores depended upon. "We pay a lot less attention to that label that has to be around our neck or on our derriere," Kurt Barnard of *Retail Trend Report* said in 2001. Wall Street's Bear Stearns titled a report on the industry, "To Live or Let Die? Department Stores: A game plan for success." Not much of a success foretold. The "game plan" was simply that Federated and May Department Stores would gobble up the weaker sisters.

In another departure from traditions dating back to the heyday of Field the First, Shedd, and Selfridge, the store cut back the commissions it paid to some salespeople. Former Field's president Daniel Skoda called the move shortsighted. "Reducing commissions is one of the last things you do to cut costs, because you're dealing with your most loyal, career-oriented and aggressive people." Although Nieman-Marcus and Nordstrom paid commissions to almost all salespeople and Saks Fifth Avenue maintained a hybrid system, paying a base salary and a bonus pegged to sales, Target defended the move on the grounds that retail workers were increasingly short-term employees. Other cost cutting measures adopted during the 2001–2002 recession included job reassignments.

As for the *Sun-Times* and its seven-story headquarters on the Chicago River, New York's Donald Trump and the paper's present proprietor, the Canadian media giant Hollinger International Inc., which also owns the Jerusalem *Post*, the *Daily Telegraph* of London, the Ottawa *Citizen*, and CanWest Global Communications, announced plans to demolish the coffin-shaped building. In its stead, they planned to build a combined office and luxury apartment tower that once more would make Chicago the home of the world's tallest building. At 1,500 feet, the Trump Tower Chicago would stand 17 feet taller than the Petronas Towers in Kuala Lumpur, Malaysia, which in 1996 usurped Chicago's Sears Tower (1,450 feet).

It was perhaps fitting that the latest chapter of the Field saga would play out in showbiz.

LOS ANGELES

27

THE CRUNCH

THE HALF-BROTHERS WERE A STUDY IN CONTRASTS. MARSHALL Field V was the Eastern preppie (Deerfield Academy, Harvard), Ted Field the bearded and restless dropout from Anchorage. Marshall was attractive, well-tailored, and conservative, with a self-deprecating wit. He was the active chairman of Field Enterprises and, for ten years, the publisher of the *Sun-Times*. He lived on an estate in Lake Forest with his second wife and three daughters and was president of the Art Institute of Chicago. Ted was a cross between Jay Gatsby and Jerry Garcia, playing in garage bands and drifting in and out of colleges, building up credits but never enough to graduate. He didn't have the signature first name and chose not to be part of the legacy. He had not grown up in Chicago, where the name was on a museum and the family owned a newspaper empire. He was awkward and lonely, and in 1975 married the daughter of one of Marshall's secretary's friends. She was Judith Erickson, the daughter of Forrest Erickson, a Chicago dentist. They were both twenty-three. The bride's mother called the marriage a Cinderella story.

Though Ted wasn't due to inherit his share of Field Enterprises until he turned twenty-five, he had little trouble persuading the trustees to dole out money for racing cars. After an accident at the Riverside, California, speedway mangled his left hand, he bankrolled Danny (The Flyin' Hawaiian) Ongais, an eleven-time Indianapolis 500 starter. Ted burned through $1 million a year on the racing circuit. The three-man team of Ted, Danny, and Hurley Haywood drove a turbocharged Porsche in 1979 and won the $100,000 24-hour Pepsi Challenge race at Daytona, beating a field that included Paul Newman.

Around the *Sun-Times*, Ted was known as the weirdo, Marshall as the wimp. The big crunch did not come on June 1, 1977, when Ted turned twenty-five and came into his share, but five years later. As we know, Marshall and Ted each owned 42.5 percent of their father's estate, worth about $260 million for each ($730 million in today's money), with the remaining 15 percent divided between the Field sisters. Field Enterprises had made a number of shrewd investments, including buying a handful of television stations. Ted, however, was unhappy. "I'd go to these board meetings in Chicago," he would say, "and all these conservative board members would look at me as if I was some kind of freak—because I was young, lived in California, liked to race cars, and wanted to enter the movie business. Not to mention the beard and the hand." By 1982, he had had enough.

In an odd replay of their great-great-grandfather's arm-twisting bargain with Levi Leiter 101 years earlier, the complex agreement drafted by their father's lawyers gave either brother the right to buy out the other at a price matching the highest actual bidder for Field Enterprises, or to force a liquidation. "The way I approached it was probably overly aggressive," Ted would admit. "I wanted to hire a very tough Wall Street–type law firm and I came marching in and said, 'This is what we want.'" As Marshall didn't want to go $260 million into debt to buy out his half-brother, Ted gave Field Enterprises eleven months to liquidate itself. "Tradition and sentiment were dying and there was no one to play taps," wrote *People* magazine in reporting the breakup of the Field media empire.

The dismantling began with the sale of Chicago's WFLD station to Metromedia for $140 million. Next to go were Detroit's WKBD to Cox Communications for $70 million; Boston's WLVI (Gannett, $47 million), San Francisco's KBHK (United TV, $23 million), and seven cable franchises to American Cable TV for $20.5 million—$300 million in all. Peddling the forty-two-year-old *Sun-Times* was painful for Marshall. Potential buyers, including Affiliated Publications, the publisher of the *Boston Globe*, and the *Toronto Sun* Publishing Corporation, were reluctant to bid for the paper, which was an also-ran to the *Chicago Tribune*, circulation 750,000. Marshall V had named James Hoge publisher in 1980, and Hoge and friends scrambled to patch together a $63 million offer. A defeated mayoral candidate, Bernard Epton, said he was interested in buying the paper and that his first act as the new owner would be to fire Hoge and columnist Mike Royko. First National Bank of Chicago was helping Hoge and his group find investors. Hoge's group was $7 million short of Rupert Murdoch's bid when the Australian newspaper czar offered another $30 million for the Field Newspaper Syndicate. Murdoch was famous for buying ailing newspapers in major cities, taking them downmarket, and restoring them to financial health if not promi-

Marshall Field V. *(Field Foundation)*

nence. In recent years, he had purchased the *New York Post,* the *Times* and *Sunday Times* of London, and the *Boston Herald-American.* Ted's mother, now the editor of the *Christian Science Monitor* and living in Boston, was against the sale to Murdoch, but Ted wouldn't listen.

"Ted wanted to maximize the price," said Marshall when the deal was consummated. "It was our agreement that we would sell to the highest bidder. I didn't want a big fight with him." To inquiring journalists, Ted responded that carrying the family torch was not his obsession. The *Wall Street Journal* took a hard look at the sellout. "Ted Field's eagerness to break up Field Enterprises may have cost the brothers a pretty penny," the *Journal* wrote when it was all over. "By selling their UHF stations and World Book publishing operations before a runup in media and publishing prices, one former associate estimates, the Fields failed to realize as much as $1 billion." As it was, the brothers came away with $260 million ($340 million in today's money) each. "The only real tradition is that each succeeding generation shouldn't blow it," Marshall said. "If you can leave the family for-tune a little bigger than you found it, that's what counts."

Both made money in entertainment. Marshall bought Muzak, the leading purveyor of background music, and the classroom newspaper *My Weekly Reader*. While Ted acquired Panavision and made a $90 million profit by selling the camera leasing company again, Marshall fine-tuned Muzak and the school newspaper.

Steven Spielberg's *Indiana Jones and the Temple of Doom* was the hit to beat in 1984 when Ted made his Hollywood debut as the producer of *Revenge of the Nerds*. Directed by Jeff Kanew, this goofy, predictable frat comedy in the vein of *Fast Times at Ridgemont High* and *Animal House* featured a cast of unknowns and grossed a handsome $91 million. The sequel *Revenge of the Nerds II* earned a thumbs-down from the *Sun-Times'* Roger Ebert. "These aren't nerds. They're a bunch of interesting guys, and that's the problem with *Revenge II*. The movie doesn't have the nerve to be about real nerds."

Ted decided he could not afford to divorce Judith, his wife of eight years, get into filmmaking, *and* bankroll Ongais all at the same time. As he divorced and founded Interscope Communications, he sent Ongais a note at the Miami Grand Prix: "I'm not going to drive anymore; the cars and the team are yours if you can find a sponsor."

The leading junk bond artists and corporate raiders, T. Boone Pickens, Carl Icahn, Ron Perelman, and Sir James Goldsmith, came knocking. Sir James got Ted's attention—and investments. Born in Paris to an English father and a French mother, Goldsmith first generated headlines when he eloped with Isabel Patiño, a Bolivian heiress whom he married against her father's wishes. She died in childbirth, and Goldsmith faced his first of many court battles when he sought, and won, custody of his baby

Ted at the wheel. *(Radar Pictures)*

daughter. He had few equals as a buyer, molder, and seller of companies and made audacious raids into the United States, buying the forestry product group Diamond International and bidding for Goodyear Fire and Rubber. Ted was in on the hostile Goodyear bid and profited handsomely when the company persuaded the raiders to give up by making them an offer they couldn't refuse. The next hostile takeover target they looked at was BAT Industries. Ted was ready to invest $40 million in Goldsmith's $21.7 billion leveraged buyout offer. The people on State Street were not amused by the idea of Ted Field becoming a part owner of his great-great-grandfather's creation.

Under chairman and chief executive officer Philip B. Miller, Marshall Field's was in the middle of a $120 million renovation of the flagship store, itself a part of a $2 billion city renewal of Chicago's historic shopping district. Miller let it be known that neither Sir James nor Ted Field was welcome. Mayor Richard Daley sent off letters to President Bush and Secretary of State James A. Baker, urging them to scrutinize the Anglo-French financier's bid and the effects it might have on the 55,000 BAT employees in the United States. Miller changed his tune once the takeover was a fait accompli, saying BAT acquired "Field's as a long-term quality investment, and they're treating it that way."

Ted's evolution in Los Angeles show business was fast and furious. By 1992, he had produced twenty-eight films. His box-office hits included *Three Men and a Baby*, *The Hand that Rocks the Cradle*, and *Class Action*. He lived like a mogul at Greenacres, the Beverly Hills estate he bought for what was considered the bargain price of $6.5 million. Harold Lloyd, the silent film comedian, built Greenacres in 1928 to imitate the 17th century Villa Gamberaia near Florence. Ted renovated the forty-room fortress mansion with fountains to rival Tivoli and installed Italian Renaissance and baroque art to complement the architecture when he moved in with his second wife, Barbara Stephenson Field. The paintings, which included such Viennese and Florentine masters as Veronese, Bellini, Pontormo, Bronzino, and Tiepolo, got him into trouble with California tax authorities. The state claimed he owed $2.6 million in so-called use taxes. He countered that he was a dealer, not a collector, and therefore exempt from the little-known Depression era use tax, originally designed to protect California retailers when residents shopped out of state to avoid paying sales taxes. He sold the collection at a Christie's auction in London in 1991. A daughter, Chantelle, was born to Ted and Barbara, but their marriage lasted less than three years. Two years later after they split up, Greenacres became too big a symbol for all that had troubled their marriage. He sold it for $18 million, bought actor Michael Landon's

Malibu beach house for $6 million, and had it gutted and rebuilt.

While some snickered at the rich boy buying his way into Hollywood, others approved. Said David Geffen, the record company tycoon and future partner in Dreamworks, in 1990: "Ted's got big balls, and deep pockets, and he's going about it exactly the right way." Marshall bought Funk & Wagnalls Encyclopedia, founded in 1876, and sold it again to Primedia before online search engines made the twenty-nine-volume print edition obsolete. He also bought out Ted's interest in the Boston real estate firm Cabot, Cabot & Forbes. *Forbes* magazine estimated the brothers' fortunes to have nearly doubled—Ted's from $250 million to $400 million and Marshall's from $260 million to more than $450 million.

For eight years, Marshall didn't speak to Ted.

28

EACH GENERATION
SPEAKS FOR ITSELF

LIKE THEIR FATHER AND GRANDFATHER, THE TWO-HALF BROTHERS
each married several times. Between them they sired one son and
nine daughters. Ted's first wife, Judy Erickson, with whom he had
a daughter they named Danielle, was a young woman lost in Ted's
Hollywood. Second wife Barbara was a society queen who, when
they split up, lost a legal challenge to their prenuptial agreement.
Ted nevertheless bought her and their adopted child Joan Rivers's
former house in Santa Barbara. Susie Bollman was seventeen, the
daughter of Ted's race car builder Barry Bollman, when they first
met. She was twenty-four when they met again, and as soon as
Barbara was out of the picture, they married. Susie became the
mother of three daughters, Britanny, Candice, and Chelsea. Ted
did not marry the mother of his youngest daughter, Emily, born
in 1993.

Brothers and sisters: (left to right) Barbara, Joanne,
Marshall V, Ted, and Kathy. *(Field Foundation)*

Marshall has stayed in Chicago. His son, Marshall VI, was one
year old when his parents divorced in 1969. Ted hired a succession
of Hollywood talents and by 2000 his Radar Pictures (as
Interscope was renamed) had produced fifty films, including
Jumanji, Mr. Holland's Opus, and *The Runaway Bride.* As a record
company, Interscope handled bands like Nine Inch Nails, No
Doubt, The Wallflowers, and Then The Morning Comes until
the 1999 shakeup and downsizing that consolidated it, A&M,
Motown, Mercury, Island, Geffen, and MCA Records as part of
Polygram Music. Going on fifty, Ted appraised his own evolution.
"I haven't forgotten my philanthropic obligations. Other than
that, everything about my life is unconventional or not establish-
ment."

The sense of dynastic continuity is remote for Ted, and he
doesn't care to define himself as a Field. "Sometimes kiddingly I
refer to myself as the black sheep because I've been involved in

controversial entertainment art forms," he said in 2001. "I believe that music pulls us in around the urban campfire. I was a child of the 1960s in the sense that music to me has to have edge and be about something. Rap music has been for a time more interesting than rock music, but I think rock has to come into its own very shortly. I've been involved in controversial movies. I've been active in several controversial political causes, fought archconservatives. I don't hobnob with bankers. I find that I relate to musicians, to actors and directors. People have written about how I give glamorous big parties with thousands of people. Nothing I was supposed to do."

Still, the legacy is there. "You can't help but be aware of the family if growing up in a city like Chicago where your name is on a museum, where you've owned a newspaper . . . You can't miss it. But I chose never really to be part of it. I have tried to separate myself from the family history in lots of ways. But at the same time, it would be unrealistic to think that it is not always looming there."

There is no Marshall Field Foundation plaque on the door of the fifteenth-floor offices on downtown Chicago's Wacker Drive. And for good reason. When the Marshall Field Foundation address was in the phone book, too many dissatisfied department store customers called up or stormed in demanding to speak to the boss. As a young man, Marshall felt inhibited by his name. He had been taught not to flaunt his money. He also knew there were things he wouldn't do because he was a Marshall Field. He mellowed later in life and in 2001 said he had little sense of taking on the family mantle or passing the torch to Marshall VI. He found it healthy that America doesn't build dynasties. "New dynasties," he said the year he turned sixty. "Bill Gates. They will come out of some other business. That's the way it should be. I have a feeling of respect and responsibility for the family name in this town because I chose to make it my home. But for Ted's and my generation, that's the end as far as the big deal goes."

He has jokingly mocked the Field dynasty, telling the Los Angeles *Times*, "They all started out with nothing in those days and the biggest crooks won. It was the name of the game. I was just lucky to come from a line of *successful* crooks." Since his son and Louise Wales Field only have a daughter, Chloe (born 1993), and he believes she is the only child they will have, the question of a Marshall VII has come up at family reunions. Marshall VI has asked his father what his feelings are if he and Louise don't have a boy; he has answered, "It doesn't bother me at all." When his daughters jump into the conversation, he tells them, "If you really want a Marshall Field all you have to do is marry a wimp, keep your own name, and insist the child be named after you and you can have another Marshall Field. It's become a joke, really."

With his six daughters, Ted shares the feeling. "Children should define their own path. I believe each generation speaks for itself."

NOTES AND SOURCES

OF THE MARSHALL FIELD FAMILY MEMBERS, ONLY MARSHALL FIELD III and his sister Barbara Field Benziger published books (see Bibliography). The Chicago Historical Society is the repository of the Field Foundation papers.

Documentation supporting quotes in the narrative is cited below.

1. A Place to Linger

Amelia Bloomer, "Women are in bondage," quoted in Ida Husted Harper: *The Life and Work of Susan B. Anthony*, 3 vols., Indianapolis and Kansas City: Bowel Merrill, 1898–1908, vol. ii, p 116. Thomas Goodspeed, She "might wander," Goodspeed: University of Chicago *Biographical Sketches*, University of

Chicago, vol. 1, p. 28., Jan. 1922. John H. Young, Ladies "should not monopolize," in Young: *Our Deportment or The Manners, Conduct and Dress of the Most Refined Society*, Detroit: F. S. Dickerson, 1885, p. 153. Mary Harlan Lincoln, "I raised it in my garden," quoted in Robert W. Twyman, *History of Marshall Field & Company*, Philadelphia: University of Pennsylvania Press, 1954, p. 29. Lloyd Wendt and Herman Kogan, "Whether the shopper," Wendt and Kogan: *Give the Lady What She Wants: The Story of Marshall Field & Company*, Indianapolis: Bobbs Merrill, 1943, p. 229. Marshall Field, "We endeavor to throw," quoted in *Dry Goods Reporter*, No. 40, Jan. 8, 1910. Field, "I was determined," Theodore Dreiser "Life Stories of Successful Men," *Success*, No. 12, *Dec. 8*, 1898. Stanley Field, "When you came to see," Field, Marshall Field & Company Archives, "Stanley Field Marks his 60th Year," Aug. 31, 1953.

2. Silent Marsh

Marshall Field studied, "with the dry passion," quoted in Chicago *Tribune* magazine, Sept. 18, 1983. Mary Evelyn Smith on young Marshall as "a handsome young man" and Deacon Davis's letter, "The bearer," quoted in Wendt and Kogan, op. cit., pp. 46–47. Joseph Field on Marshall's "unusual business talent," and John Farrell, "As a young clerk," quoted in Twyman, op. cit., p. 11. F. B. Cooley, "He appeared," F. B. Cooley in letter to A. B. Jones, Oct. 10, 1898, Chicago Historical Society, Marshall Field Foundation Papers. Farwell, "He seemed to have," quoted in T. W. Goodspeed, *University of Chicago Magazine*, vol. viii, 1922, p. 42. Potter Palmer, "If I learned," quoted in Harold I. Cleveland, "Fifty-Five Years in Business: The Life of Marshall Field," *System*, July 1906, pp. 23–24. F. B. Cooley, "I stoped [sic] buying," Cooley letter to M. F, April 17, 1863, Chicago Historical Society, Marshall Field Foundation Papers. John Tebbel, "Perhaps she sensed," in Tebbel, *The Marshall Fields: A Study in Wealth*, New York: E. P. Dutton, 1947, p. 25.

3. Partnerships

William McCormick, "Dear Brother," McCormick letter to C. H. McCormick, Dec. 14, 1864, McCormick Historical Association, Chicago. Potter Palmer, "Why, boys," quoted in Wendt and Kogan, op. cit., p. 70. *New York Times*, "the awful prevalence," quoted in Donald Miller, *City of the Century: The Epic of Chicago and the Making of America*, New York: Simon & Schuster, 1996, p. 264. Marshall and Leiter advertising, "Our intentions are," Field & Leiter Spring Catalog, Marshall Field & Co. Archives, 1870. "Cloth suitable for pants," quoted in Wendt and Kogan, op. cit., p. 94. Mrs. Edward T. Stotesbury, "The only thing," quoted in John F. Stover, *The Life and Decline American Railroad*, New York: Oxford University Press, 1970, p. 76.

4. Fire, Panic, and More Fire

The 1869 Economic Report, "within five years more cotton," quoted in Encyclopedia Britannica, 1966 edition, vol. 22, p. 774. Fire history, "Mr. McCormick, the millionaire," quoted in Chicago Historical Society, *The Great Chicago and the Web of Memory*, The Ruined City, p. 1, quoted in Chicago Historical Society, The Great Chicago Fire, *Queen of the West Once More*, p. 1 Deacon William Bross, "The capitalists," quoted in Wendt and Kogan, op. cit., p. 113. The "Cash Boys & Work Girls" sign quoted in Twyman, op. cit., p. 39. *Chicago Evening Tribune*,

"Down State Street," *Evening Tribune*, Nov. 3 and 6, 1871. *Chicago Tribune*, "a little strychnine," *Chicago Tribune*, July 12, 1877. Field and Leiter letter, "We see no cause," quoted in Wendt and Kogan, op. cit., p. 132. Marshall Field, "Trade is fair," quoted in *Chicago Times*, Oct. 19, 1873. Marshall Field, "The business of a salesman," quoted in Wendt and Kogan, op. cit., p. 192.

5. Instincts

Field & Leiter advertising, "it outrivals," quoted in Wendt and Kogan, op. cit., p. 156. Robert Twyman, "Prices on some leaders," Twyman, op. cit., p. 53. Robert Twyman, "Marshall Field and Company," Twyman, op. cit., p. 65. *Chicago Tribune*, "The general expression," *Chicago Tribune*, Apr. 29, 1879. Marshall Field, "Hire another office boy," quoted in *Chicago Tribune*, Sept. 15, 1927.

6. Marshall Field & Company

Levi Leiter, "Your record," quoted in Wendt and Kogan, op. cit., p. 136. Marshall Field, "We have been large," and Frederick F. Cook, "Mr. Storey does not," quoted in Wendt and Kogan, op. cit., p. 169. Karl Marx, "No great movement," *Chicago Tribune*, January 5, 1879. Mary Leiter on being glad to be "back on terra cotta," quoted in Marian Fowler, *Below the Peacock Fan: First Ladies of The Raj*, New York: Viking, 1987, p. 241.

7. Paid to Think

Robert Twyman, "Marshall Field and Company was in Chicago, op. cit., p. 65. John Shedd, "Sir, I can Sell anything." Marshall Field & Co. archives, two-page Shedd biography. Shedd, He "had an amazing" and "The great highway," Marshall Field & Co. archives: "A Famous Will and a Living Institution," company typescript. Levi Leither, "You have to suspend," quoted in Tebell, op. cit., p. 54. Twyman, "Despite this rapid," in Twyman, op. cit., p. 66.

8. Mile-a-Minute Harry

Harry Selfridge, "a comfortable resting place," quoted in Erika Diane Rappaport, *Shopping for Pleasure: Women in the Making of London's West End*, Princeton, NJ: Princeton University Press, 2000, p. 233. Homer Buckley, "There was no big front," statement, Homer Buckley, Sept. 1, 1946, Marshall Field & Co. archives. Selfridge, "As I was saying," quoted in Reginalf Pound, *Selfridge: A Biography*, London: Heinemann, 1960, p. 18. *Chicago Tribune*, "Projecting as it," *Chicago Tribune*, Nov. 26, 1897. Harry Selfridge, "Often I prevailed" and "To say that Mr. Field," quoted in Twyman, op. cit., p. 108. Marshall Field, "He may not be doing," Wendt and Kogan, op. cit., p. 215. Marshall Field, "is a dying business," statement, Stanley Field, Marshall Field & Co. general offices.

9. Nannie

Arthur Meeker, "One of the most dignified," Meeker, *Chicago with Love: A Polite and Personal History*, New York: Knopf, 1955, pp. 60–61. Arthur Meeker, "Tall and willowy," Meeker, op. cit., p. 56. Philip Armour, "Ogden was impressed," quoted in Harper Leech and John Charles Carroll, *Armour and His Times*, New York: D. Appleton-Century, 1938, p. 82. Sarah Bernhardt, "butchering of the hogs," quoted in Miller, op. cit., p. 200. Founder of the Fortnight Club, "They don't care about," quoted in Emmett

Dedmon, *Duty to Live: Fabulous Chicago*, Chicago: Random House, 1953, p. 117. The *Sunday Herald* "pen portrait," quoted in Wendt and Kogan, op. cit., p. 175. Arthur Miller, "In the grandstand," in Miller, op. cit., p. 291. Potter Palmer inviting friends to form "a community," quoted in Miller, op. cit., p. 414. Jennie Otis Counselman, "as he stepped on my toes," quoted in Frederick Francis Cook, *Bygone Days of Chicago*, Chicago: A. C. McClurg, 1910, p. 121. Marshall Field, "Imagine, leaving her," quoted in Wendt and Kogan, op. cit., p. 114. Stella Virginia Roderick, "Nannie Scott Field had leaned," in Roderick, *Nettie Fowler McCormick*, Rindge, NH: Richard R. Smith, 1958, p. 198. Nannie Field, "As I never wear," quoted in Alison J. Smith, *Chicago's Left Bank*, Chicago: Henry Regnery, 1953, p. 175. Sophia Hayden dedication, "to direct attention to [woman's] progress," quoted in Madeleine B. Stern, *We the Women*, New York: Schulte Publishing, 1963, p. 70. "Cocarettes" claim as a "nerve tonic and exhilarator," quoted in Wendt and Kogan, op. cit., p. 158. Stephen Becker, "weak, debilitated in spirit," in Becker, op. cit., p. 54. Stephen Longstreet, "Their loud excruciatingly," quoted in Longstreet, *Chicago 1860–1919: An Intimate Portrait*, New York: David McKay, 1973, p. 322. Goodspeed, "He did not measure up," op. cit., p. 28. Wendt and Kogan, "In repose, his features," in Wendt and Kogan, op. cit., p. 173. John D. Rockefeller, "We are grateful," quoted in Ron Chernow, Titan: *The Life of John D. Rockefeller*. New York: Random House, 1999, p. 353. John Tebbel, "Field's enemies circulated," in Tebbel, op. cit., p. 96.

10. Hostilities

Marshall Field, "'Dominate' is too strong a word," quoted in Tebbel, op. cit., p. 95. "It became a pastime," *Centennial History of*

Illinois, vol. iv, pp. 167–68. Paul Avrich, "The newspapers," Avrich, *The Haymarket Tragedy*, Princeton, NJ: Princeton University Press, 1949, p. 261. Julius Grinnell, "Anarchy Is on Trial," Haymarket Papers, Chicago Historical Society, "I," pp. 750–86. Melville Stone, "The identity of the bombthrower," Melville Stone, *Fifty Years a Journalist*, Garden City, NY: Doubleday & Page, 1921, p. 173. *Chicago Tribune*, "Law has triumphed," quoted in Dyer D. Lum, *A Concise History of the Great Trial of the Chicago Anarchists*, Chicago: Socialistic Publishing, 1887. Henry Demarest Lloyd, "for the violent insanity," quoted in Miller, op. cit., p. 477. Friedrich Engels, "I only wish," quoted in Kathryn Kish, *Florence Kelley and the Nation's Work*, vol. 1, *The Rise of Women's Political Culture, 1830–1900*, New Haven, CT: Yale University Press, 1995, p. 120. Paul Avrich, "After Field spoke," in Avrich, op. cit., p. 366. Joseph Medill, "a great ring that wrings," quoted in *Debates and Proceedings of the Constitutional Convention of the State of Illinois*, 1870, p. 1629. Henry Demarest Lloyd, "America has the proud satisfaction," *Atlantic Monthly*, March 1881. Marcus Hanna, "Oh hell," Thomas Beer, *Hanna*, New York: A. A. Knopf, 1929, p. 133. Tebbel, "The result seemed," Tebbel, op. cit., p. 58. David Beatty, "Darling Mine," undated letter, quoted in W. S. Chalmers, *The Life and Letters of David, Earl Beatty*, London: Hodder & Stoughton, 1951, p. 78. David Beatty, "your dear arms around my neck," letter dated Nov. 10, 1909, quoted in Chalmers, op. cit., p. 78. Peter Funk, "Marshall, you have no home," quoted in Stephen Longstreet, op. cit., p. 112.

11. Giving Back

John D. Rockefeller, "The good people," quoted in Allan Nevins, *Study in Power: John D. Rockefeller, Industrialist, Philanthropist*, 2 vols., New York: Charles Scribner's Sons, 1953, vol. II, p. 156.

Marshall Field, "I beg you will not allow," quoted in Wendt and Kogan, op. cit., p. 176. Max Weber, "Capitalism *may* even be," in Max Weber, *The Protestant Ethics and the Spirit of Capitalism*, New York: Scribner's Sons, 1958, p. 17. John D. Rockefeller, "I investigated," quoted in *New York Times*, May 24, 1937.

12. Politics

Steffens, "It was first in violence," Lincoln Steffens, *The Shame of the Cities*, New York: McClure, Phillips, 1902, p. 163. Carter Harrison, "The fact—too significant to be accidental," Harrison, *Stormy Years: The Autobiography of Carter H. Harrison, Five Time Mayor of Chicago*, Indianapolis: Bobbs-Merrill, 1935, p. 61. William Jennings Bryan, "Thou shalt not press," *Encyclopedia Britannica*, 1966 edition, vol. 4, p. 317. Description of Mrs. McKinley's inaugural gown, "a dress of silver," Wendt and Kogan, op. cit., p. 328. William Jennings Bryan, "One of the great purposes," Peter Lyon, *Success Story: The Life and Times of S. S. McClure*, New York: Scribner's Sons, 1963, p. 176. Marshall Field, "I have a little reputation," quoted in Tebbel, op. cit., p. 101. Marshall Field, "The trouble is that," Tebbel, op. cit., p. 102.

13. Delia

Marshall Field, "I see by the morning papers," telegram to Stanley Field, Marshall Field & Company archives, general offices. Delia Caton, "Mr. Field just wants me," Meeker, op. cit., p. 112. Arthur Meeker, "In one respect she surpassed," Meeker, op. cit., p. 57. Arthur Meeker, "What did you think," Meeker, op. cit., p. 59. *Chicago Tribune*, "None who beheld," quoted in Tebbel, op. cit., p. 104. "Thousands of Negroes," Howard H. Myers, "The policing of Labor Disputes in Chicago; A Case Study" Ph.D. dissertation, Department of Economics, University of Chicago, 1929, p. 557. Marshall Field, "I see by Morning," Letter to J. G. Shedd, July 4, 1905, quoted Twyman, op. cit., p. 166.

14. Son and Father

Chicago *Daily News*, "At a signal from the attendant physician," and Marshall Field, "No, he did not," quoted in Tebbel, op. cit., p. 107. Police Chief Collins, "whether the shooting," Tebbel, op. cit., p. 108. Dana Thomas, "There were fourteen," Thomas, *The Money Crowd*, G. P. Putnam's Sons, 1972, p. 34. Arthur Meeker, "It's impossible to say now what happened," Meeker, op. cit., p. 60. Albertine Field, "American wealth," quoted in Tebbel, op. cit., p. 110. New York newspaper obituaries, Jan. 18, 1906.

15. The Will

Edward Ayer, "Your story," told to author by attorney William O. Petersen. Marshall Field last will and testament, "Earnestly hoping," Marshall Field & Co. archives, "A Famous Will and a Living Institution," p. 206. The *Outlook* applauding Field for having "abstained from those gigantic schemes," *Outlook*, Jan. 27, 1906. John Shedd, "If you cannot find it," Marshall Field & Co. archives, John G. Shedd, "Short timeline."

16. Grandsons

Marshall Field II, "I do not know how," Chicago *Daily News*, Nov. 24, 1905. Lundberg, "Marshall Field II was fatally," Lundberg, *America's Sixty Families*, New York: Vanguard Press,

1937, p. 99. Marshall Field Co. spokesman, "the ravings of a drug-mad," quoted in the Chicago *Reader*, July 16, 1999. Marshall Field III, "I found Cambridge utterly," quoted in Stephen Becker, *Marshall Field III: A Biography*, New York: Simon & Schuster, 1964, p. 75.

17. Secrets and Spies

Winston Churchill, "My dear Nancy," quoted in Christopher Sykes, *Nancy: The Life of Lady Astor*, Chicago: Academy Chicago, 1972, p. 193. Marshall Field, "WANT YOU TO BE GODFATHER," quoted in Becker, op. cit., p. 84. Chicago *Tribune*, "America's richest young man," *Tribune*, April 15, 1917. Marshall Field III, "From now on," quoted in Becker, op. cit., p. 86. Stephen Becker, "He subdued his suspicions," Becker, op. cit., pp. 89–90. Government reports on Jechalski's "very slight German accent," through "We feel that Mrs. Marsh," quoted in Chicago *Reader*, July 16, 1999. Nancy Astor, "she lies for pleasure," quoted in James Fox, *Five Sisters: The Langhornes of Virginia*, New York: Simon & Schuster, 2000, p. 32.

18. How to Spend It

Marshall Field III, "I can't answer that" and "I'm not going," quoted in Tebbel, op. cit., p. 175. Marshall Field III, "The law of averages," *Literary Digest*. Stephen Becker, "It required a sense," in Becker, op. cit., pp. 105–06. David Batty, "'Shaky' Marshall," in Chalmers, op. cit., p. 409. Stephen Becker, "Very handsome," in Becker, op. cit., pp. 110–11. Scott Fitzgerald, "it became a habit," in "How to Live on $36,000 a Year," *Saturday Evening Post*, April 5, 1924. Evelyn Field, "as far apart," quoted in Tebbel, op. cit., p.

179. Barbara Field Benziger, "I was brought up," in Benziger, *The Prison of My Mind*, New York: Walker, 1969, p. 86.

19. Audrey

Marshall Field III, "We landed," Chicago Historical Society, Field Foundation legacy, box 36, item 1.

20. Evolutions

Marshall Field III, "I got rather disgusted," quoted in Tebbel, op. cit., p. 182. John Shedd, "Some departments," quoted in Wendt and Kogan, op. cit., p. 319. *New York News*, "if the fabulously wealthy," quoted in the *Chicago Tribune* magazine, Sept. 18, 1983. Arthur Meeker, "People sold their houses," in Meeker, op. cit., p. 61.

21. Roosevelt Radicals

Ralph Ingersoll, "I could not remember," in Roy Hoopes, *Ralph Ingersoll: A Biography*, New York: Atheneum, 1985, p. 202. Lillian Hellman, "a mess, badly written," quoted in Carl Rollyson, *Lillian Hellman: Her Life and Her Legend*, New York: St. Martin's Press, 1988, p. 160. Carl Rollyson, "Field would have a special appeal," in Rollyson, op. cit., p. 160. Louis Kronenberger on Field's "great elegance," Marshall Field V to author, May 5, 2001, interview. Virginia Schoales, "He was fooled," quoted in Hoopes, op. cit., p. 245. Ralph Ingersoll, "The cocky inference," quoted in Hoopes, op. cit., p. 226. Eugene Lyons, "with endless Communist organizations," *American Mercury*, Aug. 1940, p. 484. Ben Hecht quip, "Man bites underdog," quoted in William MacAdams, *Ben Hecht:*

A Biography, New York: Charles Scribner's Sons, 1990, p. 215. *PM*'s statement of principles, "We are against," quoted in Paul Milkman, "The News for Living section," in *PM: A New Deal in Journalism*, New Brunswick, NJ: Rutgers University Press, 1997, p. 41. Marshall Field III, "I really couldn't say," quoted in Becker, op. cit., p. 203. Henry L. Simpson, "France has been conquered," *Time*, July 15, 1940. Robert Rutherford McCormick, "It pays to have," quoted in Morgan Gwen Morgan and Arthur Veysey, *Poor Little Rich Boy*, Wheaton, IL: Du Page Heritage, 1985, p. 33.

22. Patriot Games

Unknown dowager, "Nothing is left any more," quoted in Wendt and Kogan, op. cit., p. 376. "Billions for defense" slogan and "the greatest thing since," *Chicago Sun-Times*, Dec. 11, 1966. Charles Coughlin, "a great liar and betrayer," quoted in Hoopes, op. cit., p. 261. Ralph Ingersoll, "Incidentally, Dash," quoted in Rollyson, op. cit., p. 164. Ralph Ingersoll, "Had I followed my preanalysis," quoted in Hoopes, op. cit., pp. 264–65. Marshall Field III, "Ralph *thinks* he'd," Marshall Field V to author. John P. Lewis, "He was not a man of controversy," quoted in Becker, op. cit., pp. 226–27. Stephen Becker, "As its publisher," in Becker, op. cit., pp. 329–30. American Legion letter of condemnation, "In 1917," quoted in Becker, op. cit., p. 289. Robert Rutherford McCormick, "Marshall Field is an authority," quoted in John Tebbel, *An American Dynasty: The Story of the McCormicks, Medills & Pattersons*, Garden City, NY: Doubleday, 1947, p. 331. Marshall Field III, "When organizations get to be," quoted in Becker, op. cit., p. 310. Admiral Harry E. Yarnell, "the greatest authority," quoted in Barbara W. Tuchman, *Stilwell and the American Experience in China, 1911–1945*, New York: Macmillan, 1971, p.

289. Franklin D. Roosevelt, "start winning for themselves," quoted in Tuchman, op. cit., p. 290. Errol Flynn, "The moon would," quoted in Kenneth Anger, *Hollywood Babylon*, New York: Dell, 1975, p. 302. *Commonweal*, "That verdict," quoted in Hoopes, op. cit., p. 212. Paul Milkman, "The News for Living section," in Milkman, op. cit., p. 87. Ralph Ingersoll, "You'll never," quoted in Milkman, op. cit., p. 88.

23. Coming of Age

Delivery truckers, "Happy birthday," Marshall Field V to author.

24. Bearing Witness

Marshall Field IV, "The war made a lot of things," quoted in Chicago *Sun-Times*, Dec. 11, 1966. Marshall Field III, "Secretary of Labor Schwellenbach," quoted in Becker, op. cit., p. 389. Marshall Field, "Only in the faith of Jefferson," and "Wherever there is a," Marshall Field, *Freedom Is More Than a Word*, Chicago: Chicago University Press, 1945, p. 33 and p. 46. Ralph Ingersoll, "I resigned one sentence," quoted in Hoopes, op. cit., p. 327. Marshall Field III's italicized quotes from 1947 Pan American world trip from his MF typescript dated 7/8/47, Chicago Historical Society, Marshall Field archives. Samuel P. Gutman, "In a recent conversation," quoted in Becker, op. cit., p. 395.

25. Cold War

Katherine W. Fanning, "I was closely associated," quoted in *Sun-Times* obituary, Oct. 22, 2000. Frederick W. (Ted) Field, "He would open," Field to author, April 19, 2001, interview. Marshall

Field III, "Dear Marsh," letter published Oct. 9, 1952. Robert Lasch, "Marshall Field III was one," quoted in the *Chicago Sun-Times*, Dec. 11, 1966. *Time* [Lattimore] "undoubtedly contributed," quoted in Thomas Griffith, *Harry & Teddy: The Turbulent Friendshuip of Press Lord Henry R. Luce and his Favorite Reporter, Theodore H. White*, New York: Random House, 1995, p. 217. Chiang Kaishek, "Mr. Lattimore has fully," quoted in Becker, op. cit., p. 451. Marshall Field III, "shows the greatest wisdom," quoted in Becker, op. cit., p. 452. Marshall Field III, "Well, Judge Polier," quoted in Becker, op. cit., p. 453. Marshall Field III, "As many of you know," quoted in *Chicago Sun-Times*, Nov. 17, 1955. Barbara Field Benziger, "This slow dying," in Benziger, op. cit., p. 95.

26. Successions

Marshall Field V, "So they made a deal," and Fiona "was just crazy," to author, May 5, 2001, interview. George B. Young, "a chancy, but wise," quoted in the *Chicago Sun-Times*, Dec. 11, 1966. Ruth Field, "We're all such nice," quoted in the *Chicago Tribune* Magazine, Sept. 18, 1983. Marshall Field V, "There was no dad" and "I never saw Chicago," to author. Marshall Field IV, "Will the vice-president," quoted in the *Chicago Tribune* magazine, Sept. 18, 1983. Ted Field, "We were not overly," to author. Katherine Fanning, "Growing Up in Alaska," quoted in the *Wall Street Journal*, Aug. 24, 1989. Daryle Feldmeir, "He knew enough," quoted in the *Chicago Tribune* magazine, Sept. 18, 1983. Marshall Field V, "The fact that you're," to author, May 5, 2001, interview. Mike Royko, "not, by any means," quoted in the *Chicago Tribune* magazine, Sept. 18, 1983. Kurt Barnard, "We pay a lot less attention," *Chicago Sun-Times*, "Body Blow," March 30,

2001. Daniel Skoda, "Reducing commissions," quoted in *Barron's*, "Field's eyes pay scale as profits slide," Dec. 17, 2001.

27. The Crunch

Ted Field, "I'd go to these board," quoted in *Vogue*, Nov. 1990. Ted Field, "The way I approached," to author. *People* magazine, "Tradition and sentiment were," *People*, Dec. 12, 1983. *Wall Street Journal*, "Ted Field's eagerness," *Wall Street Journal*, Aug. 24, 1989. Marshall Field V, "The only real tradition," *People*, Dec. 12, 1983. Ted Field, "I'm not going to drive," quoted in *People*, Dec. 12, 1983. *Wall Street Journal*, "Field's as a long-term quality," *Wall Street Journal*, Aug. 24, 1989. David Geffin, "Ted's got big balls," quoted in *Vogue*, Nov. 1990.

28. Each Generation Speaks for Itself

Ted Field, "You can't help but be aware," to author. Marshall Field V, "New dynasties, Bill Gates," to author. Marshall Field V, "They all started out," quoted in the *Chicago Tribune* magazine, Sept. 18, 1983. Marshall Field V, "It doesn't bother me" and "If you really want," to author. Ted Field, "I believe," to author.

BIBLIOGRAPHY

Allen, Michael Patrick. *The Founding Fortunes.* New York: E. P. Dutton, 1987.

Alsop, Susan Mary. *To Marietta from Paris, 1945–1960.* Garden City, NY: Doubleday, 1975.

Anger, Kenneth. *Hollywood Babylon.* New York: Dell, 1975.

Avrich, Paul. *The Haymarket Tragedy.* Princeton, NJ: Princeton University Press, 1949.

Barbour, George M. *Sketchbook of the Inter-State Exposition.* Chicago: Lakeside Press, 1883.

Becker, Stephen. *Marshall Field III.* New York: Simon & Schuster, 1964.

Beecher, Catharine E., and Harriet Beecher Stowe. *The American Woman's Home or, Principles of Domestic Science; Being a Guide to the Formation and Maintenance of Economical, Healthful,*

Beautiful and Christian Homes. Hartford, CT: The Stowe-Day Foundation, 1987 reprint of the 1869 original.

Beer, Thomas. *Hanna.* New York: Alfred A. Knopf, 1929.

Bender, Thomas. *New York Intellect.* New York: Alfred A. Knopf, 1987.

Benziger, Barbara Field. *The Prison of My Mind.* New York: Walker, 1969.

Bolitho, Hector, and Peel, Derek. *The Drummonds of Charing Cross.* London: Allen & Unwin, 1967.

Bruccoli, Mathew. *Some Sort of Epic Grandeur: The Life of F. Scott Fitzgerald.* New York: Carroll & Graf, 1981.

Carnegie, Andrew. *Autobiography.* Boston: Northeastern University Press, 1920.

Centennial History of Illinois, ed. Clarence W. Alvord. 5 vols. Springfield: Illinois Centennial Commission, 1918–1920.

Chalmers, W. S. *The Life and Letters of David, Earl Beatty.* London: Hodder & Stoughton, 1951.

Chernow, Ron. *Titan: The Life of John D. Rockefeller.* New York: Random House, 1999.

Chicago: Pictorial and Biographical. Chicago: S. J. Clarke, 1913.

Cook, Frederick Francis. *Bygone Days in Chicago.* Chicago: A. C. McClurg, 1910.

Davison, Irene. *Etiquette for Women.* London: C. Arthur Pearson, 1928.

Dedmon, Emmett. *Fabulous Chicago: A Great City's History and People.* New York: Atheneum, 1981.

_____. *Duty to Live: Fabulous Chicago.* New York: Random House, 1953.

Doyle, Laura. *The Surrendered Wife.* New York: Simon & Schuster, 2001.

Ellis, Edward Robb. *The Epic of New York City.* New York: Coward-McCann, 1966.

Emery, Edwin, and Emery Michael. *The Press and America: An Interpretative History of the Mass Media.* Englewood Cliffs, NJ: Prentice-Hall, 1978.

Field, Marshall III. *Freedom Is More Than a Word.* Chicago: University of Chicago, 1945.

_____. *The Negro Press and the Issues of Democracy.* Chicago: American Council on Race Relations, 1944.

_____. *The Relationship between Problems of Children and the Problems of Manpower.* An address before the Delaware White House, Nov. 18, 1942.

Fowle, Marian. *Below the Peacock Fan: First Ladies of the Raj.* Markham, ON: Penguin Books Canada, 1987.

Fox, James. *Five Sisters: The Langhornes of Virginia.* New York: Simon & Schuster, 2000.

Ginger, Ray. *The Bending Cross; A Biography of Eugene Victor Debs.* New Brunswick, NJ: Rutgers University Press, 1949.

_____. *Altgeld's America: The Lincoln Ideal v Changing Realities.* New York: Funk & Wagnalls, 1958.

Ginzberg, Lori D. *Women and the Work of Benevolence; Morality, Politics and Class in the 19th Century United States.* New Haven, CT: Yale University Press, 1990.

Goodspeed, Thomas Wakefield. *University of Chicago Biographical Sketches.* 2 vols. Chicago: University of Chicago Press, 1922.

Griffith, Thomas. *Harry & Teddy: The Turbulent Friendship of Press Lord Henry R. Luce and His Favorite Reporter, Theodore H. White.* New York: Random House, 1995.

The Grove Book of Hollywood, ed. Christopher Silvester. New York: Grove Press, 1998.

Gwen, Morgan, and Arthur Veysey. *Poor Little Rich Boy: The Life and Times of Col. Robert R. McCormick.* Wheaton, IL: Du Page Heritage, 1985.

Harper, Ida Husted. *The Life and Work of Susan B. Anthony*, 3 vols., Indianapolis and Kansas City: Bowel Merrill, 1898–1908.

Harrison, Carter H. *Stormy Years: The Autobiography of Carter H. Harrison, Five Time Mayor of Chicago.* Indianapolis: Bobbs-Merrill, 1935.

Heise, Kenan. *Chaos, Creativity and Culture: A Sampling of Chicago in the 20th Century.* Salt Lake City: Gibbs-Smith, 1998.

Hines, Thomas S. *Burnham of Chicago: Architect and Planner.* New York: Oxford University Press, 1974.

Hiney, Tom. *On the Missionary Trial: A Journey through Polynesia, Asia and Africa With the London Missionary Society.* New York: Atlantic Monthly Press, 2000.

Hobson, Laura Z. *The Early Years.* New York: Donald I. Fine, 1983.

Holbrook, Stewart H. *The Age of the Moguls.* Garden City, NY: Doubleday & Co., 1953.

Hoopes, Roy. *Ralph Ingersoll: A Biography.* New York: Atheneum, 1985.

Hyams, Edward. *A Dictionary of Modern Revolution.* New York: Taplinger, 1973.

Ingersoll, Ralph. *Point of Departure.* New York: Harcourt Brace, 1961.

――――――――――. *Top Secret.* New York: Harcourt Brace, 1946.

Jablonski, Edward. *Gershwin: A Biography.* New York: Doubleday, 1987.

Johnson, Claudius O. *Carter Henry Harrison: Political Leader.* Chicago: University of Chicago Press, 1928.

Kennedy, Roger G. *Architecture, Men, Women and Money in*

America 1600–1860. New York: Random House, 1985.

Kingsley, Philip. *The Chicago Tribune: Its First One Hundred Years*. Chicago: Chicago Tribune, 1946.

Kirkland, Caroline. *Chicago Yesterdays*. Chicago: Daughaday, 1919.

Klein, Maury. *The Life and Legend of Jay Gould*. Baltimore: Johns Hopkins University Press, 1986.

Layman, Richard. *Shadow Man: The Life of Dashiell Hammett*. New York: Harcourt Brace Jovanovich, 1981.

Le Vot, André. *Scott Fitzgerald*. Paris: Julliard, 1979.

Leech, Harper, and John Charles Carroll. *Armour and His Times*. New York: D. Appleton-Century, 1938.

Lindberg, Ferdinand. *America's Sixty Families*. New York: Vanguard Press, 1937.

Longstreet, Stephen. *Chicago 1860-1919: An Intimate Portrait*. New York: David McKay, 1973.

Lum, Dyer D. *A Concise History of the Great Trial of the Chicago Anarchists*. Chicago: Socialistic Publishing, 1887

Lundberg, Ferdinand. *America's Sixty Families*. New York: Vanguard Press, 1937.

Lyon, Peter. *Success Story: The Life and Times of S. S. McClure*. New York: Charles Scribner's Sons, 1963.

MacAdams, William. *Ben Hecht: A Biography*. New York: Charles Scribner's Sons, 1990.

Meeker, Arthur. *Chicago with Love*. New York: Alfred A. Knopf, 1955.

Mellen, Joan. *Hellman and Hammett: The Legendary Passion of Lillian Hellman and Dashiell Hammett*. New York: HarperCollins, 1996.

Milkman, Paul. *PM: A New Deal in Journalism*. New Brunswick, NJ: Rutgers University Press, 1997.

Miller, Donald L. *City of the Century: The Epic of Chicago and the*

Making of America. New York: Simon & Schuster, 1996.

The Mind and Spirit of John Peter Altgeld, ed. Henry M. Christman. Urbana: University of Illinois Press, 1960.

Mosley, Nicholas. *Efforts at Truth: An Autobiography.* London: Secker & Warburg, 1994.

Myers, Howard H. "The policing of Labor Disputes in Chicago; A Case Study," Ph.D. dissertation, Department of Economics, University of Chicago, 1929.

Nash, Jay Robert. *People to See: An Anecdotal History of Chicago's Makers and Breakers.* Piscataway, NJ: New Century Publishers, 1981.

Nevins, Allan. *Study in Power: John D. Rockefeller, Industrialist and Philanthropist.* 2 vols. New York: Charles Scribner's Sons, 1953.

The Oxford Companion to Art, ed. Harold Osborne. Oxford: Clarendon Press, 1970.

Ozment, Steven. *Ancestors: The Loving Family in Old Europe.* Boston: Harvard University Press, 2001.

Packard, Vance. *The Ultra Rich: How Much Is Too Much?* Boston: Little Brown, 1989.

Parachristou, Judith. *Women Together: A History in Documents of the Women's Movement in the United States.* New York: Alfred A. Knopf, 1976.

Peck, Bradford. *The World A Department Store.* Lewistone, ME, and Boston: B. Peck, 1990.

Plante, Ellen M. *Women at Home in Victorian America: A Social History.* New York: Facts on File, 1997.

Pound, Reginald. *Selfridge: A Biography.* London: Heinemann, 1960.

Randall, Ruth Painter. *Mary Lincoln: Biography of a Marriage.* Boston: Little, Brown, 1953.

Rappaport, Erika Diane. *Shopping for Pleasure: Women in the Making of London's West End.* Princeton, NJ: Princeton University Press, 2000.

Roderick, Stella Virginia. *Nettie Fowler McCormick.* Rindge, NH: Richard R. Smith, 1958.

Rollyson, Carl. *Lillian Hellman: Her Life and Her Legend.* New York: St.Martin's Press, 1988.

Sharp, Dennis. *The Illustrated Encyclopedia of Architects and Architecture.* New York: Whitney Library of Design, 1991.

Sherwood, Mary Elizabeth Wilson. *Manners and Social Usages by Mrs. John Sherwood.* New York: Harper & Brothers, 1884.

Skidelsky, Robert. *Oswald Mosley.* New York: Holt, Rinehart & Winston, 1975.

Sklar, Kathryn Kish. *Florence Kelley and the Nation's Work.* vol. 1. *The Rise of Women's Political Culture, 1830–1900.* New Haven, CT: Yale University Press, 1995.

Smith, Alison J. *Chicago's Left Bank.* Chicago: Henry Regnery, 1953.

Steadt, William. *If Christ Came to Chicago.* London: Review of Books, 1894.

Steffens, Lincoln. *The Shame of the Cities.* New York: McClure, Phillips, 1902.

Stern, Madeleine B. *We the Women: Career Firsts of 19th Century America.* New York: Schulte Publishing, 1963.

Stone, Melville E. *Fifty Years a Journalist.* Garden City, NY: Doubleday & Page, 1921.

Stover, John F. *The Life and Decline of American Railroad.* New York: Oxford University Press, 1970.

Tebbel, John. *The Marshall Fields: A Study in Wealth.* New York: E. P. Dutton, 1947.

_____. *An American Dynasty: The Story of the McCormicks, Medills and Pattersons.* Garden City, NY: Doubleday, 1947.

_____ . *Inheritors: A Study of America's Great Fortunes and What Happened to Them*. New York: G. P. Putnam's Sons, 1962.

Teichman, Howard. *George S. Kaufman: An Intimate Portrait*. New York: Atheneum, 1972.

Thomas, Dana. *The Money Crowd*. New York: G. P. Putnam's Sons, 1972.

Trzebinski, Errol. *Silence Will Speak: A Study of the Life of Denys Finch Hatton*. Chicago: University of Chicago Press, 1977.

Tuchman, Barbara W. *Stilwell and the American Experience in China, 1911–1945*. New York: Macmillan, 1971.

Twombly, Robert. *Louis Sullivan*. New York: Viking, 1986.

Twyman, Robert W. *History of Marshall Field & Company*. Philadelphia: University of Pennsylvania Press, 1954.

Washburn, Charles. *Come into My Parlor: A Biography of the Aristocratic Everleigh Sisters of Chicago*. New York: Arno Press, 1934.

Weber, Max. *The Protestant Ethics and the Spirit of Capitalism* (trans. Talbot Parsons). New York: Charles Scribner's Sons, 1920.

Wendt, Lloyd, and Herman, Kogan. *Give the Lady What She Wants: The Story of the Marshall Field & Co*. Indianapolis: Bobbs Merrill, 1943.

Williams, Alfred H. *No Name on the Door: A Memoir of Gordon Selfridge*. London: W. H. Allen, 1956.

Young, John H. *Our Deportment; or The Manners, Conduct and Dress of the Most Refined Society*. Detroit: F. B. Dickerson, 1885.

Magazines and Newspapers

Ainslee's Magazine. Richard Linthicum. "Marshall Field, Merchant." Feb. 1902.

American Magazine. J. B. Griswold. "You Don't Have to be Born with It." Nov. 1931.

American Mercury. Eugene Lyons. "The Strange Case of PM." Aug. 1940.

Atlantic Monthly. Henry Demarest Lloyd. "America Has the Proud." March 1881.

Barrons. Eddie Baed. "Field's Eyes Pay Scale as Profits Slide." Dec. 17, 2001.

Business Week. "Field Eyes Books." Oct. 7, 1944.

Chicago Daily News:

Items on death of Marshall Field II, Nov. 23, Nov. 24, and Nov. 27, 1905.

Story of Marshall Field's will, Sept 11, 1943. "Sun Cleared of Misuse of Paper Quota." Jan. 11, 1945.

Chicago Evening Tribune. "Down State Street." Nov. 3 and 6, 1871.

Chicago Sun-Times. "The Sun-Times Story: A Silver Anniversary." Dec. 11, 1966.

Chicago Tribune. July 12, 1877.

Chicago Tribune magazine. "The Field Dynasty: How One Family Helped Change the Face of Chicago." Sept. 18, 1983.

Cosmopolitan. Charles S. Gleed. "Captains of Industry: Marshall Field." June 1902.

Country Life. Geoffrey Hellman. "Full Length Portrait of a Country Gentleman." April 1934.

Debates and Proceedings of The Consitutional Convention of the State of Illinois, 1870.

Dry Goods Reporter, Feb. 20, 1897, and Jan. 8, 1910.

Entertainment Weekly:

"Head of the Class: *Entertainment Weekly's 9th Annual Power 101.*" Oct. 30, 1998.

"A Wild Mess Following the Largest Music Merger." July 23, 1999.

Forbes. Joe Queenan. "Why Can't Billionaires Grow Up?" Oct. 13, 1997.

Fortune.

"Marshall Field & Co." Oct. 1936.

"Battle of Chicago," Feb. 1942.

Harper's Weekly. Amos W. Wright. "Marshall Field I." March 21, 1891.

Internet Wire. "DirectWeb, Inc., Appoints Ted Field to Board of Directors." June 16, 2000.

Life. Oct. 18, 1943.

Literary Digest. "Captain Marshall Field Returns to Work." March 27, 1920.

Mother Jones. Foundation for National Progress report. April 1996.

Nation, The:

"Here Comes PM." June 7, 1940.

   Reply to Milton Mayer. March 14, 1942.

New Republic:

"PM." April 22, 1940. Wilson Whitman.

"Marshall Field, the Native's Return." Nov. 2, 1941.

Newsweek.

"PM." June 24, 1940. "PM's Second Wind." Oct 20, 1940.

"Prelude to a Chicago War." Oct. 20, 1941.

"Husky Infant in Newsdom." Dec. 15, 1941.

"Marshall Field III." Sept. 20, 1943.

"Field Museum." Sept. 27, 1943.

"Election of a Queen." Dec. 28, 1953.

Outlook. Jan. 27, 1906.

People. Dec. 12, 1983.

Publisher's Weekly:

"PM." March 20, 1940.

"Marshall Field III." Oct. 7 and Nov. 4, 1941.

Saturday Evening Post:

Scott Fitzgerald. "How to Live on $36,000 a Year." April 5, 1924.

Mrs. Marshall Field III. "Breaking Into a New Game." March 5, 1928.

"They Told Barron." June 17, 1930.

"Muddled Millions." Feb. 15, 1941.

Jack Alexander. "Do Gooder." Dec. 7, 1941.

Science. Stanley Field. "Address at the 50th Anniversary of the Field Museum." Sept. 24, 1943.

Success. Theodore Dreiser. "Life Stories of Successful Men" Dec. 8, 1898.

System: Harold I. Cleveland. "Fifty-Five Years in Business: Marshall Field." July 1906. Alfred Pittman, "A Business that Endured." Nov. 1919.

Time:

"Field from Glore," July 8, 1935.

"Marshall Field Train," July 8, 1935.

"Birth of a Daily," Jan. 22, 1940.

"France has been conquered." July 15, 1940.

"PM." July 29, 1940.

"Marshall Field III." July 6, 1942, and Aug 10, 1942.

"Favorite Sons." Jan. 15, 1945.

"Gentlemen of the Press." April 16, 1845.

"Southern Invasion." Aug. 6, 1945.

"The Colonel and His Friends." Aug .6, 1945.

"Death in the 24th Ward." March 8, 1963.

Vogue. Michael Shnayerson. "Ted Field." Nov. 1990.

Wall Street Journal. "Field's Odyssey." Aug. 24, 1989.

INDEX